Dear Baseball Gods
A Memoir

By Dan Blewett

To Maddie,

Throw cheese!

D. Blewett

ISBN: 1727813936
ISBN-13: 978-1727813937

TABLE OF CONTENTS

DEDICATION

Mom and Dad,

It was 9:35 p.m. as the ballpark lights pierced the night, bleaching my white jersey as I jogged toward the mound. It was 2-1 in the eighth as you nervously held hands in the bleachers.

Maybe it was Monday. Could have been Tuesday. But for 22 years, there you were.

No matter how I pitched, the post-game script was the same:

"Good Game!"

"I Love You."

Those five words gave me the strength to do all of this.

Love, #13

A Resolute Man Will Find a Way.

- Roye Templeton

Prologue - Dear Reader, What did you do with that?

I graduated from college in 2009 with a double-major in philosophy and psychology. As far as I knew, I was the only athlete in the philosophy department. Typically, though, I just explain that I have a bachelor's in Philosophy. In my mind, it's my *true* major, the area of study that has most defined me as a person. When I wrote this book I was trapped between these pages, and philosophy helped me find myself so I could resume my life out there. I was exceptional at moving forward...until I stopped. The biggest chapter in my life had ended, and it was unclear who I was and what I should do next. The uncertainty felt familiar. When I'd explain to someone in college that I majored in philosophy, I was predictably met with the same, slightly judgmental question:

"What are you going to do with *that!?*"

"I'm not sure." I'd reply.

Years later, when casually talking about my college days, the question shifted into the past-tense: "What were you planning on doing with that?"

I'm pleased to tell you that a decade later, I've finally discovered the answer: *this.*

I began playing baseball when I was eight years old. Up until the day I retired, it was abundantly clear who I was: *a ballplayer.* At 31, hanging up my cleats was the hardest decision I ever had to make. My metal cleats would never again clack up and down the dugout steps and there would be no more jogs across those familiar white chalk lines. Baseball was no longer my beacon and I felt lost. The green grass, the smooth leather baseball in my hand, the face-off with thousands of hitters—those were things that defined my existence. Now, having given all of myself to a game that no longer wanted me…what would I do? What purpose did I have? Who was I?

It dawned on me that my five years reading Plato, Descartes, Aristotle, Sartre, Lao-Tzu and others might just have prepared me to dig up an answer to that all-consuming question. As I started to peel back the layers, I was reminded about just how deep baseball is. The lessons it taught me had perhaps even prepared me for my difficult transition out of it. On game day, we athletes leap out of bed, eager to jog into the sun and pit our best against that of others. We lace up our cleats, tuck in our jerseys, straighten our caps and hustle til the last out not just because it's what we do, but because it's who we are.

After my rookie season in professional baseball, my life took a major turn. I met a girl late in the summer who I wanted to be with. When the season concluded, I moved back to the twin cities of Bloomington-Normal to try a relationship with her. Having grown up in Maryland, I reveled in the strangeness that, in a flash, I suddenly lived in Illinois, a unique state with a very different culture than that of the northeast. In college, I had become certified as a personal trainer. When I needed a job that off-season, teaching young athletes how to get bigger, faster and stronger seemed like a natural fit. The relationship with the girl didn't last long, but the business that I started did. Dan Blewett Sports Performance was later re-branded as Warbird Academy when a new friend, Lucas Cook, became my business partner. Our tiny strength training facility, located in the back of a large baseball academy franchise, grew each year until we were forced to expand to a bigger location. We became a full-fledged baseball academy and it kept me incredibly busy as soon as I landed back in Bloomington each off-season.

Our friend, the honorable judge Jim Knecht, brought his grandson to me in my earliest years in business. Standing 5'10" with a slim build, Jim's signature is perhaps his scholarly, round-frame glasses. To this day, he is still the only man to walk across our academy's grungy threshold in a three-piece suit. Realizing one of the town's most esteemed elders trusted us, I found myself going out of my way to steal a few minutes of conversation with Jim. We became friends and he provided us with advice and mentorship, along with a never-ending supply of new vocabulary words. Lucas and I slowly grew into our britches as business owners.

Each summer while I chased down my dreams, Lucas ran the business in my absence. It was special to be able to leave our tribe each summer and return with new things to teach the hundreds of young athletes who awaited my return. I lived this dual life—player and business owner—from 2010 until 2017. Even with unwavering support from Lucas and all of the kids we worked with, it was hard finding balance and keeping my attention properly focused. I felt guilty being away, and we had numerous challenges that pulled me away from my personal goals. Our academy disrupted the long-standing status quo of baseball in our smallish town, and new competitors sprung up each year. We had bootstrapped our academy from the beginning and so decisions involving money always had the potential to ruin us. Jim and others helped us tip-toe around countless landmines when we finally expanded into a larger facility. As I sat down with him, reflecting on many of the stories in this book over coffee and tea, he summed up the experience simply: "You and Lucas have had an intense five years." It was exactly the right way to describe it. Our foot was on the gas every moment since we first opened our doors.

Though it gave me purpose helping young players find their way, I couldn't turn off my personal desire to make it in baseball. I wanted to pitch in the Major Leagues and I deeply believed that my story would end there, in triumph. I tended both my own goals and those of the amazing kids I worked with, some of whom are mentioned in this book. We were in it together, running the same race…I was just a bit further down the road. Then one day, it happened—I realized I had to hand off the baton, that I was getting passed up by young pitchers I worked with. What I began struggling to do, they did with ease. I didn't have youth on my side anymore. My arm and body were falling apart as I slowed to a jog, then a walk and finally a standstill. My race was over.

It felt like one of those final chase scenes, where the hero is running through the forest as bullets whiz by and you're optimistic that he'll get away one more time. Then, as he hurtles out of the woods into a clearing, he stops. He's surrounded—there's a wall of troops. He *knows*. One day, after fighting and refusing to let go, I looked around and I *knew*. What I didn't know was how I'd let go and how I'd move on. My inspiration came in the form of a letter that I'd write to my parents.

When I was a kid, the librarian from my elementary school called my mother. She was upset that for weeks, I hadn't been choosing a library book to read.

"But Daniel has been bringing his own book to read during his library period. He *is* bringing it, right?"

"Yes, he has." The librarian replied.

"So why is it a problem? He's reading—isn't that the point?"

"Yes, but for weeks he has not made any effort to branch out and try new books. I want everyone to try a library book. I've explained this to them."

"Have you noticed what he wears to school each day?" My mom asked. She hadn't.

"Every day, Daniel wears a baseball-themed t-shirt and a baseball cap. The reason he brings his own book is because he's already read every biography on baseball players that you have. Baseball is his favorite thing—it's all he wants to read about."

My parents live in Maryland, half the country away from Illinois. I couldn't just text or call to let them know that *that* little boy was finally taking off his baseball cap for good. This whole baseball thing was way too big. It was my whole life and a huge part of theirs, as they supported me endlessly the entire way. I finally settled on a letter—a *real* letter—through which I would thank them and explain my decision. The concept wasn't too foreign, as I had sent updates throughout the final four years of my career in a weekly email newsletter. Family, friends, clients and some of my blog readers were offered a chance to sign up for it to keep track of me each season. I received lots of love, support and encouragement, and many of the kids I trained sent me their own season updates. It only felt fitting that I officially say goodbye by writing to my parents. With that first letter, I decided I could tell my whole story in the same way.

Every letter in this book is written to someone who either impacted me or whom I hope to impact. Some of them you'll get to know in other parts of the book, as the stories interweave and interlock with one another. Pseudonyms are used for only a handful of people. I have no scores to settle and everyone, including those I describe conflicts with, changed my life for the better. We grow from conflict and most of mine were with myself, anyway.

As you dive in, I hope you read each letter as if it's written for you. The great ballplayers I read about during my library periods in middle school? I tried to live up to the standard of hustle, grit and greatness they set for all of us. I wasn't always successful but my cleats—like my arm—were tattered and worn when I finally hung them up. This is my story.

Dear Baseball Gods, I'm not a spectator.

It was June 27, 2012 and I was in Rockford, Illinois. It was one of those days when the sun was impossibly high in the sky, taunting us with its inescapable rays. I always believed I would know when it was time to walk away from the game, that my inner monologue would spell it out like a neon sign at the end of a long, dark alley. Seeking relief from the sun, I sat cross-legged in the shade of what looked like a Christmas tree, inexplicably planted in the middle of an open field. I peered down at the wispy green grass, darkened as it too enjoyed a reprieve from the oppressive heat. *Is this really it? Is this the end? Is it really my time?* As I pondered my fate, I surveyed the fractured pieces of my baseball career, scattered around me like shards of glass. With too many to count and without any glue, my disappointment turned into sobbing. My sunglasses fogged, the rushing wind not enough to dry them. A month ago, the end was impossibly far off. It couldn't possibly be here by now...*could it?*

"Are you in a wind tunnel right now? I can barely hear you."

"I'm in the middle of a field sitting behind a tree. It's really windy."

"Well...what's up?" Andrew asked. He definitely had never seen or heard me cry. As I attempted to respond, the words remained stuck in my throat—uttering them would make it even more real. *Get it together. You're tougher than this...aren't you?* My eyes welled up and spilled over as I held my gray flip-phone to my ear, waiting for the composure to reply. Andrew was my best friend, one of a handful of people who had wished me well and shoved me off to sea when I signed my first pro baseball contract. I told them I wasn't coming home for a long, long time.

The news had come moments prior during batting practice. I had been awaiting the results of my MRI, and the doctor finally got ahold of Liz, our athletic trainer. Liz and I were close—she had taken care of me that season in the training room, trying in vain to keep me on the field. I repaid her with snarky jokes that connected with her dark sense of humor. While I was out shagging BP with the other pitchers, she called me over to the dugout, this time with an expressionless face I rarely saw. "The Doctor is on the phone. He wants to talk to you." I sat down on the wooden dugout bench and took the call.

"Hi Dan. Thanks for speaking with me." He told me his name but I immediately forgot it.

"Hi Doc. No problem. I appreciate the call."

I listened, watching as our infielders cautiously fielded ground balls. The field had been baking in the sun and was, to put it lightly, *rough*. Balls were taking fast, unpredictable, aggressive hops and the grass was parched, starting to brown ever so slightly. I was hot and thirsty; everything—myself included—was overcooked.

"Dan, it was hard to read your MRI. To be perfectly honest, I've never read the MRI of a pitcher who's had a prior UCL reconstruction." Reconstruction of the ulnar collateral ligament , or UCL, is better known as *Tommy John Surgery*, eponymously named after the first player to receive it—Los Angeles Dodgers' pitcher Tommy John. The pioneering Dr. Frank Jobe subsequently saved thousands of pitchers' careers with the procedure after Mr. John first agreed to be his crash test dummy. Hurlers were reborn thanks to Dr. Jobe, myself included. I had already undergone the procedure once, four years prior, in 2008. I was told I would never need it again.

"The problem is—he continued—that there's so much scar tissue from your first procedure that I'm not 100% sure of my diagnosis. But, I'm sorry to say I'm 99% certain that you've ruptured your repaired ligament. I'm pretty sure you'll have to go through Tommy John Surgery again if you want to keep pitching."

Ordinarily, I didn't trust doctors from small towns and Evansville, Indiana was a small town. But this orthopedic surgeon—who I hadn't and never did end up meeting in person—was articulate and deliberate in his choice of words. He projected a voice that felt both empathic and kind; I trusted him. He hadn't just glanced at my MRI—I got the impression that he searched it like a maze, trying to find a way out for me. And I could tell that he was disappointed that he hadn't. I thanked him for the call and handed the phone back to Liz. I took a deep breath and walked back out to left field.

This was *my* year. My first seven starts of the season couldn't have gone better by any metric. I was leading the league with a 1.06 earned run average (ERA) along with a number of other pitching statistics. I had struck out 51 batters in 42 innings and was only giving up an average of three hits per outing. I was proud to be considered the Ace of the Evansville Otters pitching staff, the first time in pro ball I'd earned such a distinction. In my second start, when I took a no-hitter through to the eighth inning, it was clear that the work I'd put in the previous offseason had paid off. My mind and body were in harmony as I executed game plans each night with an aggressive confidence. Soon enough, I would no longer be a lowly Independent League player, and I could brush that pesky chip off my shoulder. I began seeing MLB scouts in the stands, radar guns fixed on me. It was a season of redemption and newfound confidence. And with one phone call, it was all for nothing.

It took a minute, but Andrew waited, patiently, in silence, to hear why I had called him. I finally got the words out:

"My elbow ligament is torn…again. The doctor called just now and said I needed Tommy John a second time."

"Jesus, dude. I'm so sorry."

I sputtered and blubbered as I tried to dry my eyes. "It's…it's okay."

It was *not* okay.

Andrew and I were best friends in preschool. When we graduated, however, we enrolled in different elementary schools and I didn't see him again after that. Later on, we only knew we were friends because our moms told us so. We moved on and lived separate lives…or so we thought. Over a decade later, I found myself sitting in a classroom on the top floor of the University of Maryland-Baltimore County athletic center, waiting for orientation to start. It was the first official day for me as a Division-I baseball player. Our coach took roll, rattling off names from his list of thirty or so players. Finally, he got to mine.

"Dan Blewett?" Here!

A guy in the front row cocked his head around, as if he was confused to hear my name.

Andrew Sacks? Here!

My head did the same sideways tilt upon hearing his—*wait! I know him! We're both on this team?* We exchanged incredulous looks. Then, I spoke up:

"Do you know that we used to be best friends as kids?" He remembered.

Andrew is 5′10 with a wide back and a slight bow in his legs. Projecting a calm energy, I always found myself a little shocked at how quick he was when he'd take off into a sprint. I'm two inches taller but he takes the crown as the better athlete. He's also more socially adept, in part because he'd jump right into a pick-up basketball or football game and make friends through competition. I never cared much for other sports—pick-up or organized—and tended to keep to myself in my free time. I always needed a bit longer before becoming "one of the guys," and I'll admit that I'm still not great at it. We decided to be roommates sophomore year and were assigned to a quad in a nice new dorm building.

The connection we had as little kids apparently endured through 13 years of separation, leading us both to excel at baseball. We lived eerily similar lives in a silent parallel. Just to cap off the weird coincidences, I was a pitcher and he was a catcher, which meant we'd be working together as battery mates on the field. What always united us, though, was our similar overall affect—sitting around, we could be perfectly content to not say a word, neither of us feeling awkward or anxious about it.

Andrew transferred a semester later. Playing time was in short supply and he didn't see eye to eye with the coaching staff. He ended up finding a good fit at Frostburg State, a school up in the mountains near both the Pennsylvania and West Virginia borders. We talked only occasionally, seeing each other during winter and summer break. We could go six months without a word, yet pick right back up like we'd seen each other yesterday. Nothing had changed. Years later, when I had my first contract in hand, he was there to help send me off.

I made my debut a month after that and it meant everything to me. It was a combination of a million emotions—excitement, terror, nervousness and elation. I had done it. When the game ended, I went out for pizza with my parents and my host family. As we waited for our two large pies, I got a call. It was Andrew.

"Hey man, I listened to your game. Five and two-thirds innings! I just wanted to call and tell you great job."

"Thanks, man." There was a unique inflection in his voice, a tone of pride and excitement that I had never heard from him before. His voice was *different*.

"Yeah, I just…I'm just really proud of you, buddy."

He called me at the beginning. I called him at what might have been the end.

The four-year anniversary of my first Tommy John surgery was just a few months away. That day—August 25, 2008—marked the end of my collegiate career. It's a simple, quick procedure in which the doctor first removes a tendon from a small, vestigial muscle in the forearm. Then, holes are drilled through two bones—the ulna (inside of the forearm) and humerus (upper arm), after which the tendon is pulled through the bone tunnels. Once weaved through in a figure-eight configuration, the tendon is stitched and anchored, once again linking the two bones together. If all goes well, the tendon heals just as well as the native tissue that snapped under the strain and stress of bases-loaded jams, long toss sessions and high pitch-counts.

I had never worried about my first surgery failing. I had one of the nation's best surgeons, had been diligent with my rehab, took care of my body, and did everything in my power to stay healthy. Yet here I was—nearly four years later—on the sidelines yet again submitting to an arm that no longer worked. Since spring training, my fastball—a heavy four-seamer that sat at 91-94 miles per hour—had been dipping into the 87s by the third inning. My control slipped from good to average to poor. All of a sudden, I was walking six batters per nine innings—an abysmal doubling of the acceptable rate of three batters per nine. The version of myself that was blooming—about to get signed and do great things—was rapidly peeling away. I attempted to manage my arm troubles by not throwing between starts, thinking that I could get ahead of what we thought was severe tendinitis. A cortisone shot from a different team doctor provided a temporary masking effect, but eventually wore off. What was revealed—beneath the worn-off medication—was a season-ending injury.

As I sat by that tree I thought back to the words imparted to me by one of my mentors, Coach Fred Cantor. He was my strength coach in college, and built me from a kid who had never touched a barbell into a force in the weight room. Coach, a heavyset, balding former football lineman who was about as wide as he was tall, was hard on me. He had a quick wit, making jokes and snapping about technique corrections that were too lightning fast for anyone to respond to. At times he was unrelenting, singling me out from across the weight room to "GET IT RIGHT, BLEW-IT!" while seemingly ignoring everyone else. He broke me down but would build me up just before I hit my breaking point. It was a cycle that repeated for years, and I became tough, coachable and resilient because of it. I later realized that he singled me out because he saw something in me, and wouldn't let me slip through the cracks.

I thought back to the time in college when I stood sheepishly in his doorway, hoping to avoid a conversation about how I'd blown a huge chance to earn a bigger role on the team. It was my sophomore year as I stood outside his office, leaning against the door frame in my heather gray UMBC t-shirt and black mesh shorts. I looked down, watching my hard work pool, circle, then slowly flow down the weight room floor drain.

"BLEW-IT! Come in here!"

"Yes." I looked at him, expressionless, hoping I'd be shooed away as quickly as I was summoned.

"Tell me about the weekend. You pitched, right?"

I had indeed entered a baseball game, but it was unclear if the mess I had made would have been accurately described as "pitching."

"It didn't go well," I said. "I was supposed to go four innings but didn't make it out of the second." I chose not to elaborate further and turned my gaze back to my shoes. Ordinarily, a gap in conversation meant he'd fire off some joke at my expense.

"Well, Blew, I don't think it's the end for you."

I looked up.

"With what you've done and your desire, I think the final chapters are yet to be written." He paused as I looked him in the eyes, taking in a deep sincerity that I rarely saw. "I believe you'll come back from this. I really do." I nodded ever-so-slightly, glanced down at my strength program and walked out to begin my workout. I had writing to do.

Sitting in the shade of that tree in Rockford, I hung up with Andrew and called my parents to break the news. My parents were equally crushed by it as I hung up the phone for the final time that day. I was now alone and needed to do what I always did: sort things out in the silent confines of my head. I closed my eyes, hoping maybe I'd get lucky and open them to find out it was all merely a nightmare. I then thought back to Coach Cantor's words. I repeated them in my head: *The final chapters are yet to be written. The final chapters are yet to be written. MY final chapters are yet to be written.* I opened my eyes; I was still beside that tree, still rooted in a horrible reality. I reached to my back pocket and tucked Coach's words neatly inside; they'd be needed someday soon. I checked my phone for the time and realized I couldn't go back into the clubhouse looking like I'd been crying. Guys would perhaps understand, but nonetheless it wasn't my intention to show weakness in front of them. It was 90+ degrees and blindingly sunny, so I decided a good sweat would cover up my lack of composure. Rain and sweat could mask pretty much anything. Then, I turned my palms up and looked at them, inspecting the callouses and fold lines. I had uneven gaps between my fingers from years accommodating a unique changeup grip, with thick yellow callouses resting beneath from nearly a decade of picking up heavy barbells. I'd done a lot with those hands in the last eight years; they'd served me well. I finally closed them—gathering up my destiny into my fists—and got up from beside that tree. I put my headphones in and jogged off, down a dusty back road that cut deep into open farmland.

Why is this happening to me?

This is a bad dream.

This can't be real.

I don't deserve this.

As I jogged, trying to make sense of it all, I wondered where you—the Baseball Gods—were at a time like this. You were supposed to protect a guy like me, saving a little magic in case one of their humble servants needed it. You could have helped the doctor find me an alternate route out of that maze of an MRI. I had been a pious disciple. I deserved better.

Where is my good luck? When do I get a break? Why is it always me and never someone else? A second Tommy John!? That doesn't happen to anybody! I swatted at the air in anger as I ran. I had been diligent. I had waited my turn. I had paid my dues and played the game the right way. I had scratched and clawed to earn playing time, suffered in the weight room, pushed through numerous little injuries and finally a surgery, then gritted through two hard years of pro baseball. This year was *my* year. It was all coming together. I was a leader, not just on my own team but in the league as a whole. This wasn't fair. Why did you abandon me?

I had turned 26 in December and did the math. I would be 28 before I returned to professional baseball. 26 was already too old to not be in Triple-A or the Big Leagues. I had tools—an above-average fastball, a sharp, power curve and a changeup that had heavy sink and arm-side run. I had the requisite ability, was learning to pitch and hitting my stride. I only needed an opportunity, but I kept hitting speed bumps. And now, here was this roadblock, an impasse that few found navigable.

As I jogged deeper through the middle of nowhere, grain silos in the distance, a new voice began speaking up.

Stop complaining. Stop whining. It's done. It's over.

It's happening no matter how much you want to whine about it. You can moan and cry or you can do what needs to be done.

It's NOT your time. You know better. Life isn't fair…you're tougher than this, aren't you!?

What happened to my arm simply happened and there was no finger to point. No one owed me anything. Maybe I had a defect in my arm, my mechanics, my pitching style—I didn't know. Regardless, I hadn't made it a habit of complaining about things beyond my control, so I certainly didn't need to start now. I berated myself a little bit more before acknowledging that making the best of it was all I could do. I was going forward—not backward.

A half hour into my jog, I remembered that I hated jogging and slowed to a walk. My navy batting practice shirt was stuck to me, my earbuds fell out repeatedly, and I had built up enough sweat 20 minutes ago. I thought about Forrest Gump and the pain that turned him into a bearded, long-distance machine. Unlike Forrest, I wasn't running from my problems; I was running toward something—*clarity. I can do this. I believe in myself.* I repeated it a few times as I started to run again, passing the barns and cornfields I had seen on the way out. The 50-foot lights from the stadium were only a half a mile away now, and I had to return with a conclusion and some semblance of composure that I could wear the rest of the night. Two more years on the bench awaited when all I wanted to do was go play. But after purging some anger—shouting into the wind as loudly as I could—I was *done.* I was done feeling sorry for myself (well, mostly), and I was done whining. I was done sobbing and I was done looking at a glass half-empty. Sure, there was not a drop of water in the glass at all, but it had been pretty darned full the last few years, even with setbacks and hard times. I started thinking about what would come next. Maybe something good could come of it…*maybe.*

I finished the homestretch as my feet burned with fresh blisters. It was nearing game time, and players were streaming out of the clubhouse as I approached. I was no longer a part of them, no longer had a game to hustle off to, no longer ran with the herd on the rocky path up the mountain to the Big Leagues. Somehow, though, I'd catch up. I stalled a while outside, wandering off as I monitored the flow of uniformed athletes. Finally, ten minutes before game time, my chance came—I slipped in and sat down in our detached clubhouse. Clubhouses are supposed to be underground, connected to the dugout via tunnel. This one, though, was little more than a glorified trailer located way out beyond right field, beyond the stadium. Since I had been on the disabled list for a week, I was used to not having any real obligations and had settled on taking a personal day. Each game, two pitchers sat in the stands behind home plate; one did the radar chart and the other the game chart. I enjoyed sitting in the stands in plain clothes and getting the straight-on view of each at-bat. From that point of view, it was easy to assess hitter tendencies, pitching strategy and umpire competence. I was also away from the griping and negative emotion that was always present in the dugout. The team had been playing sloppy baseball of late, and there was currently an overabundance of negativity.

I was going to be late to the game, that much I knew. It was hot out, so if I didn't sit and cool off for at least 15 minutes before showering, I'd be sweaty again in no time. I only brought one set of attractive street clothes per road trip, so a fresh coat of post-shower sweat wouldn't wear well if I sat in the stands in my jeans and polo.

I wasn't sure what I wanted to do. Would I sit in the stands in street clothes with the rest of the spectators? Or, would I uniform up and spend my night in the dugout? While I air-dried in my towel, contemplating what seemed like a trivial decision, it dawned on me that my choice was perhaps *bigger*—a metaphor for my journey ahead. Would my future be watching baseball from the stands? Or would it be competing alongside my teammates in the dugout? I could say that I was too old, too fragile and too tired. I could say that I'd given it my all and that I just wasn't lucky enough. I could say that I'd been through the rehab once before and the road ahead was just too long to travel a second time—no one would argue. Or, I could get the surgery, grind it out, force down the jagged pill and rebuild myself one more time.

Tossing my towel aside, I made my choice. I pulled on my compression shorts, then my navy-blue socks. I took the gray baseball pants down off the hanger and stepped in one leg at a time. I rolled up the bottoms until they wouldn't roll up any higher, which stretched and flared the leg openings, helping the pant cuffs to fit better over my shoes. I threaded the navy belt through each loop as I grabbed my maroon practice shirt and pulled it over my head. After partially zipping my pants so they wouldn't fall down, I removed my grey road jersey from the hanger, EVANSVILLE stitched on the front in navy blue with maroon trim. I pulled it over my head and shook out the shoulders, adjusting until it hung just right. I zipped up and buttoned up, sprayed my loosely-tied turf shoes with Scrubbing Bubbles, wiped them down and put on my cap. I walked over to the mirror and looked myself in the eye.

A ballplayer looked back.

Dear Teddy, You're in good hands.

I held you in my arms when you were just a few weeks old. Annie—my little sister and your mother—handed you off to me for a quick nap on my forearm before Thanksgiving guests arrived. You didn't know it at the time, as you laid in your white onesie, but we had a lot in common. We both had a blank slate in front of us—everything new, confusing, challenging, frustrating and intimidating. Though a blank slate can mean uncertainty, it also means potential. I'm still figuring out what my potential looks like at 33 years of age and I have a nagging suspicion that I might still feel that way as a frail old man. I think that's how I prefer it.

Potential, though, is complex—it's not just about how much you have, but how much you tap into. Both one's potential and how much of it is ultimately realized are highly dependent not only on a person's strength of will, work ethic and determination, but also their environment and the people around them. Who I am today has everything to do with the people around me. I've tried to make something of myself and have had nothing but help in that endeavor. As luck has it, the same people who were in my corner will also be in yours. So, I'm going to tell you what you're in for.

Your grandpa, William Blewett, was raised in Lawton, Oklahoma. He trekked out east working as a civilian mechanical and biological engineer for the U.S Army. Not only was he brilliant in his work, protecting buildings against biological and chemical attacks, but he is a decorated runner as well. We have boxes of first place trophies, medals and ribbons from races of all distances—the mile, 5K, 10K and Marathon. In his prime, he ran a 4:02 mile and a 2:30 marathon. Grandpa? Grandpa can run. He's written a newspaper column for 40 years now, has written one book thus far and has plans for numerous others. He edits my work to this day and I improve with each revision.

Grandma grew up Joann Kolarik, raised with her two sisters in a modest home in Baltimore. She met Grandpa at a Toastmasters meeting in which a best humorous speech contest was being held. She had volunteered counting votes. He was dazzled by her beauty; she was impressed with his kind smile and witty anecdotes on stage. Grandpa won the contest that night and not too long after, Joann Kolarik became Joann Blewett.

Grandpa didn't play much baseball as a kid, but volunteered to coach my older brother—your Uncle JD—when he took up baseball at seven years old. JD is built slimmer than I am and followed Grandpa in a love for running. He's also the best writer in our family of writers. I wasn't interested in baseball at first, but became curious as my brother gained a reputation as a good pitcher. They both invited me to come to a practice one day when I was six, but I felt overwhelmed and confused, threw a fit and ran home. Baseball wasn't for me, I decided, so I carried on wandering around the woods behind our house, catching little critters that I'd find in the stream, under a rock or beside the pond. I loved frogs, turtles, salamanders, snakes—you name it. I would chase down anything that could hop, slither or scurry. I asked Grandma to read me expository bedtime books; it was *not* normal. You'll probably choose more...exciting books.

"Mom, read me another one about frogs." She'd grab a field guide from the bookshelf in my room and sit down at the edge of my bed.

"The Wood Frog grows to a size of 51-70 millimeters in length. Females are typically larger than males and though they're usually a medium brown, their skin color can range from light to very dark brown." I'd sit up.

"What area of the country are they found in?"

"The northeast plus the forests of Canada. They are good at tolerating the cold."

I'm not sure how I ever slept—you know, from the excitement of those bedtime stories.

At age 8, I gave baseball another shot. I don't know what sparked it, but I dove in head first. My first coach was John Resta, a man who believed in me from day one. Years later, as a freshman in high school, I went out for the football team. John told my Dad, "If he breaks his arm playing football and can't play for the USA Baseball team because of it...I'll disown him!" I was nowhere near good enough to play on a national team, but John always felt I had something big in store for me.

He coached me for a few years, providing an initial boost of enthusiasm for the game. I learned the fundamentals, had success on the field and most importantly…had fun.

What I didn't appreciate then is how my parents and my coaches approached my participation in the game. Baseball was fun and I didn't *have* to play it. My mom and dad drove me to games, hunkered down with blankets on the cold days and cheered until the last out. It was rare that they missed one, though they did have to trade time carting JD and Annie around town to their activities. Annie played soccer and tennis, plus attended dance and sewing classes. JD was a Boy Scout, sang in the school chorus, played tennis and ran cross country and track. He was also in a few musicals because, well, he really liked a pretty girl who did school musicals.

I understood baseball and baseball always seemed to understand me. I hated school, nor did I comfortably fit into a social group. JD has always been a connector and he was well-liked in high school. Annie was, in her own words, a "chatty goober who hung out with people who didn't get in trouble." I didn't know either of them all that well and few of our interests seemed to intersect. As kids grow up—struggling to figure out who they are—it can be easy to live a life parallel to their siblings. I loved my brother and sister and we generally got along, but we were the family that could never agree on what to do on family vacations. Mom and Annie wanted to do artsy, cultural things. JD wanted to wander the world and explore and I wanted to play some sort of sport, real or invented. Dad? He just wanted us all to get along.

When I graduated from high school I made a commitment to myself. I was stern about it: *you're going to start fresh. You need to stop being a sarcastic jerk to everybody. Bite your tongue.* I wasn't in the cool crowd for two reasons: One, I had no interest in getting in trouble, which meant I had no interest in going to parties, drinking or doing drugs. I just didn't want any of that. Two, I used my wit for evil. Today, I can still be sharp-tongued if I allow myself to be, but in high school I could make the entire class laugh at someone else's expense with a poignant, snappy remark. I knew it wasn't the right thing to do each time I did it and when I realized that in college I would be starting fresh, making new impressions on new people, I decided that side of me would die. I could still be witty, but the put-downs had to stop. I had friends in high school but alienated a lot of people because at some point, they were the target of a joke. I was always aware, always felt bad when I did it. Maybe it was social awkwardness as I struggled to connect with groups; I don't really know. Either way, I decided I wouldn't be that person anymore—it really wasn't who I was.

In college I battled a few of the upperclassmen who, well, did what upperclassmen do. I'd get bullied here and there because I was one of the freshman who didn't laugh it off well—I fought back. One of the seniors, who is now a police officer, would grab my arms and pull them behind my back, telling me I was under arrest. Clamping my wrists as tightly as he could in his hands, he'd make up some infuriating, insulting charge as everyone else watched and laughed. If I had laughed along, he'd have moved along. But I didn't...I resisted arrest. He did it to pick on me and it wasn't right, but I also didn't know how to let things go—I gave it more power than it inherently had.

Later on, in pro ball, I stopped letting other people get a rise out of me or dictate how I felt. There was always a rare exception when a teammate got under my skin, but the guy who both put others down and battled everyone else was largely gone. I didn't have time for that —it was too exhausting letting others affect me in a negative way. I was also exposed to a revolving door of new alpha-male type personalities that I was expected to share a dugout with. The biggest egos in the room always tended to brawl or isolate themselves and I wanted neither—I'd had both.

Within the confines of the dugout, bullpen and clubhouse, though, lots of traits rub off. Besides collecting mentors and father figures throughout my time in baseball, I also tended to gravitate toward teammates who were a bit different than I. I stole character traits from other players I admired. One such player was Steve.

Steve Garrison pitched in the Major Leagues for the New York Yankees and we were teammates in 2015. A left-handed pitcher, he was drafted out of a private high school in New Jersey and turned pro as an 18-year-old. Players who made it to the top could have easily talked down to players like myself who were basically nobodies in the grand scheme of things. Yet, Steve always treated me—and everyone else— like an equal. As soon as I'd walk into the clubhouse and had set my gear bag down, from five lockers to my right I'd hear, "Hi Dan. How are ya?" You couldn't walk past the guy without a hello and an authentic inquiry into how your day was going. Even as his shoulder deteriorated and baseball became a grind, he remained focused on everyone else. Many people showed me the standard I had to live by as a player, how I should strive to play the game. Spending 140 games in a dugout, though, your character is equally stretched, carved and molded by those around you. My teammates shaped me as a person as I grew up so far from home. When I thought about trying to be a nicer person, really I just tried to be more like Steve. Sometimes, we need to be shown what's possible.

Teddy, though I had countless influences over the years, it became clear who the biggest two were—your Grandma and Grandpa. It started in the car rides home.

"Good game, Honey!" I'd groan as I sipped my Gatorade from the passenger seat.

"The play you made on that fly ball in the fourth inning..wow!" I couldn't believe you caught that!" I rolled my eyes at her. Why did Mom insist on being so annoying?

"You've had a lot of really good games recently. Do you know when you pitch next?"

I didn't respond.

"Well you pitched a few games ago so it's probably coming up soon."

I crossed my arms and turned toward the car window, leaning against the door. I watched the trees and 65mph speed limit signs blur past as we returned home on Interstate 95. Who knows if I actually played poorly—chances are, it was just an ordinary game where I fell short only of my own standards. Maybe I went 1-3 at the plate and popped a ball up in a big situation. I probably still played well in the outfield. Or perhaps I started on the mound and gave up a few more runs than usual. It really didn't matter what the scenario was—the script on the car ride home was always the same.

"You looked good out there, Daniel. Your curveball was really breaking. How many strikeouts did you have on curveballs?"

I shrugged and didn't respond. *Dad, stop talking to me—we lost and I walked six batters.*

"I think you're throwing faster, too. Your fastball had a really strong hiss today as it crossed the plate; I could hear it from where I was sitting."

I turned away and looked out the window. Maryland highways were always lined with a jungle of trees, poison ivy and honeysuckle. I gazed deep into them, wondering what kind of creatures lurked beyond the mess of vines and leaves. As I did, refusing to break character, I decided that maybe Dad was right—I had been feeling strong lately on the mound. Maybe I *was* throwing harder. I sat up in my seat and asked him if we could get something to eat. "Sure," he said.

In my pro days, I worked in the offseason as a strength and pitching coach. Parents and young athletes flooded in to learn how to improve their results on the field. I watched the interaction between players and their parents. Unfortunately, I commonly overheard the following:

I know what I'm doing!
Dad, I get it—STOP!
I'm trying my best.
It's not as easy as you think.
NO—I'm not doing it that way.
I hear you! Leave me alone...

I always played for myself and never had anyone else's shoes to fill —I played because I liked to play. What I didn't realize, though, is that it wasn't my choice. Whether or not an athlete plays for himself is largely external, determined by those closest to him or her. One Saturday night in college, as I walked my parents to their car following a pre-season team banquet, I apparently remarked, "I'm going to make you both proud." Upon retiring, Dad reminded me of that quote and assured me that I most definitely did. They were proud no matter what I did. My parents, always cheering at my games and always positive afterward, allowed for my passion for the game to blossom naturally. My own expectations were the only ones I ever had to face and it allowed me to push myself to the limit that I deemed appropriate. I didn't stay up late in my garage doing pitching drills because they expected it—I did that because I wanted to. The only feedback I received was "I thought you played well! Good job!" My coaches and teammates did the rest.

I saw what the other side of the tracks looked like. I had a teammate one year—a high draft pick out of high school—who had a combative relationship over baseball with his Dad. His father, a pro scout, was incredibly critical and demanded perfection in every practice session. I heard through the grapevine how they once got in a fist-fight on a community field over some casual batting practice. When I asked him about "the fight" with his Dad, his head tilted sideways, confused: "which one? There were too many to count."

In college, the only ride home was that of my parents as they commuted 50 minutes to UMBC's windy ballpark that sat recessed in a wooded area below a soccer field. Win or lose, good game or bad, I'd trudge up the grassy embankment beside the dugout to give each of them a hug. Mom smiled and provided the enthusiasm. Dad tried— but failed—to hold back a proud smile before asking specific questions about my pitching tactics: "Was that a changeup you threw to the third batter on a 2-1 count in the fifth? I wasn't quite sure." He grew more and more interested in my craft with each passing year, eventually authoring his first book not on running…but pitching. *The Science of the Fastball* was published in 2013, exploring the countless questions he asked himself while sitting in the bleachers for 20 years.

Early in pro ball, my parents' ride home was by plane the next morning. I'd come over to the rail when the game ended, signing autographs for the kids who would interject in our conversation with a ball, ticket, hat or program in hand. I'd then depart down the tunnel to shower and change, leaving them to sit back down and wait as the fans streamed out. They'd watch the grounds crew repair the field as the buzz of the electricity from the light towers became audible in the silence of the empty ballpark. We'd grab a late dinner but really it was just to feed and spend time with me, as they rarely ate. My dad was usually full on peanuts and anxiety from my outing; my mom couldn't eat another morsel after nine innings of nail-biting while sipping a beer the size of a movie popcorn container. Neither of them drink often, so it always made me chuckle. I spotted them in the stands one Friday night as I pitched against the St. Paul Saints in front of a sold-out crowd of over 7,000. Mom was holding a huge beer with two hands and I could barely see her behind it as they sat dead-center between a sea of Saints fans wearing blue and white. I was the starting pitcher for Fargo wearing black, grey and red. Pitching in St. Paul is incredible, their ballpark always packed tight with engaged, excited fans. That night, I imagine they felt like I was a lone gazelle out there completely surrounded by growling lions and yipping hyenas. I have no doubt they were more nervous than I was. I had been struggling in Fargo but threw a gem that night.

It's human nature to slowly but surely take for granted the things we have. It was normal for me to have parents who cheered and asked nothing more. Baseball was a fun thing I did and they left it at that. The only one who had delusions of grandeur of becoming a name-brand player on TV? It was me. They were happy when I was happy and left me be when I wasn't. If I wasn't responsive, they didn't belabor the point and many car rides home were silent. But that was okay. My highs never got too high and my lows never got too low. Over time, I developed this wide-aperture lens through which I viewed the game and my life. Through it, only the positives and only my path to my goals remained in focus; the negatives were blurred in the background. That lens? It was ground in the passenger seat of those car rides home.

My web of support has been unique, each of our clan contributing a different type of silk. Uncle JD boasts about the exploits of his younger brother to anyone who would listen. Wherever he works, people hear about me. If I finally met one of his friends or co-workers, it was always, "you're the ballplayer, right? I've heard a lot about you." He and I have had a strained relationship at times, brought on by differences in personality and our failure to understand each other. Through it all, he continued to brag. Through it all, I continued to be flattered by it though I never told him so.

Your mother, Annie, grew up from a dorky little girl into a quirky, hilarious, yet still dorky woman. She is without a doubt the one who keeps our family intact. With a unique disarming quality, she mediates and extinguishes family turmoil. If she tells me I'm wrong, there's a 98.3% chance I'm wrong, so I shut up and listen. I probably shared more of the "real" story with her than anyone else, however even she got the outsider's version too often. When I needed it, she'd send me "good juju" from across the country. I'm not precisely sure what good juju is but I will testify that it has magical powers. When she's stressed with anxieties big and small, I talk her down. *No, Annie, a plane will not crash into my house before this book is complete. Nope—not Mom and Dad's house, either. Don't worry. Go back to bed. Call me in the morning if you need.*

Both she and JD went out of their way to attend my games when they could. When your Dad, Ryan, came into the picture, the crew in the bleachers got bigger. I handed off the torch as calmer of irrational fears. Your mom is smart as a whip but just needs someone to laugh at the wacky place her mind goes every now and again. Soon after, though, conversations contained mostly gushing her love for your dad. Your parents are very different, sharing a happy yin and yang of stoicism and free-spirited energy. I don't know your Dad that well yet; it's probably because he and I both have a tough outer shell. His demeanor—stoic, pragmatic, deliberate—is probably what helped him become a leader in the military. We seem to approach problems and life in general in a similar way. One day, he and I will be in a situation to get to know each other. He was the first expansion of our family and that, in turn, brought us you.

Your grandma, though—who I refer to as Mom—is perhaps the one who changed the most as I grew up. She and I butted heads in high school during my teenage years. I never got in trouble, we just didn't see eye to eye. The turning point, however, was my senior year when I was stuck in an AP Chemistry class that my teacher—we'll call her Mrs. Williams—wouldn't let me drop. I registered for it in error and tried to drop it in the first week but she refused, keeping me in class for an entire semester. I, in turn, refused to do any of the exhausting amount of work. I showed up to class as instructed but when she slid me a worksheet, I slid it right back. There was no good reason I shouldn't have been allowed to drop that class. Mom called her about it one day. Basically, the teacher told her that I was a bad kid and that I wasn't going anywhere in life. She did *not* accept this response.

It was the first time I can remember her going into "Tiger Mom" mode, though I'm sure there were other incidences. When I got accepted into UMBC at the end of the year, a small honors university, she brought it back up, saying something to the effect of "suck it, Mrs. Williams!" It was a departure from "go Daniel!" and an entrance to "get out of my son's way." Things changed after that. We were no longer opponents; she was on *my* team.

We also butted heads over Church. In college, as I got deep into philosophy, I distanced myself from it as she grew closer. Five years later, however, her views started to change. She continued growing spiritually, though organized religion became less a path to her enlightenment. At some point, there was no longer anything contentious left and our world views mostly converged. In my eyes, Mom became wise and worldly. I have a suspicion she was always that way.

What makes one man confident and another not? What makes one woman give up while another keeps going? Much of it is unseen and intangible, a confluence of factors that trickle together to form a life well-lived. You've got a heck of one ahead of you. I've been lucky to have a great family, each member a tributary feeding me strength, wisdom, affirmation and good juju into the river that was my love of baseball. At some point, you'll need more than just passion. At another, you'll need someone to remind you who you are. New things are coming for both you and I, but that means only that more support will flow our way.

Teddy, I think we're all excited to find out what your thing in life proves to be. No matter what it is, your Grandma and Grandpa won't miss a performance. Uncle JD will brag about you at work, your mom will send good juju from the bleachers while your dad holds her hand. I'll buy ice cream and tell you how well you did, even if you don't want to hear it.

Dear Jon, It's about to get fun.

I know that it ate you up as you waited for that long overdue growth spurt, wondering if it would ever happen as your teammates starting pulling away. Finally, there it was—you shot up six inches and 40 pounds like a magic beanstalk. We knew that your work ethic would allow you to hang around just long enough…and it did. It would have been wonderful had it arrived earlier, as we both know your place at the next level would have been changed dramatically. If there's one thing I learned over the years, though, it's that the long road is usually the better one to take. More potholes, more fallen branches, more speed bumps and road blocks. A long first road makes all the subsequent ones feel shorter. With all of us, we need a spark to make major changes in our compass heading. You had a stronger work ethic than I did at your age, though we both shared a common love for the game. Back at age 18, my spark came in the form of an honest assessment from the only college coach who ever came to watch me play. Everything changed and I realized that the only road I had available to me was going to be, well, *long.*

It was a clear, warm night as I stood atop the mound at Harford Community College in my home state of Maryland. It was early June and I was 18 years old. A few days earlier, I had graduated from high school without committing to a college. The idea of going into the military interested me, but I wasn't a soldier at heart. There I was, with a high school diploma in hand and no future direction, staring down my catcher as the light towers buzzed and drenched the field in light. Harford's diamond was set deep from the road, trees looming beyond the outfield wall. At night, the lights illuminated it in such a way that we felt like there were no other people on earth. It was just us, our mitts and the crack of our wood bats as we were cradled in utter blackness on all sides. It felt special, like our own field of dreams. On that night, I'd take a new fork in the road as a man named John Jancuska (pronounced Jank-uh-shay), settled into his lawn chair behind the plate. He was there for one reason—to watch me pitch. It was my last chance to jump onto a train that had left the station for most players long ago. I felt I had a good chance if only because I was naive to all of it. I had a special skill that—unbeknownst to me—would become my fare for passage through that gate to college baseball guarded by Coach Jancuska.

From middle school into high school I worked for a man named Duane Rhine, who owned Grand Slam USA, the only baseball facility in my county. Duane—one of only a handful of people to refer to me as "Danny"—gave me the first pitching lesson of my life when I was 14 or 15. My Dad, not a baseball player in his youth, asked him to teach me how to throw a curveball. A few lessons later, it was taking shape.

"Danny—you've been practicing a lot, I can tell." I had indeed—throwing and hitting baseballs were really the only things I did in my spare time.

"It's starting to break *really* hard—if you keep at it, you're going to make a lot of hitters look silly. Just remember to always throw it *hard*—otherwise, it will pop up out of your hand and won't look like your fastball." I nodded and Duane went back to his end of the 70-foot indoor pitching tunnel. I gave him the curveball signal with my glove, kicked and delivered.

Duane, a strong player in his day, took me under his wing and taught me about the game. He had attended Louisburg Junior College, a high-caliber program in North Carolina. After his time playing second base at Louisburg, he got an offer to play at North Carolina State but instead elected to return to Maryland. He missed his home state and took an offer to play infield at the University of Maryland Baltimore-County (UMBC). When my senior year of high school was nearly complete—with little fanfare and a constantly aching arm—I wasn't sure what to do. My mom bumped into Duane at a charity fundraiser and asked for his advice on the college baseball recruiting process. Having not seen me much because of the busy spring schedule, he told her that if I called him, he'd help. I picked up the phone the next morning.

"So what do you want to do, Danny? Your mother says you want to play in college."

"Yeah, I was thinking I'd look for a Division-III school. I looked up a few of them but I'm not sure I could play there; no one has contacted me except one community college." Duane scoffed.

"You're not gonna play D-III baseball; you can play at the Division-I level. Let me make a call to my former coach. He and I are still close and if I ask him to come look at you, he will."

"Really? You mean Louisburg?" I asked.

"I actually already called them; their roster is full. But I'll call Coach Jancuska at UMBC. He'll come out to watch you; I guarantee it."

Sure enough, Coach J called me a few days later to arrange a date to watch one of my games. My final high school game had just concluded, so he agreed to come see me pitch at Harford in the old mens' league. He explained what he was looking for in a high school pitcher:

"If you're 84 to 86 [miles per hour], you show good command of your fastball and a second pitch, we may have a spot for you here at UMBC. Alright?"

College coaches were mysterious. I had heard of other players my age being recruited to play college baseball, but I didn't understand why I wasn't one of them. What was the mystery behind these men who magically appeared for some but not others? I was good, right? *Really good*, I thought. I was always one of the best on all my teams. But these coaches—these specters of men who appeared out of the fog, radar gun in hand—never materialized at my games. I later learned that I was merely a medium-sized fish in a small pool; in the vast sea of college baseball I was, well, a minnow. Nonetheless, I had spoken with a real-life college coach and he was coming to my game. Excited, I told my coaches at Bel Air High School about the situation. "All I have to do is throw 84-86!" I declared. Despite not knowing for sure, I *did* have cause to believe I could throw that hard; an umpire had praised my arm years before my talk with Coach J.

It was a sunny afternoon in the summer before my freshman year in high school, and I was pitching for the Yankee Rebels, a mid-tier team in the most competitive summer league in Maryland—the Baltimore Metropolitan League. Playing "Metro" was a big deal back then. I was facing off at our home field against the top team in the league, the Maryland Mariners. It was me against their ace, and we were locked in a pitchers' duel.

About four innings in, the Mariners' starting pitcher came up to bat. It wasn't intentional, but I absolutely smoked him on the elbow with a fastball. He was holding us to just one run, and it was an unwritten rule that hitting the opposing pitcher was a no-no. But, a fastball got away from me and it was no glancing blow—it hit him solid, making that loud, dead sound that baseballs make they strike bone. I felt bad about it, but it wasn't intentional; off to the hospital he went.

A few innings later, I crossed up my catcher who had called for a splitter, one of my secondary pitches at the time. The fastball I threw instead whizzed by—failing to break like my catcher anticipated—and got no glove at all. It struck the umpire's bare forearm, dropping straight to the ground after transferring all of its energy into him. After another hitter or two, he called the field umpire over to examine the golf-ball sized lump that had grown on his forearm. Just like the pitcher before him, off to the hospital he went.

I gave up one hit and struck out 12 batters in a complete game 2-1 loss. We made a few misplays and they pushed the winning run across late. It was a waste of one of my best amateur games, but we all played our hardest. My Dad beamed and put his arm around me as we hiked up a steep hill, then across the soccer fields toward our car. We barely made it 40 yards before the remaining umpire stopped us. No, he wasn't looking for vengeance.

"You know, your son has a really good arm. I umpire high school games in the MIAA—are you familiar with it? All the big schools like Calvert Hall, Curley, John Carroll, and Mount Saint Joseph's play in it; it's the best high school baseball conference in the state."

We both nodded our heads that we knew of it—big leaguers Mark Teixeira and Gavin Floyd were both Mount Saint Joe's alumni. Today, my close friend, Scott Peddicord, is the head coach there. I told the umpire I had been planning on going to Bel Air High School, an academically excellent public school but nowhere near the caliber of MIAA schools in terms of sports prowess. He continued:

"Well, you're one of the hardest-throwing pitchers I've seen for your age. Do you know how hard you throw? I'd guess you're in the low to mid-80s, and I've umpired a lot of games. For a 14-year-old, that's excellent. You're good enough to play in that league. You should consider visiting Calvert Hall; it might be good for your baseball career."

We both shook his hand and told him we'd check it out. My Dad did, in fact, take me to Calvert Hall for a visit. I felt uneasy about it and I knew he felt uneasy about the price tag. It just didn't feel like the right thing for me or for our family. Maybe it *was* a great opportunity but four years later, I earned my diploma from Bel Air High School. As I told our assistant hitting coach about the phone call and opportunity with Coach J, he muttered a dismissive "Uh huh." I wanted to tell anyone who would listen that I had a chance, though I wasn't close with him like I was our head coach and pitching coach. After constant arm problems in high school, I probably didn't throw much harder as a Senior than I did as a Freshman. He knew that I didn't throw 86 miles per hour.

A few days later on our agreed upon date, there sat Coach J, radar gun aimed through the fence at my chest. He wore a black polo shirt, khakis and a black baseball cap embroidered with UMBC in white letters with a gold outline. I shook his hand before the game and then nervously began my pregame routine with the adult-league team I was playing for. Despite the nerves and the gravity of the situation, I pitched like I knew how to pitch—nothing more and nothing less. After I was done, I slipped out of my cleats and asked Mike, the team's coach, if I could go out to talk to Coach J to see how I did. Mike agreed and I walked—sweaty and nervous—behind the 25-foot tall backstop to find Coach J. He was all packed up and extended an arm to shake my hand as I approached. His thick five-o-clock shadow and wide jaw were intimidating.

"Hey, Dan," he said as I shook his hand. Coach always greeted a person with his or her first name—it was something he would sternly remind me of for the next five years if ever I greeted someone with a mere "Hey." "The number one thing people want to hear when you meet them is their name," he'd say, almost as if I was in trouble. There at that field, I awaited his evaluation:

"You did a good job. You were 78 to 81, touched one 83 on the radar gun."

My heart sank.

"But." (There was a but!) You have perhaps the best curveball I've seen in the last 20 years. I've been coaching and scouting a long time, and your curveball is outstanding." I waited for the punchline.

"You're going to have to get a lot better, and I don't have any money to give. But, I have a spot on the roster for you if you want to play at UMBC. That curveball will get Division-I hitters out right now, though your fastball and command are below-average. However, if you work hard and get to 84-86 with that curveball, you'll really have something and could become an accomplished pitcher at UMBC."

The assistant coach from Bel Air was right—I didn't have 84-86 in my arm—but yet so was Duane, the man who had taught me the curveball that saved my career. I went back into the dugout after Coach J departed and shared the good news with the guys, many of them former collegiate and pro players themselves. They got up and gave me congratulatory high-fives and bro-hugs as I tried, in vain, to contain my excitement. I now had *direction*, catching up with and jumping into the last open freight car on the college baseball train. I had no idea what D-I baseball looked like, but I figured I'd learn and pull myself up to that level. I realized how narrowly I had made it through, how naive I'd been, and how far I was from making the next leap, which would come four years later. If I ever hoped to be the Major Leaguer I'd dreamt of since I was a kid…things had to change. I had to find a way to not only pull myself up to the D-I level, but exceed it. A week later, after visiting UMBC and finalizing my admission, I received a life-changing document in the mail: the summer strength and conditioning workout. As I leafed through it, I decided I would do it exactly as they asked, and give it my all. The clock was ticking on my baseball career, and so I shed my childhood skin right then and there, leaving it in a heap on my living room floor. A man slithered out and stood up, ready to get to work.

Looking back, I think for the right person, sneaking in with just enough to get by can be a blessing. When they're backed into a corner, wolves show their teeth. Arriving on campus a few months later, it became clear where I stood in the pecking order: *the bottom.* Sure, all freshman start at the bottom, but I was one of the few who arrived with no scholarship and no investment made in my success. Anything I wanted to accomplish in the game I would have to earn, and earn in fewer chances. They'd give the guys with scholarship money repeated opportunities to fall and get back up in hopes of getting their money's worth. As a recruited walk-on, I could easily fade into the bench without costing the team a dime. Though the coaching staff always treated me as an equal and never made me feel second-class, I made it a personal mission to prove my worth. I could catch up. I had put in the work that summer, exactly following the workout given to me. I ran the required three miles three times per week and performed the push-up and sit-up routine afterward. It was a rather basic plan I'd later realize, but it was also the first formal strength and conditioning work I'd ever done. I had never really heard of sports performance training and though I lifted weights in class at school, it was never explained to me as an essential part of an athlete's routine.

On our first day of team workouts, we gathered on the red-rubber track that encircled the bright-green astroturf field used for field hockey and lacrosse. We all stood nervously in our heather-grey UMBC Baseball t-shirts, waiting around under a clear blue sky for our timed mile-and-a-half run to begin. As I stood anxious to prove that I had, in fact, done the summer workouts, I turned to another freshman who was of a similar build. I had weighed in at 172lbs, of which I carried a disproportionate amount in my chest, back and legs. My dad had the same broad chest and wide back, even when he was at his lightest during his marathon-running days. I was a medium-sized kid, not *big and strong* as they often described athletes, but not skinny and weak, either. Standing at 6'2 or so with light skin, dark brown hair and a square jaw, the guy next to me introduced himself as Brian Duffy from New York.

I asked Brian what he thought of the summer running plan, to which he replied in his thick Queens accent, "Ah I dunno. I didn't really do it." I was stunned. *This was college baseball,* I thought…*this was serious! How could he not do it?* Coach then herded us together and explained the task—one and a half miles for time, with the purpose of exposing those who hadn't done the workouts in the summer. Despite knowing that I was well-prepared for the run and had nothing to hide, I was nervous and amped up. With clipboard and stopwatch in hand, Coach J walked off to position himself for the start of the race. As we all leaned on the line in tense anticipation, he finally blew the whistle. We burst off, a grey blob of athletes slowly putting distance between one another. I got off to a good start but didn't pace myself very well and paid for it after the mile mark, when I started to drag. I was in the top 25% of the pack, but didn't know exactly how well I had to do to prove myself. *Do I have to win this? Is 8th place okay? There's no way I can catch those few guys. Am I going to be in trouble?*

The term "scared freshman" is real thing—I was in a new world and wanted to make a good impression, but had no idea what was expected of a Division-I baseball player. Brian and I were at a similar pace for most of the run. His black turf shoes beat away at the pavement in front of me, but as mine started to slow his didn't. He pulled away and his long legs propelled him faster and faster in the final bend of the track.

Brian beat me by about 70 meters—a solid 15 seconds—and he hardly broke a sweat doing it. I was pissed. My dad had run the marathon in the Olympic trials, and I actually put in the work getting into good running shape. I thought I had two things on my side—good genes and a decent volume of running from the summer. But it didn't dawn on me yet that maybe I just wasn't as athletically gifted as some of my new teammates. Brian didn't have to try very hard to smoke me in that run. His 80% beat my 110% and there was nothing I could do about it. I grew up in a bubble thinking I was pretty good and felt justifiably confused when no college scouts attended my baseball games. I just didn't *know*, but was quickly learning what the rest of the world looked like. I hated that feeling of losing despite putting in more work. Ten years later as we got a drink and caught up in Chicago, I told Brian the story. He loved it.

"I was just messing with you and trying to play it cool."

"What do you mean?" I asked.

"I *did* the running—I was scared to not do it just like you were. I just didn't know you yet, so when you asked me that, I just acted like I hadn't. I'm not sure why I did that (he laughed) but I'm glad now that it got you all fired up."

"Yeah, you jerk. I was pissed—*really pissed*—thinking I got smoked by a guy who didn't even try." He leaned back in his chair and laughed harder. Brian was a good teammate, a hard worker and a good friend. He unknowingly pushed me as I tried to emerge as the best pitcher in our graduating class. Either way, his innocent lie on that track was a blessing—my competitive spirit burned and it fueled me to work harder.

Later that winter, after I had made it through fall cuts (a few players were let go) and was safely on the team, I starting to get a little more comfortable in workouts. One day in our badly-dated weight room, a plank contest broke out. Guys were challenging each other, and I faced off with Brian, who had become my throwing partner during the fall. In the center of the long, narrow weight room, white power racks lining one side with benches and machines lining the other, we got down on our toes and elbows. I often felt overshadowed by Brian, as he was taller, threw a bit harder and was a recruited pitcher on scholarship. I hated feeling like I was the shorter, slower-throwing, non-scholarship version of him. He was more graceful in team agility drills and earned more respect from the upperclassmen. But in that weight room, planking on the dingy, unpadded carpet, I decided I could even the score.

"Okay, ready? Start!" We were off as our official held a stopwatch, keeping time and giving us updates. "One minute!…two minutes!… three minutes!…four minutes!" We finally reached the five minute milestone in our contest, neither of us wavering. I'd glanced up at him periodically, my head just a few inches away from his, to check his resolve. I had made my mind up that if I had lasted *this* long, I could last another five seconds. Then, I'd last another five seconds. And after that? Five more seconds. I was *not* going to quit. My strange 19-year-old brain decided that intimidation was in order, to make sure that he knew what *I* knew. I looked up at him and gave a battle-cry, a loud *Ahhhhhhhh!* that only lacked a chest-pounding for full effect. A few minutes later, when he gave in and collapsed to the ground, I was vindicated—it was the first time I was better at him at anything. And of course, years later we discussed that infamous plank contest.

"Blewett. When you screamed at me during that plank contest freshman year…you know how weird that was, right?" I laughed.

"Yeah, I feel a little embarrassed about it now. But it obviously worked—you quit a little bit later."

"I did; we planked for a long time. But I just kept thinking the whole time after you screamed in my face…what was *wrong* with this guy?"

Maybe I had a screw or two loose, but really I was just changing, growing into my work ethic and new reputation as a guy who hit it hard in the weight room. Learning the lifts was exciting as I started to grow bigger and stronger with each passing week. It continued to take time, but I was making progress and I vowed to not waste a single day.

I was one of the last pitchers on the depth chart as a freshman—if not *the* last—but I never dwelled on it. I knew who the upper class starters were, the five guys who would eat up most of the innings. I also knew who threw harder than me and all those basic details that a baboon could figure out. Yet I refused to acknowledge that any of these guys were better than I, at least in a permanent sense. They currently possessed a level of skill that I didn't, but the idea that they were *better*? *Better* felt too permanent, too absolute. At best, they were better *today*.

I closed the gap by working hard on the field, in the weight room, and doing pitching drills and shoulder exercises in my apartment at night. I was running my own race, not much paying attention to those who were beside me or behind me. For those in front, they were still merely stepping stones on the way to an even brighter, even more distant future. There was never a time when I wanted to *be* one of them —I always believed that inside me was a greatness no one else had. The way I saw it, the future was up for grabs and it was up to me how fast it got here. My eyes were set on the day when I'd finally be the best version of myself. The thing was, though, that I didn't really know how to accomplish that. I didn't know how to do, well, much of anything.

I first wanted to know what I could do to make my results in the weight room come faster. To do this, I stood in Coach Cantor's doorway as he scribbled out workouts on plain white paper with a felt-tipped black marker.

"Hey Coach."

"Blew-it what do you need?" He glanced up and then right back down at the workout he was creating.

"Well, I have a few questions. Do you have a minute?"

"No. But, go ahead."

Every time I approached Coach Cantor, he would yell at me for disturbing him, trying to get me to go away. I came to learn that he didn't really want me to leave, and I never went away. He had a packed bookshelf that contained pretty much every book on strength and conditioning in existence.

"What should I be eating to maximize my workouts? I've heard about whey protein, but I don't know anything about it." He looked up, then pointed to his bookshelf.

"There's a book over there—it's got a red spine; do you see it? Give it to me." I grabbed it and handed it to him. He leafed through it before extending it to me.

"Go home and read this. When you're done with it, bring it back." So, I did. A week later, I returned.

"Hey Coach."

"BLEW-IT! WHAT DO YOU NEED?" I handed the book back to him.

"I don't want this! Put it back on my shelf." I did as I was told.

"The book was helpful. I ordered some whey protein and some maltodextrin to mix with it for a post-workout shake. I'm also thinking of taking fish oil—the book said it was something athletes could take to recover faster from workouts. Do you think that's true?"

"Absolutely. I take 10 grams of fish oil every day," he replied.

"Okay," I said. "I also wanted to work out on days when the team doesn't have official lifting. Could you write me extra workouts?" He agreed to write me two additional workouts each week.

"I also want to run on my own an extra day or two. Is there a book you'd recommend?" Once again, he pointed at his shelf. I slipped out one book, then another, then another. He sent me home with five different books that day as he explained who wrote them, what they were about, and how they'd help me. Twenty training, pitching and nutrition books later...I was making progress faster than ever. My clock was ticking slower and I was gaining on the upperclassmen faster.

A day didn't go by without a "BLEWETT!" bellowing from Coach's lungs. I didn't get mad and I didn't feel slighted, nor did I really care that he singled me out. Rather, I just complied with his orders as he barked them and did my best to remember proper technique before every set and every rep. Even as a junior when I was leading the pack in conditioning drills, he'd get on me to run faster; I decided I'd win by a bigger margin rather than complain. Other guys found him abrasive and dismissed his advice, but one thing was abundantly clear to me: whether it was a book, a public tongue-whipping or a rare bit of encouragement, he always gave me what I needed.

Entering my first spring season, I had transformed from that 172lb kid into a 185lb man, and was excited to see if my velocity had climbed. In our road series against the College of William & Mary, toward the end of the year, I had a strong relief appearance—I came in under the lights and shut the door in a sharp inning of work. After the game, Coach J told me that—according to his internal radar gun—I had thrown fastballs that he believed were around 85 mph. I took him at his word, excited that my typical 80 or so was finally ticking upward. Against Delaware in the final homestand of the season, one of our pitchers sat in the stands behind a scout with a radar gun. He reported back to me afterward that my fastball sat at 84-87...87! It was a big number only three measly miles per hour away from 90, that magical milestone that every pitcher dreamt of. I was intoxicated by the feeling that I could control my destiny. I went home that summer vowing to get even stronger, even bigger, and to put in harder, longer running workouts. It felt like I was an overnight success, even though it was far from the truth.

That next fall, entering my sophomore year after a productive summer, I came back throwing even harder—86 to 89 miles per hour. I hit my first 90 the following year, then my first 91 shortly thereafter. I was suddenly one of *those* pitchers—guys who threw 90—mythical creatures who, when I was younger, always seemed to walk taller and wore the fancy Oakley sunglasses that I never had. *Those* guys were special. Yet somehow, I had become one.

Jon, the thing I learned was this—life is easy when your destiny is within your grasp, when outcomes are controllable. I found my spark that night at Harford Community College, and every hour in the weight room, on the track, and in my basement doing pitching drills yielded a consistently measurable, tangible result. Who *wouldn't* work hard when the payoff was clear? When there's an observable ratio of work to payoff, any rabbit would put in the effort, knowing for certain that they'll get their carrot. Even though the physical effort was exhausting and the hours long, it was easy compared to the alternative: working without knowing if there would ever be a payoff. I had many, many harder years and it was the helplessness, the uncontrollable injuries and the waiting game that reminded me how easy it was to put in healthy hard work. I never trained harder than when I was in college, but life was also never easier.

When you and I met, you were a 130lb, 5'2" 13-year-old who loved catching baseballs more than perhaps anyone I'd ever met. When I was preparing for pro ball that year in 2015, your hand shot up when I asked around for a catcher. *But you're just a little kid...*I thought to myself. *I'm gonna break your thumb with my curveball...*"Don't worry about Jonny," your dad said. "He's never caught pitching that fast before, but he can do it." Your crazy dad was right, and you blew me away with your ability at such a young age.

Yet, that was easy for you—thats who you are. What *wasn't* easy was years later, when you were almost 17 and still only 5'6" and 140lbs. You waited in agony for a growth spurt that was years overdue. No matter the work you put in, no college scout could see past your lack of size. "Nice receiver—good actions behind the plate, but he's too small." Your teammates hit their growth spurts and got their college offers. Not you. You had to wait til the bitter end. It was completely beyond your control, completely unfair and hard for all of us to watch as it ate you alive. But it finally happened, and you shot up. It was a little late, but you punched your ticket and your foot's in the door. Now—as a 6'2", 210lb 18-year-old—the results will start to pour in.

You paid your dues and stuck it out and now your destiny is squarely in your hands. The hard part is over. All you have to do now is keep being you. It's about to get fun.

Dear Jim, I was pious.

Though I was eager to be away from the nest, at times it was difficult growing up so far away from home. When you first brought your eldest grandson to my academy in Bloomington, seeking the baseball-specific training I had to offer, you were merely a client. Yet, when I found myself in need of business advice, I sought you—the honorable Judge Jim. From then on, I always found you in my corner providing sound, objective advice. One of our bonds is a shared love of words. Whenever I think of festooning a house for a party or bloviating on my soapbox about pitching, I'll think back to our conversations about English, philosophy, religion and life.

Pious has been one of my favorite words since I learned it in college while reading *Euthyphro*, the well-known Socratic dialogue written by the philosopher, Plato. *Euthyphro* was the story of a conversation between Socrates—who was jailed for being a poor servant to the Gods—and Euthyphro, who had brought charges against his own father for murder of a servant. The two discussed the nature of why the Gods loved certain deeds and despised others. The very acts that we deem as "good" and "holy"—were they good because the Gods approved of them, or did the Gods approve of them because they were good? For me as a college sophomore, this chicken or the egg debate about the nature of piety was—to put it lightly—confusing. To be pious means to be devoutly religious, dutiful and loyal. In baseball, we know that there are certain unwritten rules, ways of acting and playing the game that definitely fall within the scope of being pious or impious to the Baseball Gods. The Baseball Gods favor those who hustle, and send bad luck to those who don't. And if we want to stay in the good graces of the Baseball Gods…we better at least understand who they are and what they look for. And so I can't think of a better person with whom to discuss this topic than one of my favorite scholars.

I was playing summer baseball following my junior year of college, pitching for a team in a Washington D.C. suburb called the Silver Spring-Takoma Thunderbolts. John Duffy—known as "Duff"—was my coach, and he was a *baseball guy* if there ever was one. In his mid-30s, he was only a few years removed from his last game as a player. Duff oozed baseball savvy, probably because in his day he was one of the least physically talented pitchers in any bullpen. He was open with us about his playing career, and when we had down time we'd pick his brain for little stories and snippets of his life. On the first day of team activities, with all of us gathered around in the outfield, he introduced himself:

> "Alright, so in a minute we'll go around and I want everyone to introduce themselves. But as manager, I'll go first." He raised his left hand high as he began: "I'm John Duffy; originally hail from Audubon, Pennsylvania; I was a left-handed reliever in my day; attended the University of Richmond and graduated with a double-major in Finance and Economics. I also went back and got my MBA in Finance. After college, I was signed by the Boston Red Sox and played one year in their Minor League system, after which I went on to play independent baseball, retiring after nine seasons. I played for Thunder Bay, Allentown, Bridgeport, Fargo, Atlantic City, Somerset, Sioux City and got to see a lot of the country playing baseball, something I'm very grateful for."

Duff was a guy who kept coming back even after being released countless times, and who would find a way to stick with a team and win games. He bounced around with numerous clubs until he was 31 years old. Standing 6'2" tall with wide shoulders, a rounded jaw and salt and pepper hair, he earned a very peculiar nickname in college —"the pink bunny." One day just as we were walking back from running pre-game poles, we complained about how much running, well, *sucked*. It was within earshot of Duff and he couldn't resist jumping in the conversation.

"What do you guys have to do at your schools for conditioning when you get back? Do they give you a running test?"

"Yeah," I replied. "We have to do a timed mile-and-a-half, sometimes a three-mile; it just depends on our coach's mood, I guess."

"What's the time limit?"

"Usually 10 minutes for the mile-and-a-half or 24 minutes for the three-mile."

"Oh man! That's it? You guys have it easy! Back when I was at Richmond, we had to run two miles in 12 minutes or less. If guys failed, they'd have to keep running it until they finally broke 12 minutes." My buddy and I both made a *yuck* face.

"That's pretty fast," I replied. "I'm a pretty decent runner and I think that would be pushing it for me. A six-minute mile is *movin'*."

Duff scoffed. He was tall with long legs, but never struck me as much of a runner.

"You guys know why they called me the *pink bunny?*" We shook our heads.

"At my best, I ran back-to-back five-minute miles...crushed the team running test." He reiterated: "Back-to-back five-minute miles." They said I was like the Energizer bunny, and my face gets bright red when I exercise—it's the Irish in me. I'd take off ahead of the rest of the team whenever we had conditioning, and they'd yell at me *there goes the pink bunny!*"

Duff spoke with a moderate Pennsylvania accent, drawing out his words ever so slightly and using the turn of phrase "jammed up" way too often. If your car broke down and you couldn't make it to dinner on time, you were *jammed up*. If you were low on money and couldn't make next month's rent, you were *jammed up*. And if you picked a fight you couldn't finish...you were definitely *jammed up*.

He lacked that shiny, proper veneer that was common to all my former coaches. Duff wasn't offensive, but also didn't take crap from anybody. Though he maintained absolute power and none of us would dare cross him or break team rules, we were comfortable asking him personal questions about his playing days.

"Hey Duff—what was your favorite place you played?"

"Fargo. Up there, the Redhawks [Fargo's team] are basically the Yankees—people love the team, they get big crowds and you get treated like royalty. I had a great host family, this couple that set me up with basically my own basement apartment. Everything about Fargo was first class, the team was always good and they cared about winning."

"What kind of pitcher were you?"

"I was basically what they'd now call a lefty-specialist. I'd come in and get lefties out or pitch to two hitters in a tight spot. I could pitch every day of the week and they always needed guys who could do that, so I always had a job. If they asked me to pitch, *I pitched*—and I was proud of that."

In my first season playing for Duff, I was finishing rehab from a partially torn UCL and was barely useful. My elbow and I were like a bickering old couple with relationship problems. I'd go out and work all day to give him more pitching velocity, but that very velocity left him constantly cranky and hurting. It was the second time I had a partial tear of the UCL in my pitching elbow (the first being back in high school) and this time it had all but killed my junior season. The only bright side was that as an injured player for the T-Bolts, I got to spend a lot of time in the dugout watching the game and absorbing Duffyisms.

When one of our pitchers made a clutch pitch to get out of an inning: "You see that guys!? That's how you do it [he clapped as the team streamed back into the dugout]—*that's* pitching—showing them who's got the bigger pair."

When we lost but played well: "I'm proud of you guys; you went out and competed your balls off today. We came up a little short, but baseball is a game of details, of inches, of little mistakes. If we keep doing the right things, the Baseball Gods will reward us."

And when the conversation moved to our personal lives: "We're a family. If you guys ever need something, if you're ever in trouble, if you're ever jammed up…you call me."

He'd talk about how we had to puff our chests out and dig deep as players. He explained how important mental toughness was, how conducting ourselves like professionals was *everything*, and how baseball was a game that had to be respected, played the *right* way. Because I was more of a bench coach than a player, I took his word as gospel and started—for the first time—to really *think*. I was never a dumb player, but I had never been challenged to mentally navigate my way through a game. My baseball IQ slowly began to increase.

It was Duff who first mentioned the Baseball Gods. One day, an umpire made a horrific call that cost our squad an out that led to two runs scoring. It was an egregious error, an unthinkably bad call. "Safe!? Are you kidding me!? You can't ask for help!?" The umpire stood by his pathetic decision as Duff challenged him, asking in an oddly calm yet still aggressive manner, how he could make such a dumbfounding, terrible call. The very next inning we threatened, advancing runners to second and third with two outs. The game was getting late and we needed those runs back *now*. Our right-handed hitter at the plate was battling for his life until he finally made contact, a loud wooden *THOCK* sending a not-gonna-get-the-job-done routine ground ball bouncing toward the shortstop. As if on cue, the Baseball Gods intervened.

On maybe the sixth bounce—as it just entered the dirt—the ball hit a tiny rock, vaulting into the air over the charging shortstop's left shoulder. It trickled into left field as both runners sprinted home. We in the dugout cheered as our boys scored and cruised in for high-fives. Duff—with a huge smile on his face—shot over to all of us: "You see that!? Do things the right way and the Baseball Gods will come through for ya!" It was very good timing indeed, though I wasn't sure how the Baseball Gods changed the physics of a bouncing ball. Fearing they could read my dissenting thoughts and would smite us, I took it back and doled out more high fives.

As the season wore on, we heard more and more about how the Baseball Gods rewarded hard-nosed players who played the game the right way. Those who put in the work, hustled, ran out ground balls and treated their coaches, teammates and umpires with respect were rewarded with the lions share of good luck. Baseball is a sport fraught with luck—both good and bad—and so any sensible player would want to be in the good graces of the Baseball Gods. Yet, a question remains: what exactly does piety look like in our nation's pastime?

To be pious, again, is to be devout—to be faithful, to do things that are pleasing, honorable and noble in the context of one's religion or God. Piety in the eyes of the Baseball Gods, however, is a bit different. Annie Savoy, the main female character from the legendary baseball movie *Bull Durham,* believed in the church of baseball above all others.

To Annie, piety was supporting the team—rain or shine—and taking care of players in a way that lifted their spirits. She hoped to help them break out of slumps and appreciate baseball for all the little things it provided. For players and coaches, piety is perhaps best understood as the embodiment of three major qualities: hustle, grit, and diligence. Baseball is hard, and these three qualities are equalizers.

I learned firsthand how amazing Lou Gehrig and Cal Ripken Jr's consecutive games played streaks were, only after I played a 140-game season myself. Every pro ballplayer walks out onto the field despite nagging aches and pains, awful nights of sleep on overnight bus rides, blazing hot sun and draining mental fatigue. But to never miss a single game…for well over a decade? Unbelievable. Unthinkable. Gehrig and Ripken showed tremendous grit, doing whatever it took to suit up every single day. The Baseball Gods were pleased—a game of baseball is precious and should never be wasted.

Hustle—the aggressive, competitive pursuit of the next base, the ground ball in the hole, the ball in the gap—hustle is really what embodies the spirit of baseball. It's the burning, competitive will to win that drove people like Jackie Robinson to run at 110% no matter the score or situation. He hustled because his team needed it, because the fans demanded it, and because he believed in it. The will to outcompete his opponents and prove himself to his detractors drove him to sprint with every available fiber in his being. Hustle is a special quality that is too often ignored or thrown by the wayside by young players who don't understand how much of a separator it can be. A player who never gives up, never gives in, and sacrifices his body on every play can—and often does—change the outcome of a game.

Then there's *diligence*—the willingness to put in the tedious daily physical and mental work that is required to not be crushed by the weight of the game. Slumps abound in baseball, and thus staying positive, keeping a routine and staying "within" oneself is critically important. Mental diligence—to one's craft, one's strengths and one's weaknesses—is as important as the physical work. When a player tries too hard, attempts to force success, gets down on himself or tears down others during a time of struggle, he loses his way and the game swallows him whole. But when a player arrives at the ballpark early, learns who he is as a player, hones his craft on a daily basis with focus and open-mindedness, helps his teammates along, and puts in the work to stay healthy and physically prepared…the Baseball Gods smile and reward him. A few more bloopers fall in for diligent hitters and a few more borderline strikes go in favor of a diligent pitcher. The Baseball Gods want us to succeed. Or so I thought…

That season, Duff and the Baseball Gods both watched as I methodically rehabbed my elbow with dedication and care in hopes of being back on the field better than ever. I wanted to make good use of my injury time and repair problems that would have gone unfixed had I been pitching every day. Just as I hoped, I arrived back on campus that fall in great, healthy shape. I was throwing harder than ever—creeping above 90 for the first time and impressing MLB teams who came to scout the squad. The sun was shining on me and I approached the next season excited to perhaps hear my name called in the MLB draft.

The following year, however, I suffered another big blow—my third career UCL tear, this one at the very end of the season in the conference tournament. I was pitching in front of a lot of scouts, and had to walk off the mound in front of them. My doctor, however was still optimistic about rehab—he thought I could again avoid surgery. This time, however, his diagnosis came with a warning:

"Let's give this one more shot. I don't think your ligament is completely torn, so we can try rehab again. But—if you have *any* pain at all during the return-to-throwing program, it'll be time to go ahead with surgery."

I called Duff and broke the news. He picked up the call with what was apparently my nickname...

"Dangerous Dan Blewett, how are ya?"

"Eh, not great. I wanted to give you an update since we last spoke. I know you heard about the game, but I finally saw the doctor."

"And?

"He thinks I can rehab again. It's a good thing—don't get me wrong —but I'm gonna be Coach Blewett again for a while this summer—I'll need to do my throwing program and rehab, but it's going to be a while before I can pitch."

"Don't worry about that," he said. "Just come back and you can rehab with T-Bolt Nation like you did last year. When you're ready to get in a game, we'll get you in a game."

"Alright. Thanks Duff, I'll see you in a few weeks."

Over a month later, June reared its head and I was a few weeks into my rehab program. I could tell that my elbow wasn't right. As I threw one afternoon in Alexandria, Virginia, Matt, one of my tall, right-handed teammates, asked me how rehab was going.

"It's going okay. I've done this a bunch before, but something just feels different this time."

"Like, it hurts? What do you mean?" I looked away from him to catch the throw coming in from my partner in the outfield.

"It's not really pain, it just feels loose. When I throw longer distances or really let one go, there's a looseness in my elbow that really weirds me out. It doesn't hurt, but it feels like the bones are spreading apart. It's hard to describe." I stepped and made my long throw into the outfield.

"Well hopefully it gets better. You look like you're throwing it well; you're up to what [he looked into the outfield toward my catch partner]...180 feet now?"

"Yeah. I'm about ready to jump on the mound. Honestly, I'm pretty nervous about it because of this. But, we'll see."

A few days later I started throwing off the mound again, and after a few weeks of that I was ready for my first game. I had gotten through those bullpen sessions okay, but I still had to test it in games. Would I be alright?

I can still smell the air from that humid evening. It rained just a few hours before we arrived and the outfield grass had a thick, somewhat sweet bouquet. We were playing at the University of Maryland's ballpark and Duff and I agreed that I'd make my appearance in one of the middle innings. Sure enough, in the sixth, I was told to get hot and hopefully bail our first reliever out of trouble. I knew that I had to be honest with myself and let go; holding back wouldn't tell me what I needed to know. I warmed up quickly in my white baseball pants, royal blue jersey and blue cap. With each throw my arm inched closer to full speed. After throwing about a dozen fastballs as hard as I could, my elbow started to itch. Sweat dripped down my brow as I looked up at the clouds, barely visible in the navy blue sky.

I ignored it and continued to throw. The itch became an ache; the ache became slight pain; the slight pain became concerning pain. As the umpire ran down the left-field line to wave me into the game, I made peace with my career:

This might be it. This might be the end. You can't. hold. back.

...Please, just let me get through this.

I took a deep breath, flipped the ball to a teammate and jogged toward the mound as the sky inched just a little bit more black. I didn't want to admit it, but I knew what was about to happen. I promised myself, though, that no matter what went down, I would leave it all out on the field.

If this is it, we're going down swinging.

The last pitch of your career...it can not. be. scared.

If any single pitch left my fingertips with pain, it was over—I'd be going under the knife and no one knew if I'd ever pitch competitively again. I agreed with the voice: On that mound in College Park, I would put on my toughest mask and let it eat.

As I stood on that tall, tan mound, the Maryland campus looming majestically beyond the brick ballpark, nothing was the same. Familiar adrenaline flooded my veins, and the plate appeared to still be but 60 feet, six inches away. However, the umpire wore a black cloak I hadn't noticed before; the hitter swung a sickle as he prepared to time my fastball from the on-deck circle. Fear set in. The reaper had been waiting…and I was trapped.

I flicked my mitt upward to the catcher, signaling my first fastball. I kicked and delivered. As that first pitch left my hand, I decided that the Baseball Gods didn't exist. I had been pious—I worked as hard as anyone I knew and deserved to pitch healthy. Throughout my career—despite making huge leaps and bounds in ability—I kept succumbing to illness or injury, culminating on that mound in College Park. As my fastball tracked down the catcher's mitt, sharp pain shot deep into my elbow. I looked up at the sky and let out a deep, deflating breath.

The bases were loaded and there was no one out. Duff hadn't intended for me to enter a messy inning, but the previous reliever gave up four singles in a span of about seven pitches, so it had to be dealt with. There I was—just a few pitches in—wanting desperately to get back off that mound. With each pitch I threw, the pain intensified.

Do not let up. This could be your last day on this mound. Do NOT let up.
The voice was getting angry.
You're not going out like a coward. You're NOT a coward.

I again obliged and stomped on the gas, asking for more of what felt like a screwdriver being jammed into my loose, unstable elbow. Mercifully, the hitter swung, and as I watched his pop up rise high into foul territory on the first base side, I cursed at it to stay fair. *Please, please…drift back.* Alas, no—it bounced just out of reach in the bleachers. Ugh. *God—that couldn't have just blown back in? A few feet?* I rolled my eyes. A few pitches later, still hoping for a miracle, I somehow got a swing and miss, recording a strikeout for the first out of the inning. Now with one out, a mere ground ball could end it via the double play.

It wasn't just pain that hindered me at that point—I had no command whatsoever. So the gameplan was just, well, heave the ball as hard as I could, hoping the hitter would just beat it into the ground. Somehow, the next hitter did exactly that—the righty hit an absolute missile one-hopper at our shortstop, who promptly picked it and started an easy double play. Jams in baseball are funny like that sometimes—everyone in the ballpark is tense, biting their nails on the edge of their seat. Then, with one pitch—just like *that*—it's over. I appreciated the good luck on the scorched line drive, but there was little joy in getting out of that inning. That jam was all I had left.

I walked to that dugout slower than I ever had, perhaps savoring my time between the lines, or perhaps trying to further delay the inevitable. I sat down in the dugout and put my hands behind my head. Duff walked over and asked how it felt. Mentally exhausted, I glanced up at him out of the corner of my left eye—it was the only answer he needed. "That bad, huh?" I nodded. *That* bad.

Why did Duff speak of the Baseball Gods so highly? Why did he give them any praise at all? He saw what was happening to me, a good kid who tried his hardest. How could they let that happen? I had been diligent. I gritted through a lot of hard times and was a good teammate through it all. I hustled on and off the field and went down swinging on the mound. I gave it my all. But still, the Baseball Gods just watched, complicit, as I called my doctor and scheduled the end of my baseball career. With infinite power to intervene, they just watched.

A few days later, as I started looking at my fate through a new lens, I thought maybe—just maybe—there was something bigger in store for a 5'11", right-handed walk-on from a school no one ever heard of. Maybe, the Baseball Gods knew something that I didn't.

Dear Keller, Grow tall.

It was a really happy day watching my sister get married. She was as smiley as I've ever seen her, making googly eyes at my now brother in-law, Ryan. Ryan's tough to get a smile out of…except when he's around my sister. Watching those two was the highlight of my day. In a close second, however, was playing ball with you and your little brother. It was a wedding, after all, so we improvised, using a balled-up table napkin and some scotch tape. The tape didn't hold real well, but we made do. Though uncle JD has watched you and Tyce grow up, I've been traveling the country and only get the cliff notes from your mom. She says you continue to develop into quite the pitcher and I've seen video that proves it.

You're going to grow up into a vastly different sports world than I did and baseball is changing more rapidly than ever. Some of the changes are good and others…not so much. As you, Tyce and I played our made-up game, all of us in suits, I was reminded both how innocent the game is and how much it changes as we age. I'll always want to slip away from a crowd to play pick-up napkinball—it's infinitely better than doing grownup things. My childhood friend, Kevin, and I played every day after school and never got tired of it. We made it what we wanted and it never felt like work. Later though, as organized baseball became more serious and I was no longer a child, having success at the game was what made it fun. Yet, it began to feel like work.

As I worked toward my goals as a ballplayer, I started to figure out what kind of player I was and who I might become. I watched older players strut around, confident, and wondered if I'd ever feel the same way. Lots of people helped guide me in the right direction, but I still felt…small. Would I ever feel like one of those big, tough players in a leadership position? In trying to make sense of it all I learned one lesson that unified all the others and carried me further than I could have without it. You've got a little brother to look out for, to teach and help along. To do all of that, you'll first have to learn who *you* are. Once you do, you'll provide for him and so many others in your life just by being the best version of Keller. You won't have to try, you'll just *be*.

When I was a junior in college, our team hired a new pitching coach named Tim O'Brien. Tim loves baseball more than almost anyone I'd ever met and came to the ballpark each day with a smile on his face, ready equally to coach us up and learn from us. To Tim, working with a new player is like a zoologist discovering a new species—it both excites him and inspires looks of awe. Even though he's worked with thousands of players spanning multiple decades, he maintains the position that each of us is unique and capable of teaching him new things about pitching, hitting and baseball as a whole. With a salt-and-pepper mustache, a lanky build and sloping shoulders, Tim made deep eye contact and listened as if you were giving him the combination to the vault at Fort Knox. When working on new techniques, his signature question was *how did that feel?* He wanted to know exactly *everything* about the new drill or movement we were collectively trying to learn. And when a player would go off and come back—returning from an event, season, or other type of learning experience—his question would be, *what did you learn?* He'd then put his elbow on the table and install his chin to his fist as he eagerly awaited the answer, dug-in and ready to listen. The man is a sponge.

When I turned pro, he came out to a handful of games each season. He had a glimmer in his eye when at the ballpark, much like the little kids that ran over seeking autographs. Tim didn't need an autograph, but he did come prepared with the same question in hand: *what did you learn?* We'd grab a bite to eat and catch up but it was always a one-sided conversation in the exact opposite of most—Tim didn't want to talk about Tim, he just wanted to know what wisdom I'd acquired.

"What was it like playing for a manager who won a World Series?"

"What's the difference between hitters at this level compared to last year?"

"Has your approach on the mound changed at all?"

"Are you staying healthy? How's the arm?"

Then, like an effective worker bee, he'd take it back to the hive and share with the players he coached. If he could find a new way to approach an old, persistent problem, then he was on the right track to help his team get better and win more games. If there was one overarching answer to Tim's signature question it was this: I learned that I had to deeply understand and become the best version of myself. Only then could I maximize my efforts and my potential.

Everyone wants to fit into a mold—we don't want to stick out and we don't want to be different...that is, until we *want* to be noticed. When we suddenly find it impossible to get noticed by being ourselves, we feel helpless. We doubt our ability and depart from the very things that brought us near the spotlight in the first place. The old adage is, *dance with who brung you.* It means simply, what got you here is good enough now that you *are* here. Don't change at the last minute; stick with what's been working. This is much, much easier said than done.

Though the philosophy department was small, I was only close with one of my professors, a man named Dr. Roye Templeton. He was a tall, light-skinned African-American man with a lanky build and a booming, forceful voice. He always reminded me a little bit of Muhammad Ali. As far as I knew, I was the only athlete who majored in philosophy. I kept mostly to myself, rarely raising my hand in class or contributing to discussions. I didn't really know why I was a philosophy major, nor did I feel like I fit in. Mostly I just sat and listened, internalizing and trying to make sense of the dense, difficult reading as best I could. Dr. Templeton only lectured for 30 of the allotted 50 minutes. One day, after a typically short class, I stopped at his lectern after other students had departed. I had a question.

"Hey, Dr. Templeton."

"Hey, Dan! How are things going? You're a baseball player, right?'

"Yeah, I am." I wore my baseball jacket a little too often to class, like most of us arrogant athletes. "And I actually had a question about that —do you think the mindset of the Samurai can apply to baseball players?"

He looked me deep in the eye. "Absolutely."

Over time, Dr. Templeton and I developed a rapport. I took more and more of his classes, and occasionally began meeting him in his office to talk sports and philosophy. He taught lots of subjects, but as a lifelong student of the martial arts, it was clear that his classes on the philosophy of sports and of the Far East were his passion. I had been assigned a dozen books written for these ancient warriors, including the *Art of War, Tao Te Ching, Hagakure, The Book of Five Rings,* and *The Unfettered Mind.* They spoke directly to me as an athlete, though I still felt I needed approval to use them for baseball. I sought his help in clarifying them. He and I would discuss the teachings of the Samurai and how it pertained to both our lives. One day I sat in his office on a pedestrian afternoon, hoping to learn a thing or two that could help me stop pitching so darn badly.

"We've talked about the concept of Wu Wei in class. Do you remember it?" I nodded that I did as he continued.

"Wu Wei is *non-action*. And through non-action, we create our best performances in all walks of life. What the Samurai knew—all too well —was that if they pressed, if they tried, if they fixed their mind on their opponents sword or their response to it...well, that would be *it* for them. The sword was so fast that if they had to think to act, it was too late."

"So it's about letting the mind go and just reacting?" I asked.

"That's right. You don't *try* to act. And by not forcing action, you let your body take over and do what it knows how to do, what you've trained it to do."

"That's one of the hardest things about pitching, something I struggle with. I feel myself at times trying to control my motion to make sure everything is perfect. I feel how it tenses me up and it only makes things worse. Some of my hardest, cleanest fastballs come on 3-0 counts when I know the hitter isn't swinging. I just relax and the ball comes out faster—it's really weird, I'll throw 89 on a 1-2 count and 91 on 3-0." Dr. Templeton leaned forward.

"*That* is a perfect example. Your body knows what to do. So let it do it! When you have a mindset of non-action—of Wu Wei—right action appears because the mind isn't interfering with the body."

As an athlete, it takes a long time and a lot of failure for it to become abundantly clear what you are, and what you are *not*. The same is true for any occupation or walk of life. We can't do it all and though we learn from others, we can't always imitate successful people with any kind of success ourselves. We all have to use our own machete, blazing our own path while walking our own pace. Even as we learn from mentors and peers, it remains difficult figuring out which bits of wisdom we can use and how we can best use them. In the forest, what's food for one animal is poison for another. We have to keep trying new things, discarding what doesn't work, and re-evaluating in hopes of understanding each new version of ourselves.

Two years later, I was in Dr. Templeton's office during summer session, this time to break bad news.

"Hey, Dan! What's new? How you doin?"

"Eh. Not great. I mentioned a month ago how I hurt my elbow and how I thought I might still be able to rehab it. Rehab didn't work...I'm scheduled for surgery on August 25th.

"So what does the timeline look like?"

"Well, a lot of pitchers seem to be back in games in a year, sometimes a little less. But with the season ending in May, I'd need to be back in nine months to have a chance to pitch at all. I think if I work really hard maybe I can do it, but it doesn't look good. It might be the end."

Dr. Templeton, leaning forward in his burgundy office chair, took a deep breath and looked down, mulling over his response. He spoke deliberately or not at all, and this was no exception—it was clear he was choosing the *right* words. Finally, he looked back up at me and in a very direct but understanding tone, presented words that I would carry for the rest of my life:

"A resolute man will find a way."

His eye contact and projection of the words was very precise; he didn't just *say* the words, he *gave* them to me—in the same way an aging warrior might bequeath his sword to a worthy young apprentice. We sat there in silence for a moment as I took yet another internal step toward my eventual comeback. Dr. Templeton didn't need to elaborate or explain; those seven words were enough, and they applied no matter the situation. I'd find a way back from surgery and into pro baseball, even though I'd miss the draft. All of us have a remarkable ability to adapt, re-imagine and re-invent ourselves. Much of the time, though, it's not outright re-invention that drives us forward. Rather, it's a deeper, more profound understanding of parts of us that we didn't comprehend before. It's digging deep into every last line of the instruction manual to find one more button to press, one more obscure function we didn't know we had.

To successfully come back from the surgery that awaited—to shed my old skin and heal up after surgery—I had to become more in tune with who I was, what made me successful in the past, and perhaps things that were unknown or unrealized before. I had to extract every bit of my potential to keep going, to catch up as I lost ground to my peers. As we climb the ladder, we're challenged more by this unique task—fully squeezing every last drop of ability and translating it into wins on the field, on the court, or in life.

Dr. Templeton and I sat a little while longer and I began to talk about how I'd grown up in my time on campus.

"You know, it's weird—when I was a freshman four years ago, I looked up to the upperclassmen. They looked so confident and in-charge and I wondered if I'd ever feel the same way. Here I am—the same age as they were—and I don't feel that way at all. I still feel mostly the same as I did then." I paused for a moment as I glanced out the window.

"I know that I do all the same things they did. I know I set a good example for the freshman now, and I probably *am* the same as the guys I looked up to. But, I don't feel the way I always assumed they did. They looked so confident and strong; they were leaders. I know that I am those things, but I don't *feel it.*"

In Dr. Templeton's class on the martial arts, a good portion of the reading was allegorical poetry, written on the tenets of Taoism. I liked Taoism, because its principles were simple: live the way of nature—flow though life's events quietly, calmly, without forcing things to happen. Live as if you're a leaf floating down a creek—go where the water takes you and revel in the freedom of powerlessness. After internalizing what I said, he responded:

"Think of the oak tree. The oak provides shade, food, clean air and shelter to all the animals in the forest. Does it try to do all of that? Heck no! Just by being itself, it provides so much to so many." I exhaled. He continued.

"You've set an example for others, you've put in the work and you've shown how a player can rise from the bottom to the top. You don't have to try to be a leader; your teammates have already seen your example. Just be yourself and you'll become whatever you're meant to become. Just remember the oak tree. It doesn't try to be what it is, *it just is.* In being itself, others benefit."

Much of the philosophy I read and contemplated was hard to make sense of. Sometimes, it was because the concepts were just so…*out there.* Other times—as was the case with Dr. Templeton's words and the Taoist literature he loved to share—it was the simplicity of the message that was hard to make sense of. Was I supposed to stop being ambitious? Should I sit at home instead of pushing myself to train harder and do more? What did it truly mean to float down the creek of life? I couldn't just wait for things to happen, could I? Wouldn't life just pass me by? Wasn't a strong work ethic a *good* thing?

It took almost 10 more years to figure it out, but in the end it was a matter of collecting little pieces of knowledge about who I was. Finally, the broad but simple concept became clear: if I knew myself, I could maximize myself. When Tim would ask, "what did you learn?" I'd reply with more things I came to know for certain I was either good at or *not* good at. In 2012, I began writing email updates home to my family and friends. I called the series of 60 emails *You're My Boy, Blew*, a reference to a line in the movie *Old School*. It felt fitting because those emails were read by the people who cared about me most. What I didn't realize, though, was that they'd become a time capsule of my growth over the years, the way I changed and adapted.

When you know yourself—both as an athlete and person—you'll know where to apply your effort so that it has maximum effect. Then, tackling the obstacles that pop up becomes easy—like the leaf flowing mindlessly down a creek. When you know your process, you trust and apply it whenever a new challenge comes. We can't try to be someone else. In trying to become more than we are, we become *less*. Whether or not we grow into a tall oak tree isn't something we can decide. When a Cherry Blossom tree tries to grow into an oak, it sets itself up for failure. Though it will never be as tall or as wide, one can put on a beautiful display that an oak could never match.

As athletes rise through the ranks, the gap between them narrows. The intangibles, however—the inner strength, the confidence, the focus, the professionalism—those things speak ever louder. They bring the previously invisible up above the crowd, making a difference when there are few to go around. Those with silent strength, who compete and accept failure, who show an eagerness to acquire knowledge of self—they grow taller and taller in a crowded forest.

Dear Baseball Gods, I shook my head.

Don't worry—in the end, I saw the humor in it, too. That's in part because 2008 was such a hard year. I was a "Redshirt-Junior," which meant I was entering my fourth season but still had two more years of college eligibility left. The previous season, my elbow was hurting and landed me on the bench, resulting in a "medical redshirt." Yet, I had bounced back better than ever. My skill as a Division-I pitcher was finally coming together, and I was excited to possibly hear my name called in the MLB draft that upcoming summer. On scout day, the radar guns pointed at me read 89-91, which meant that I finally had enough velocity to be considered. My elbow had healed and some mechanical adjustments I made were paying off. The Colorado Rockies liked what they saw, and I sat down with them for an interview a few weeks later. I was crazy excited. A Major League organization was interested enough in me to drive in a higher-up scout for a meeting. They told my coach that all I had to do when the season arrived was repeat my performance, and they'd likely draft me. The future that was always so far in the distance...it was suddenly right in front of me, filling my field of vision.

That winter, I both worked harder and worried more than ever. The pressure I created for myself to basically *not screw this up* was really, really heavy. Reaching that 90mph mark with consistency was what put me on the map, and thus every day I woke up anxious it would disappear as mystically as it arrived. My ability hadn't actually appeared overnight—far from it—but nonetheless, I worried.

Entering college as a freshman, I pitched at 78-81 with an occasional 82 or 83. The next fall, I was 86-88, touching an 89. The year after that, I was 87-90. And entering my fourth fall at UMBC, I was 89-91. I had crept up each season with hard work and improvements to my pitching mechanics, improvements that came about mostly by trial and error. I didn't know exactly what I was doing, but was unafraid to tinker, put in work and see what happened. It paid off.

Like a kid waiting for Santa, I counted down the days until the season arrived. I was slated to be the opening day starter when the season began in late-February. What was different, though, was that there were scouts in the stands watching me. On a cold opening day, with howling winds and near-freezing temperatures, I turned in a pedestrian performance, giving my team five or six innings in a losing effort. But it was opening day, and no one put too much stock into what was always a potentially rusty outing. A few more mediocre starts later, on the phone with my parents, they could tell my mind was somewhere else.

"Daniel, is everything okay?" It wasn't. The very thing I had feared was happening.

"I don't know. My velocity has been falling in each start, and my forearm starts cramping earlier and earlier. Something is wrong, but I'm not sure what."

"So you have sharp pain when you're pitching?" Mom asked.

"No, not sharp pain—it just gets tight, kinda sore, and starts to cramp; my arm doesn't like to straighten when it starts happening. I mean, I guess it's good that I can keep pitching through it, but if my velocity keeps dipping the scouts will stop showing up." I hung up the call a few minutes later and let out a long sigh. My dream felt like it was slipping away.

I thought at first it might have just been the cold, northeast weather. As my velocity decrease persisted, though, symptoms started to become more obvious. The muscles surrounding my elbow got more and more irritated, and it was clear something had to change. My results on the mound were heading south and I'd be no use to anyone if I didn't figure out what was going on.

My next start was a big one at home against Manhattan College. It was a cold, blustery day and a scout from the Milwaukee Brewers was watching me warm up in the bullpen. I felt like such a rock star; I had a scout watching my every move, following me around even before the game had begun. I went through my pregame routine, dressed in our white pinstripe home uniform, trying to act like I wasn't fully aware of his presence at every moment. Yet, I did what I always did while puffing out my chest just a bit more. At game time, the wind was gusting out to center field at 20 miles per hour. I yanked off my black puffy jacket that had buttons—no zipper—and 1980s-style yellow and black striped elastic cuffs. It seemed like we lagged behind modern fashion by about a decade, but at least the jacket was warm and did the job. The scout took his place behind the plate and had his radar gun, stopwatch and clipboard beside him in the bleachers. I jogged out from our black cinder block dugout to meet my destiny.

I started the game off okay, getting hit somewhat hard but throwing strikes, which was something I did better than ever. Despite having mediocre control as a high-schooler and underclassman, as an upperclassman I rarely walked more than two batters in a start. Scouts needed to see a pitcher display good physical tools, velocity, and off-speed "stuff." Beyond that, one had to throw strikes, compete hard and induce swings and misses. If a pitcher couldn't make a college hitter swing and miss regularly, how in the world would he make Minor League and Major League hitters miss? The answer was that he wouldn't. They needed to see dominant stuff from a college pitcher to believe that he had a chance to one day pitch in the Big Leagues.

I didn't strike anyone out in the first two innings. *Not good.* Then, in the third or fourth I gave up a well-struck but wind-aided home run to right-center. *No big deal*, I told myself. *These things happen.* I refocused on the next hitter and got ahead with a fastball. Then, trying to get to 0-2, I left a little too much of my second fastball over the heart of the plate. The free swinging Manhattan hitter took a hack and the ball went up. I watched helplessly as that one, too, cruised out toward center field, calmly sailing out of the ballpark. I stood with my fist clenched in my glove as he rounded the bases, irritated that I'd allowed back-to-back home runs. I focused my aggression on the next hitter, who didn't know what he was in for. I was going to ruin his day. Two home runs in a row? They'd pay for that. They were done scoring for the rest of the afternoon. I rocked and fired. He swung…*hard.*

My vindictive fastball crossed the plate about letter-high and the hitter promptly crushed it. It was *not* wind-aided, though the wind did make it even more of a no-doubt home run, one that our centerfielder took one look at before stopping to watch. It soared deep into the 30-foot tall trees beyond our 16-foot fence. Back, to back, to back—three home runs in a row. When I looked up in the stands following that third homer, the scout was gone. My heart sank and I kept pitching, though I wasn't sure what for.

It didn't get better. I pitched in front of fifteen scouts in Florida a few weeks later, in March, and I watched through the chain-link fence as most of them turned their radar guns off following my first inning. It was never a good sign when they didn't have the gun pointed at you. Once they gathered enough data showing you didn't throw hard enough, they wouldn't waste the energy to hold up the two-pound plastic device. A lot of them left after a few innings even though I ended up pitching well, going eight-strong against Eastern Kentucky. I was getting crossed off list after list and I worried my opportunities to win them back were dwindling. My body was revolting against me and everything was slipping away.

My forearm felt terrible the day after that Florida start. I spent the next few days constantly bending and straightening my elbow. I hoped that the next time I'd bend and straighten it, it would feel better. *Is my forearm healed yet? What about now?* That was the game I was playing all day, in lieu of enjoying the Florida weather. Ruminating only makes problems worse, but I wanted to wake up the next day to find it back to normal, as if it was just a bad dream and nothing was ever wrong. As a sophomore in high school, I first hurt my elbow and thought my life was over. I threw with a chronic ache in my arm for the rest of my high school days, and pitching wasn't fun. The relationship between my elbow and I had always been a tumultuous one.

By the time conference play began in April, my arm began cramping in the second inning and my velocity was stuck at 86-88, nothing even close to the 90s that I had been posting in the fall. I took a week off and stopped throwing between starts; it helped. The additional rest boosted my recovery, and I hit some 90s against the University of Maine as May approached. This was good timing, as the Maine series was just a week or two before the conference tournament, which we were poised to make for the first time in school history. We played in a weak conference but were coming into our own, a cohesive and hard-nosed team with good hitters leading the charge. I was slated to pitch the first game against Stony Brook, which meant I'd match up with their ace pitcher, a guy named Tom Koehler, who would later pitch in the Majors. Tom was the top prospect in the conference, a hard-thrower with a wipeout slider. We faced off in the final week of the regular season, him beating me 2-1 in a well-played game. When the conference tournament finally arrived, he brought a lot of scouts to the yard as we faced off in Farmingdale, New York. I was finally feeling healthy and ready to even the score.

It was a beautiful, clear night to play baseball under the lights.

Farmingdale College was a neutral site, and the baseball field was set back in the woods, surrounded by forest and clearings where a family could picnic. It was a nice complex, and we played on a turf field with dirt cutouts for the mound, plate and bases. I wasn't exactly sure why a Division-I tournament was held at a Division-III venue, but it was nice enough. Since America East Conference baseball not was not a sought-after ticket, the stands were filled mostly with parents, girlfriends and fifteen or so pro scouts.

I had been feeling strong—my arm felt as healthy as it had all season. The scouts kept their radar gun fixed on me for the entire game; none put theirs down like they had in Florida. With two outs in the sixth inning, we were down 4-3 and I had runners on second and third. It was a pivotal moment in the game and I knew I had to strand both runners. With just a one-run deficit, we could still potentially scratch across a pair of runs to come out on top. But if the gap spread, we'd have a tough time getting to Koehler for three or more runs. I don't remember what the count was but I remember the pitch—a curveball. As it left my fingers, tracking into the zone for a strike, a strong vibration shot down the inside of my forearm. It was as if my forearm was a guitar and someone had strummed it. I didn't know what to think—it wasn't painful, but it was very...strange. I stepped off the mound and took what felt like an eternity trying to discern what had happened, and what I should do next.

I looked off into the distance, a thousand yards beyond first base. It was a beautiful little park, the tall trees in the background now barely visible in the blackness of night. I had a pit in my stomach, terrified to find out what was going to happen next. What *was* this new sensation? *Am I okay? Do I call the trainer out to look at me? Am I done? Can I even throw another pitch? Is my elbow injured?* I took a deep breath, deciding at last that I'd throw the next pitch without drawing any attention to myself. I wasn't calling for the trainer and I wasn't walking off that mound. I wasn't a coward, and I was going to throw the next fastball as hard as I humanly could. Yet, I also felt like I had just poked a sleeping bear. The bear whipped his head around and stared straight at me. As I accepted the sign from my catcher, I took the deepest breath of my life. Something bad was about to happen. I kicked and delivered.

As the fastball rolled off my fingertips—crossing the plate high for a ball—the same sensation shot down my arm a second time. *What is going on? What is this feeling in my arm?* I didn't know, but I now had a goal: get off the mound before my arm blew up. I made a conscious

59

effort not to shake, look at, or make any abnormal motion with my elbow; I'd ignore it and hope it played dead along with me. I threw another pitch, now with two strikes on the batter and got the same sensation along with a foul ball. The right-handed hitter fouled off another pitch, prompting me to call Tom, my catcher, out to talk. I covered my mouth with my glove as we had a short, one-sided conversation:

"Is my velocity the same?"

"Yeah," he replied.

"Is my curveball the same?"

"Yeah."

"Did you notice anything different?"

"Not really. Why? You okay?"

Slightly reassured that I was the only one privy to the situation, I committed to finishing off the hitter. Years later, Tom revealed that he knew something was up, though he didn't know what. He heard slight fear in my voice and knew it was a defining moment for me. He was right.

The right-handed jerk at the plate kept fouling off fastballs—each of which was more difficult to locate than the last. Even though my velocity appeared to be holding, my control was not; I had little idea where any pitch would end up once it left my hand. Maybe I was overthrowing to compensate for the fear I felt. Finally, after what felt like an eternity of foul balls, he kept one fair. A hard grounder bounced between our third baseman and the line. I watched as the ball rolled disastrously into the left-field corner. Both baserunners cashed, ruining my chance to get off the mound unscathed. Now down 6-3, the game had been broken open and it was time for me to get off that mound. Toward the end of that 10-pitch at-bat, the guitar strumming turned into pain, and it was clear I could no longer be effective. After I got the ball back, I walked the plank over to the first base line to get my coach and trainer's attention. With a simple gesture, I killed my hopes of turning pro. I pointed at my elbow, prompting Coach J and our trainer to walk out. He escorted me back into the dugout, across the white line for the final time in a UMBC uniform. The sound of my name being scratched off the scouts' lists was so loud, I couldn't hear myself think. The day was May 22nd and I was no longer a college baseball player.

The next morning, I awoke to a healthy dose of swelling and pain, both of which confirmed that my guitar had played its final note. This time, I didn't need to straighten and bend my elbow all day to figure out its status—I knew it was ruined. I visited the doctor a week later and to my surprise, he once again diagnosed me with only a partially torn UCL. He was optimistic I could rehab again, so I shipped off to summer baseball with John Duffy and the T-Bolts and gave it my best. When it failed on that miserably painful day in College Park, Maryland, I found myself on the operating table just a few weeks later. On August 25, 2008, the doctor skillfully drilled, weaved and stitched a hamstring tendon from a deceased fellow into my woeful elbow. I was good as new...if having the strength and capability of a newborn qualified as "good."

As my mom drove me home from surgery on that August morning, I was in shock. I looked down at my elbow, heavily wrapped to the knuckles in Ace bandages and suspended at a right-angle in a dark blue sling. *How did I end up here?* Frayed ropes eventually snap, and my elbow had been fraying since I was in high school. Yet this funk, this depression, emanated from more than just one lowly joint—it was as if half of me had died. I could no longer do the things that made me who I was. Not only could I not throw a baseball, I could barely even make a fist. My identity was in pieces, but the doctor didn't suture those back together.

In the coming months, sorrow slowly yielded to optimism. I had to take on a second major in school (Psychology) and return for a fifth year. I was previously on track to graduate but wanted to do my rehab at school, using up my last year of eligibility as a fifth-year senior. I knew that staying with the team and training staff would give me structure and purpose. Most pitchers recovered in 12 months or more, but I'd be demolishing that—I planned on returning to the mound in a mere eight months. Tim O'Brien fed my belief: "If anyone can do it, it's you!" T-O-B, as we called him, would be my biggest cheerleader to get back on the field.

Eight months later, as my super-senior year in college wound down, I found myself on the University of Vermont's field, long-tossing as far as I could. I felt strong and the ball was jumping out of my hand as I stretched out to well over 300 feet. When I returned home, jumping on the mound with the radar gun, I hit 90mph again—right at the eight-and-a-half-month mark. I smiled. It hadn't been easy, but the progress back to that huge milestone had been steady. To now make the leap to pro baseball, I needed lots more 90s to show up. Though the velocity was about back, there was a lot more to pitching than just speed. Could I go out and pitch an inning from the bullpen? Could I warm up fast if called upon in a pinch? Could I command the strike zone and mix up my offerings with curveballs and changeups? Was it all there? My bid to get into a real game for at least one inning—to not miss my entire last season—was suddenly looking more complex than I had previously thought. Upon returning home from Vermont, Tim and I had a discussion on the meaning of the one inning I desperately wanted.

"Hey Dan, I have something I'd like to discuss with you." Tim was always very clear and plain in his manner of speaking. "Sure," I replied. "What's up?"

"About this inning that you're seeking before the season ends. What do you hope will come of it?"

"I just want to prove that I can beat this. It doesn't have to take 12 months."

"I understand that. It looks like you're close. But what's the upside? Is it worth it if you go out and hurt yourself? Is an inning worth jeopardizing the whole surgery?"

If he had lived in the Wild West, Tim would have been a good horseman. He knew when and how to get the horses—his pitchers—to run harder and give their strongest effort when it mattered. But he also knew when to find shade, a pasture and a stream for them to rest. Pulling on the reigns was just as important as kicking the spurs. At the time, I was the horse who would run until I died of exhaustion unless someone pulled my reigns and forced me to rest.

A week later, as our last home-stand of the season approached, so again did Tim. He wanted my permission for something he'd set up without my knowledge, after we'd collectively decided I wouldn't enter a real game.

"Dan, I did something without your permission, so I'd like to make sure it's okay with you before I go all the way through with it." I raised my eyebrow. "Okay?"

"I've arranged for you to throw out the ceremonial first pitch on Senior night. The guys in the booth know about it, as does the rest of the coaching staff. I'll tell the players if you're okay with it. I know it's not what you wanted, but it's a small something to go out on. Would you be okay with that?" I nodded. I was okay with it.

Before the game began, I walked out to the mound in my white pinstripes. Our tiny crowd stood and both teams took their places in front of the dugouts. The PA announcer explained my battle with Tommy John surgery and the purpose of my ceremonial pitch. As he shared my career statistics with the crowd, I felt a tinge of embarrassment. Being a great rehabber seemed to be the bulk of my legacy. I was a very below-average pitcher in the record books, and it was unclear what tangible contribution I had made to the success of the team. In 155 career innings, I amassed a 7-15 record and a 6.18 ERA —downright abysmal numbers. But, I continued to focus on what mattered most—the future. Those numbers didn't define me, nor did the reputation of being constantly injured. On the mound with everyone watching, despite being healthy enough to throw it hard, I lobbed that first pitch. I then wiped a tear from my eye and walked off. That lob would *not* be my final pitch.

A few months later, in late July, I was hoping to sign a contract with an independent professional baseball team before the season ended. Because I went undrafted, I'd have to earn a contract in a professional league not affiliated with Major League Baseball—they called this Independent Baseball. If I did well there, an MLB team would sign and transfer me to one of their Minor League teams, where I'd be in the feeder system to the Majors. But, since all minor and independent leagues ended in early September, I had to figure things out quickly. My velocity kept climbing, and I was slowly but surely getting some feel back for my changeup and curveball. It started to look realistic that I could catch on for the final month of the indy season. I was just a thrower back in May, but was becoming a pitcher again toward the end of that summer.

It was a hot July night, and I was pitching for the Susquehanna Arsenal, one of the adult-league teams that I played for back in high school. It was the same team that I pitched for when UMBC came to recruit me, so this eerie feeling of déjà vu was in the air. Starting a late-night game under the lights, I fired in fastball after fastball at 91 and 92 miles per hour. I was looking good and feeling good. In the second inning, however, a big hitter named Arnold laced a double into the right-field gap on a fastball low and away. I thought nothing of it, until he jogged into second base declaring aloud that he'd "hit that 86 mile-per-hour college stuff all day." My blood boiled.

As I returned to the dugout, I pulled my catcher aside and explained what happened. I told him to be prepared for Arnold's next at-bat. I was *not* going to be disrespected by some guy in a meaningless game, not after all the work I had put in to get back on that mound. On the first pitch of his next at-bat, I was going to hit him with a fastball as hard as I could.

Arnold was *not* a small man. He was probably 6'2 and 240lbs and had an intimidating presence in the box. He was a catcher and should have known what was about to happen. A few innings later, he strolled up to the plate. I scowled at him, my adrenaline high, knowing what I was about to do. I shook *yes* to a fastball, then lifted my leg, reared back and uncorked a missile. It cut through the air with a hissing sound that was audible in the bleachers. But, I didn't get it in far enough—my catcher reached up to snatch it out of the air, a few inches from his chin as he leaned slightly out of the way. I vowed to do better.

The next fastball I threw absolutely as hard as I could. As it whizzed by him—about 10 inches *behind* his head—he appeared to get the message. He dropped his bat, turned toward me, pounded his chest, then threw his arms up overhead as he yelled, "WHY YOU THROWIN' AT ME!?" His eyes got wide when all 185lbs of me stormed toward him, pointing angrily as I replied, "BECAUSE YOU'RE OUT THERE RUNNING YOUR MOUTH ON SECOND BASE!"

He did *not* expect this.

My catcher wrapped his arms around Arnold as I rapidly approached the plate, menacingly speed-walking and cursing at him. The man had a solid 50 pounds on me, but I didn't care. I'll never forget his eyes as I rushed the plate—they got wide, revealing an initial reaction of fear and surprise, after which he immediately switched into tough-guy mode. The benches cleared as we continued cursing loudly at each other in the area in front of home plate. He punched at the air, "I'll mess you up!" but was unable to escape my catcher's bear hug. Everyone else tried to calm the situation, and as it died down I was ejected. I packed my things and headed for my car as steam poured from my ears, floating up toward you in the blackness of night. You'd have liked me standing up for myself, though I was in the wrong breaking the unwritten rule to never throw at a guy's head. Go for the knee or the ribs, just don't go head-hunting.

It turned out to be a blessing that my night ended right then and there. After the melee, walking back to the parking lot in darkness, my elbow started to swell. It hurt to extend it and I worried that I was headed back to the surgeon's table. When I let that fastball go behind his head, I had felt my elbow joint "gap" a little bit. I knew that unforgettable, disgusting feeling; I remembered it well from the previous summer before I underwent surgery. I went home in a panic. *Did I re-injure my arm? Am I getting surgery again?*

I saw my doctor and he assured me that I was fine; his work was still intact. He prescribed rest and medication. A week later, on anti-inflammatories and observing six weeks of rest on what the doctor claimed was mere tendinitis, I got a phone call from Duff. He had been busy trying to find me a team to sign with. As luck had it, one of his close friends was the hitting coach on the Joliet Jackhammers, an independent team near Chicago. They were struggling and needed another bullpen arm to finish out the season.

"Mr. Blewett! How's the elbow?"

"Eh, it's okay. What's up, Duff?"

"Well, I've got good news. I have a buddy who's the hitting coach for Joliet in the Northern League. They're struggling right now and need an arm or two to finish out the season. He's looking for guys and I told him I had one, but wanted to call you first. If you go there and pitch well for the final three weeks of the season, you can probably lock up a spring training contract with them for the 2010 season. What do you think?"

I could have collapsed right there in the grass. I had just completed a long run and was standing in the grassy center area of Harford Community College's track when he called.

"Well, I actually hurt my arm again. It's okay, but I tweaked it two weeks ago throwing at a guy's head."

"Really? What happened?"

I recapped the story for him and he laughed—that was *exactly* the kind of pitcher Duff was, someone who didn't take crap from anybody. I was becoming a little more like that myself, and despite being disappointed that I had hurt myself in the process, he had the tone of a proud father.

"Well, I'm glad you stuck up for yourself—you own that plate and you can't let guys show you up on the field. I'm sure your teammates respected you for that."

"Yeah, I guess so," I said.

"But—if a guy charges the mound on you in the future, here's what you do: You take your glove off and put it in your throwing hand. Then, you wait for the guy to get close. When he's within a few feet, you throw the glove at his face—*hard*—and then you hit him in the jaw with your glove hand. Never—I repeat—NEVER punch a guy with your throwing hand; you'll break it and that'll be the end for you. But here's the thing: no one will just take a glove to the face, so when you throw it at him, he'll duck and that'll be your chance to get the first punch in. One punch is all you'll really need to defend yourself before everyone else gets there to break it up."

It was classic Duff. I explained that I was shut down for the year and would have to wait until 2010. Nine more months of hibernation before I'd get my chance. It was a cruel joke—the offer was there and all I had to do was accept…but I couldn't. I hung up the phone, cursed the sky and went home. If that was *your* doing from above—some sort of cruel joke—it wasn't funny.

Waiting was always the hardest part, but I suppose I had gotten used to it. Years later when I retired, my accumulated injury time tallied up to about five seasons' worth. Though it never got easier, it did become more predictable. I got better at setting goals and slowly crossing days off the calendar, taking it one step at a time. Watching my teammates go out and play in the sunshine was hard, but all a person can do is suck it up. Complaining doesn't get any of us anywhere, so I mostly stayed silent and controlled what I could. There certainly were days when I was a grumpy, unsupportive teammate, but I tried my best not to be that guy. I didn't want to bring others down, and often just being neutral to everything was my best armor. I'd get my chance, I just didn't always know how.

That winter, Duff made a call for me to that same hitting coach—Josh from Joliet—only this season he had latched onto another team, the Normal, Illinois, Cornbelters. Josh put in a good word for me to their manager, Hal Lanier. A man named Rick Forney, who was also a manager in an independent league, gave pitching lessons in the Baltimore baseball academy where I worked as a strength coach. Rick obliged when I asked him to watch one of my bullpens, and he was impressed enough to call Hal—*his* former manager—on my behalf. Rick had been a standout pitcher for the Winnipeg Goldeyes when Mr. Lanier managed the team years prior. Baseball will always be a surprisingly small fraternity.

I was playing for a barnstorming team, the Gildea Raiders, and sitting in the dugout when my cellphone rang. The Raiders were managed by Bob "Goose" Gildea, a former pro pitcher now in his 50s who had built a successful landscaping business. He then somewhat retired into helping ballplayers like me find a place in pro baseball. I always referred to him as my agent when I mentioned him, but he technically wasn't. Rather, he was my friend, advisor, and a well-connected mentor who had a key to any door. He later worked for a major agency helping foreign players make the leap to the Major Leagues.

Duff had told me that Hal seemed interested and that I should be on the lookout for a phone call from a Florida area code. When my flip-phone started buzzing with an unknown area code, my heart immediately started racing. Was it *that* call? I picked up the phone.

"Hello, Dan? This is Hal Lanier, manager of the Normal Cornbelters. How are you?" I replied that I was *great*.

"Good, good. Well, I've heard your name from a number of good sources—from Josh and from Rick Forney—did you know that Rick played for me? He now manages the Winnipeg Goldeyes." I replied that I *did* know that.

"Well, Rick and Josh both spoke very highly of you. There was one other, though I can't remember his name. A scout maybe? Guy named Duffy? I can't remember, but either way—I want to extend to you a contract with us. We are an expansion team in the Frontier League, which is a great league for rookies like yourself. Would you be interested?"

"I'm *definitely* interested," I replied as calmly as I could.

"Great! I'll fax over the contract. You're in Florida, right? I would have loved to come see you throw over there, but I'm too busy this weekend. But I'll fax the contract to your hotel. Just send me the number later and I'll have it faxed over."

With that phone call, I was a professional baseball player. More precisely, I had a spring training contract and a chance to make the opening day roster. I walked back to the dugout, where we were embroiled in an exhibition game against the Detroit Tigers' A-Ball squad. I couldn't hide my smile, which poked through as I told our fearless leader the good news. Every bit of 6'5" with white hair, a beer belly and wide frame, the only thing bigger than Goose was his personality. He had a confident walk that could part the Red Sea, along with a strong, deep, booming voice. When he spoke, the room fell hushed. I never saw him in action, but I can imagine he was an intimidating figure on the mound. As I told him about my phone call, a big grin spread across his face. He stopped everyone to announce the good news to the team.

"Hey guys, listen up. Danny here just got his first contract—just this very moment. This is the exact reason we're all here: to help each one of you get your foot in the door. This is a big day for him so make sure you give him a pat on the back."

We were all there in Florida to prepare for the season and get signed by a new club. For some, it was one more chance. For others like myself, it was that first opportunity.

Two months later, I was sitting on the bench in my uniform, my heavy jacket draped over my shoulders. I was in the dugout of historic Bosse Field, the third-oldest ballpark in America still in use. In 1915, Bosse Field held its first professional game, and I could feel the ghosts the first time I stood in the ballpark. There was a special gravity you felt everywhere on the grounds. I was waiting for my turn after our half-inning up at bat was finished. The ballpark was a big oval, wrapping fans gently around the diamond in thickly-painted, green wooden seats. At the top of the concourse was *Support the Racine Belles!* painted in old-timey script, alluding to the famous women's ballclub that called the ballpark home in the movie *A League of Their Own*. The Tom Hanks movie was the town's claim to fame, and rightly so—it boasted timeless sound bites that would outlive even the archaic ballpark.

The crowd of 4000+ fans roared as their hometown Otters recorded the final out of a clean inning, signaling that it was my turn to pitch. I had made the team, earned a Normal Cornbelters jersey, and was about to make my pro debut as a starting pitcher on the second game of their inaugural season. We opened up with a week on the road before returning home to our brand-new ballpark in Normal, Illinois. I took a deep breath and peeled off my jacket. I buttoned my top jersey button to keep my heart from beating out of my chest, and cautiously ascended the steep concrete dugout steps. I had waited a long time to feel the grass beneath my metal Nike cleats as I jogged out between the lines. I threw my eight warmup pitches without sensation; I didn't feel, see or hear much of anything. Adrenaline was all I felt until that final warm up pitch was complete, my catcher sailing a strike down to second base. After the ball was tossed around the infield and placed in my mitt by the third baseman, I patted my hand with rosin and walked up the mound. There in front of me was my catcher, the umpire and a professional hitter as he made himself comfortable in the batters' box, along with Mom, Dad, and the sweet older couple—Denny and Dory —who took me in as my host family in Normal.

I gazed around the ballpark, trying to take in the moment if only for a second. Atop that mound in Indiana I wondered, *How is this going to go?* There was so much that could happen and so much potential that would be unlocked with my first pitch. After all the workouts, running, pitching drills in my garage on Friday nights, the disappointment of falling short of expectations in college, the surgery and recovery, the pain, the anguish, and the dreadful waiting…all of it led me there. The only thing left for me to do was throw the pitch.

As the hitter narrowed his gaze and my catcher put down signs, adrenaline swooped back in. Suddenly, the busy ballpark was empty of fans. The sun was just about to set as it peeked over the stadium shell, and all I could make out was a round piece of leather approximately 60 feet away. My feet started to move on their own. Then, my leg. My hands rose up, then down, before each going their separate way. My legs pushed me sideways toward the three men waiting down range. Then, a familiar sound rang out.

CRACK! The ball found the leather mitt.

STEEEEEEEEEEEERIKE!

Those two sounds set me free. A huge weight sheared away, sliding off my shoulders like a glacier into the ocean. All the fans were back in their seats and I heard my team in the dugout cheering for me. "Atta boy, Blew!" I was a professional pitcher and my first pitch—after two arduous, exhausting years away from baseball—was a strike. Now back in control of my body, I focused on my next pitch, which I decided would be another fastball. I stepped, kicked and delivered. This one too was a strike, only it didn't reach the catcher's mitt.

HISSSSSSSSSSS.......THOCK!

A mere blink after it left my hand, the right-handed leadoff hitter barreled it up, sending a line drive on a bee-line back at me. The hiss from the seams slicing the air was deafening as the shiny white ball struck me square in the left thigh, hitting me so hard that I barely flinched to protect myself. It ricocheted off my leg into the grass toward the first base line. *Go get it!* My mind raced as I hustled over, picked it up and flipped to first to record the out. As my infielders threw it around the horn, I rolled my eyes. *Is that how this is going to go?* Welcome to pro baseball, Dan.

No longer in an adrenaline coma, I settled in. Five innings later, I found myself locked in a 0-0 pitching duel. In the sixth, I got two quick outs before walking their 3-hole hitter on four straight pitches. Two-out walks are a huge no-no. Their cleanup hitter then doubled, plating the first run of the game and ending my day. Hal sauntered out and asked for the ball, giving me a pat on the butt as I descended the mound. I walked off down 1-0, but we'd later come back to tie it up. The reliever who replaced me gave up another hit and run before retiring the side, marking the statistical end of my day. My line for my first start was nearly six complete innings with four hits, two runs, three walks and two strikeouts. Not a bad first day on the job.

As I sat in the dugout watching the rest of the game with ice on my elbow, my pulse still high from the adrenaline, I thought about the last day I was on the mound. That conference tournament game in Farmingdale, New York took place in late May. Here I was, two years later, sitting in the dugout in the third week of May. What *was* the date of that game against Stony Brook? I vowed to look it up when I got back to the hotel later that night.

After pizza with my parents, Denny, and Dory, I got dropped off at the team hotel and sat down with my laptop. My folks would fly home the next day, and I had 98 more games to go. As I searched through the UMBC baseball archives for the last game I had pitched, I took note of the date displayed in the upper-right corner of my white Apple iBook laptop. The dig through digital data was deep, but finally I found it. The night I blew out my elbow and ended my college career was May 22, 2008. I went five and two-thirds innings that day before pointing at my elbow in front of all those scouts in Farmingdale. My eyes widened as I quickly glanced back at the date in the corner of my laptop. *No way. Couldn't be.* I had just pitched five and two-thirds innings on May 22, 2010. Two years to the day. I smiled and just shook my head.

Dear Jason, It's the eye contact.

In today's society, it's harder than ever to look people in the eyes, especially when you have to break news that they don't want to hear. The norm nowadays is silence—we just fade away or ignore people when we've decided to move on. I'm guilty of this myself, as is pretty much everyone else. In the baseball world, everyone remarks how small the community is. Even though millions of kids play the game each year, at the higher levels it seems like everyone has some connection to everyone else. "I played with him back in Rookie ball." "He went to college with my buddy." "I pitched against him in Double-A."

You should be good to other people solely because it's the right way to act, the right way to treat them. But if that's not reason enough, don't forget that what goes around comes back around. As a 16-year-old pitcher, you likely have no idea how important simply looking someone in the eye can be. Being honest and taking responsibility for your actions will come back to benefit you in the long run. I learned this in two of my first seasons, when taking heat like a man and being honest with one of my coaches ended up making a huge difference in both our lives.

It was August of 2010 and I was in St. Louis, sitting in the visiting clubhouse waiting for the game to end. I had just returned from the disabled list, where I was shelved for a little over a week. I sat at my narrow metal locker in my sweat-drenched grey uniform, thinking about how horribly I had just pitched. My brother had driven 10 hours to watch me, and in a spectacular letdown I gave up six runs without making it out of the second inning. It was a miserable, pathetic performance. After waiting two hours at my locker for the game to mercifully end—to the tune of a 16-5 loss—the team finally streamed in. As their cleats clacked on the concrete walkway onto the thin, unpadded carpet floor, I tried to blend in with the lockers as best I could. Finally, with most players situated silently at their lockers, Brooks, my pitching coach, walked through. He immediately called on me to follow him into the coaches' office. I assumed he wanted to ask me about my finger.

I hadn't pitched in over a week because of a serious blister on my middle finger. In my previous start, back at home in Normal, I loaded the bases with no outs. As I paced on the dark green turf just behind the mound, sweat dripped off my fingertips—it was incredibly hot and so humid I could practically drink the summer air. My calloused fingers had turned into prunes by the fourth, and now in the sixth my middle finger tip began to blister. Not thinking much of it, I kept pitching. My pitch count was high, so my goal was to work out of the jam in what had to be my final inning of the night.

A few pitches and a strikeout later, my whole middle finger pad started to burn as it filled with fluid. I proceeded onward anyway, eventually punching out that hitter, too as the burning sensation increased. As the next hitter walked toward the batter's box, it was time to really bear down and finish the inning. But as I ritualistically reached for the rosin bag, I realized the fluid had spilled out and the blistered skin on my middle finger was torn wide open. I looked down at my most important finger tip, which was now just a dime-sized patch of oozing, bloody skin. I tamped down the remaining skin flap with my thumb, hoping it would act as a protective layer…it didn't.

The middle finger is the last finger on the ball on almost every type of pitch. It's like the tires on a Ferrari—if one runs flat, that big engine under the hood is rendered useless. With a raw finger that was unable to grip the ball, I really couldn't do much "pitching." So, after a moment of reflection, I formulated a plan: I'd throw fastballs as hard as I could and see what happened. I had just one hitter to go, so the "chuck it and pray" plan—which I'd gone to many times in the past when tired, hurt, or frustrated—seemed like the proper move.

After a few balls, a few strikes, and a foul ball or two that landed just in the seats, the hitter popped one up that swirled high above our dugout. Foul pop ups have a unique flight—as they go up, the backspin carries them out of play and over the seats, making them appear like they've gone foul for good. But when a high foul pop-up hits the apex of its flight, that same spin pulls it back toward the field as it descends. As I watched, desperate for an out, the ball peaked just a few rows foul, high above the spectators below. As some fans reached up and others ducked for cover, I noticed our first baseman starting to wander back toward the playing field. The ball had been maybe four rows deep as it went up, then slunk back toward the playing field in foul territory. The ball landed in our first baseman's cavernous mitt with a loud POP! as I smirked and walked off the field. My messy inning with my messed-up finger was now over.

Brooks greeted me at the top of the dugout rail with an excited pat on the butt, pumped up that I had preserved our lead. I was unhappy that I had caused that jam in the first place, but accepted his congratulations for undoing it. In his mid-50s with gray hair, a wry smile and a slightly crooked walk, Brooks was a salty old veteran. He and I had a mutual respect. Brooks liked hard-nosed players and I pitched inside to hitters, unafraid to brush them back and challenge them. I also tended to thrive in tough situations, focusing hard when runners got on base and bearing down to keep them from scoring. These were all things that Brooks lived and breathed as a pitcher back when baseball was the Wild West of beanballs and take-out slides. He hated the "soft" brand of baseball kids play nowadays and took obvious pleasure when one of ours took out one of theirs. At the conclusion of a good start, I was greeted in the dugout with a hug and a "Love ya kid." It was this very relationship that made what happened in the coaches office so unexpected.

Re-growing the skin on my finger was a process that couldn't be rushed. I had missed two starts for the finger blister, and when I took the hill that night outside of St. Louis, had declared myself ready to pitch. I was nervous about it re-tearing, though—the new skin was still thin and I could feel it as I warmed up. I was holding back a bit and the normal aggression behind each pitch wasn't there. When a pitcher pitches without 100% conviction, he usually gets killed; so was the case with me. As I was summoned into his office, I assumed that Brooks realized this and was going to greet me with a "how's it holding up?" kind of talk. I was wrong. He was *pissed.*

"Hey, Blew, sit down." I sat down as I looked across the desk at Brooks and Hal.

"I'm going to get right to the point here. What I saw tonight was an embarrassment and it will *not* happen again." He leaned forward and started waving his pointer finger at me to drive home the message.

"If you can't go out there and throw 92 miles per hour, then you need to tell me right now. And if that's the case, then maybe we need to make a change. What happened tonight will *never* happen again. If you can't go out there and have your best fastball when *you* tell *me* you're ready to pitch, then I'll find someone else who can."

My eyes got wide; I was shocked and had no rebuttal. As he finished reaming me out, I nodded that I understood. He didn't care about how my finger was doing. He didn't care if I was nervous about it. He didn't care what my reasoning was for turning in such a pathetic, gutless performance. I said I was ready—ready meant *ready.* There were no excuses to make and I was expected to do my job and do it well.

He and Hal both stared, waiting for me to say something. Finally, I did.

"You're right. Tonight was awful and I'm better than that. It won't happen again."

"Alright, then get out of here. You know I love ya, Blew." Hal laughed as I walked out.

It was an important conversation. In college, we were held to a Nerfy standard where I could go out and pitch like crap and continue to get innings because, well, who else was there? Yet as an easily-replaced Independent League pitcher, there was no place for excuses. Lots of pitchers blame the umpires, bad hops, errors, a lack of sleep, arm soreness, the slope of the mound, you name it—all of us have heard it all and said it all at some point to make it seem like it we weren't to blame for doing a poor job. But in the end, I wanted to be successful, not just at that low-level of pro baseball but at the highest one—the Major Leagues. And so if that was the standard to which the best in the world were held, then I wanted to be held to it, too. If we accept blame and make a plan to avoid the same shortfalls, we can move forward, better for it. I could have *always* done better to prevent some external event from beating me. And anyway, if I couldn't succeed in entry-level baseball, how on earth would I ever pitch in "the show?" I could accept blame because doing so made me stronger, not weaker.

Mound visits with Brooks were always about the same. I hadn't pitched competitively since 2008, during a nearly two-year layoff while I recovered from my first Tommy John surgery. Finding myself again after that long recovery—especially my off-speed stuff—proved difficult. Basically, all I could do in my rookie season with the Normal

Cornbelters was rip fastballs. I threw harder than I ever had, sitting at 90-93 mph for all nine innings. I had a hard fastball and "late life" on it, meaning that it appeared to rise and speed up as it approached the plate. My fastball was special enough that I once threw 98 fastballs in a 110 pitch start, something unheard of at any professional level. This wasn't what I wanted—had I found my curveball and changeup, I would have been a much more dominant pitcher. Nonetheless, I couldn't find my secondary stuff that year and did the best I could with what I had. My fastball carried the load and it taught me a lot about how to pitch.

Thus, mound visits with me weren't as much about strategy as they were with other pitchers. Rather, Brooksy would come out, tell me that the hitter who stood before me didn't have the bat speed to catch up and that I should ram it in on his fists. If I threw 90 fastballs in a game, at least 50 of them would be inside. Jamming hitters and exploiting slow, wooden bats, was the only reason I could get by with just one pitch. Usually all it took from him was to come out and remind me that I had a fastball they couldn't hit. Any time I lacked 100% conviction, he'd walk out in hopes of turning it back up. If in doubt, I pitched in; if I missed, I missed in.

It also took guts to pitch inside that much, and maybe the reason I embraced it was because my coaches in college didn't believe in it; they believed fervently in pitching low-and-away in almost all situations. To survive in pro ball I had to quickly un-learn all of it, because low and away meant a little extra time for a slow bat to reach my single, very predictable pitch.

I assumed getting the "feel" back just took more time after surgery. I was never really a feel pitcher and was perhaps too mentally afraid to throw my off-speed stuff with the required conviction. I'd baby my offspeed pitches and hitters would pay no mind to them. So, I just kept bringing the heat. Brooks didn't mind and it was fun challenging hitters, seeing how my power matched up with theirs.

On June 29th of that year, the headlines on the sports page of the Pantagraph read *Blewett Brings It,* highlighting my one-hit shutout in perhaps the only time my last name was parodied in a positive light:

> The pronunciation of Dan Blewett's last name (blew it) lends itself to outings when the Normal pitcher does not fare well. Monday at the Corn Crib, however, Dan Blewett past Gateway hitters all

evening. Blewett blanked the Grizzlies on one hit and struck out 13 as the CornBelters cashed in the first complete-game shutout in franchise history for a 5-0 victory before a crowd of 1,334.

It was one of the finest games I had ever pitched and one of the only times I was featured in a newspaper. I didn't play for recognition, but every once in a while...I just wanted a record that I existed, that I did something in my career. Despite the paper trophy, I was committed to continuing to get better. I didn't throw 98 miles per hour and even if I did, MLB hitters wouldn't balk at it. My fastball was my best pitch and I could barely throw my off-speed stuff for strikes, so I knew I had to figure out the rest of my repertoire sooner than later.

After my rookie season in Normal, I was traded away to a higher league to a team called the Lake County Fielders. Brooks had a friend named Tim Johnson who managed the team. The two had spent time in Arizona each off-season scouting players. When Tim explained that he needed pitching, he decided that he wanted the guy Brooks always talked about...*me*. Early in 2011, I got a call that the deal went down, that I would be joining Lake County for the 2011 season.

I was excited for the new opportunity. I enjoyed the travel and uncertainty of new places, ballparks, and people. The idea of returning to the same team wasn't nearly as attractive as bouncing around a bit. If nothing else, I wanted to see the country and what other leagues and teams had to offer. I learned a lot from Brooks and was eager to see who I'd learn from next. What I didn't realize, however, was that he and I would continue to be intertwined for each of the next two seasons. I'd save him from a disastrous career move.

A year later after that summer with the Normal Cornbelters, I was standing in a hotel room in downtown Chicago, peering out the window onto Rush street; I was stressed. The Lake County Fielders hadn't been paying us. Tim Johnson and the rest of our coaching staff had quit and I had been granted my release along with the rest of the players; the team had disbanded. A girl I had been seeing had flown in to visit me at the worst possible time and I was just about to jump in the car with her to drive to Sioux Falls, South Dakota to meet my new team, the Fargo-Moorhead RedHawks. But first, I had to call Brooks.

"Hey Blew! What's goin' on, kid?"

"Hey Brooks. I have something I want to tell you. I know I told you I'd come back and play for you in Normal, but I got an offer from Fargo and decided that I'd prefer to go there. I know that you knew I wanted to play in a higher league, so I figured you'd understand why I wanted to go with them instead. But since I told you I was coming back to Normal, I just wanted to call you and tell you personally."

He paused, considering his reply. Then, he slowly started…."Well, Blew, I actually have something to tell you, too. You might not be going anywhere…because I've been offered the manager job in Lake County. And if I take it, I'm gonna need you there; I'll need a good core of players."

I was stunned. I couldn't believe that my departure might now be blocked by none other than one of my mentors. It begged an obvious question, though: why in the world would he want to be the manager for the team that couldn't pay any of us? Something wasn't right.

"Brooks, you don't want to do that. You don't want to come up here —no one does. Lake County is a nightmare, I can't even imagine that there will be a team here a few weeks from now."

He was surprised to hear this, which confirmed that someone had been lying to him.

"Well, that's not how it was described to me. I was told that the financial situation was cleared up and that everything was moving forward."

"No, that's not true at all. Guys weren't getting paid and many still haven't. Checks were bouncing. They accused Pete—our hitting coach —of embezzling money when in reality, he was giving guys cash from his own pocket to pay their bills and buy meals. Pete was the glue that held the team together. The field is a joke—there's no irrigation and the grass is yellow and dying. The clubhouse is a trailer with these awful thin lockers. The field has temporary bleachers. There's no way it's going to get better. You can't take that job—it'll be a nightmare for you just like it was for us. Leaving Normal for that would be a big, big mistake.

He exhaled, and again paused. I could tell it was starting to sink in as he asked me a few questions. He knew I wouldn't lie to him and he could tell in my voice how serious I was. Finally, he spoke.

"I believe you, Blew. I'm gonna call them back and tell them I'm not taking the job."

I breathed out a huge sigh of relief. I had spent my last few days frantically rowing away from that sinking ship, just to see Brooks in a speedboat heading back toward the wreckage.

"I appreciate you calling me, it took balls to do that," he said. "If you hadn't been a man and called me—even with news I didn't want to hear—I'd be on my way up there tomorrow. I owe you one and when you need something, you just call me."

"I will," I said. And, I would—later on, I'd need every bit of help I could get. My reputation would follow me like a hunting dog and I'd be stuck with it good or bad. I had no idea how important those moments of eye contact would prove to be.

Dear Kevin, Just five more minutes.

We just couldn't get enough. Whether it was my backyard or yours, with real equipment or improvised, we found something to throw and something to swing. Every warm afternoon revolved around backyard baseball, and if my parents looked out our French doors into the backyard, there we were. We were creative 10-year-olds—if we got a little bored we just changed the rules.

"Hey let's go lefty-only for a while. What do you think, Kev?"

"Pitching or hitting?"

"Ah, lets pitch normal but bat lefty; then we'll switch after three innings."

"Sounds good. I'm gonna be Ken Griffey Jr."

"No! I was going to use his stance. Hmmm. Who should I be?"

There *was* no one else. Ken Griffey Jr. had the prettiest left-handed swing in the world. No one else was even worth remembering. We played *Ken Griffey Jr's Winning Run* on Super Nintendo when it was too dark to play outside. The man was a god. It didn't matter the form, we just wanted more baseball.

"Daniel! Kevin! It's too dark! Time to come in. Pick up everything so Dad doesn't run over it with the lawnmower tomorrow!"

"Five more minutes!?"

"No! I can barely even see you."

"MOM! Five more minutes." She wasn't hard to convince.

"FIVE. Five more minutes. Then you're inside for the night."

"Thank you!"

That summed up our childhood, at least for a short while. It didn't matter if we couldn't see the ball.

"Hurry up! Pitch it! I'm gonna take you deep one last time."

You stood 40 feet away and began your windup in front of the sky blue shed in my backyard. You were really more of an infielder, but obviously the two of us played every position. You kicked and delivered...*or so I thought?* I watched as, well, nothing whizzed past me. At least, I couldn't see if it did. Mom was right—it was too dark. It was time to come in and for you to go home.

But it didn't matter—a backyard baseball field cloaked in the black of night was still better than the bright lights of, well, anywhere else. To this day, I'm not sure baseball was ever more fun than it was when you and I played our epic 4-hour games on the lawn. As 11-year-olds, we just couldn't put down our bats and gloves. 20 years later, I still just wanted five more minutes, even if it wouldn't do me a damned bit of good.

A decade later, a handful of anti-inflammatory pills became the only way I could stay out longer. I didn't like that pills kept me in the game, but it was no longer the sunset that forced me off the field. We took the field, playing under the shining, buzzing stadium lights day in, day out for 140 games in 155 days, and it wore all of our bodies down. *Something* had to keep us in one piece. My parents didn't raise me to be reliant on medicine, though there isn't anything morally wrong with taking an over-the-counter pain reliever. Mom rarely gave my brother, sister or me medicine for the little things. We always seemed to just grit it out. In hindsight, I appreciate that about my parents. My grandma was the same way—she'd always whip up a placebo of seltzer water and sugar when my Mom felt ill as a little girl. It cured her on the spot.

They prescribed me Vicodin when I underwent Tommy John surgery for the first time. I took one dose because the nurse gave me very, *very* dirty looks when I told her I hadn't planned on taking any of it. "It will keep you relaxed, not worrying about your arm, which in turn will make the recovery go more smoothly." I rolled my eyes and agreed. A dose later, I swore that stuff off as not only useless but downright poisonous. When those two pills dissolved, it felt like I had a tumbleweed churning a hole in my gut. I was miserable; *never* again. Despite terrible allergies, I rarely took my allergy medicine. I needlessly sneezed and suffered each spring. My overall disinterest in medicine stuck with me well into adulthood. The day I signed my name on a pro baseball contract, however, everything changed. I had to be ready to pitch when they called my name or else I'd lose everything. I'd worked too hard for that.

A few weeks into my first season in pro ball, I was plagued with an intense, deep, throbbing ache in my pitching arm. This same pain had plagued me in high school, making it difficult to pitch more than two innings; I could barely lift my arm when I was done. It had gone away in my freshman year of college, but for unknown reasons had returned. I wrote a lot during my playing days, my Apple MacBook Pro filled with blog posts, email newsletters, journal entries and later, books. My writing time-stamped my exploits and whereabouts, a black box of sorts. I never kept a formal journal, but on the bus that season in 2010, just two starts into my pro career, I was scared and needed to sort things out. So, I wrote:

It's 11:16 p.m. and I'm on the bus, worrying about my arm. Who knows what's wrong this time, but all I know is that the dull ache that invaded my sleep last night hasn't gone away. Rather, it manifested itself in the most painful session of long toss that I can remember. I start again in two days.

A few days ago, I started against our division rival and the current occupant of first place. I'm ashamed to report that I did little to take them down and I earned a big L for my mediocre five innings of work. It could have been better had a few ground balls found mitts, but that's baseball—once that pitch leaves your hand, anything and everything can happen, regardless of the quality of the pitch you just released.

It wasn't all bad. I pitched in the nicest ballpark of my short life, and it was a pretty neat experience being in front of 4,200 fans. Back in college, we were lucky to get 150 fans, and it was an additional blessing if some of them turned out *not* to be parents. Thing is, though, the crowd never really plays much of a part in the game, at least not when I'm locked in and focused. It's a fight against only the mitt, and not a single person of the 4,200 can squeeze their way in between that 60'6" of focus. Sure, I heard the roar when I was backing up the plate after giving up an

RBI single, but I didn't mind; pitching on the road means that when you screw up, the fans are allowed to remind you about it. And anyway, I'd rather be out there giving up runs than back on the sidelines waiting to be healthy again.

We tend to want it all. Four weeks ago, I rolled into town after a 12-hour drive, and found myself scared about the prospect of getting cut and sent back to Baltimore. Sure, I knew I was good and had a spring training contract in hand, but there were no guarantees. I was faced with the task of proving myself to be figuratively above 17 guys who were all literally taller than I. Before leaving for camp, I wanted to be a Major Leaguer; when I arrived I just wanted to stay in Normal, Illinois as a part of the team. Funny how mindsets change and short-term goals take precedent.

Yet, I made the team and I even earned a spot in the starting rotation. And yet again, my mindset changed—in camp I just wanted to be one of the 24, and now I wanted to be the best of the 24. But as the season got rolling and I got a few starts under my belt, my arm started providing me with more aches and throbs than I cared to indulge. I then wanted something completely different: *to not hurt.*

It's a scary feeling when you've just left the mound from start number two and you're already in jeopardy of missing start number three. No one else knows it, but *you* know it. Sure, you can pitch with pain, but if your arm doesn't want to go along for the ride, you might not have the physical stuff to compete. If your arm decides it would rather not throw 90—and instead just go about 84—well, then, guess what? You're screwed, and people are going to figure out in a hurry that you need to be replaced.

So here I sit, an hour from my summer home,

wishing that I'd wake up to a pain-free tomorrow. It's one thing to miss a road start, but when you have 7,000 fans at home eagerly awaiting your arrival on their brand-new mound, you need to find a way to get up onto that bump and get it done. But it's not just this upcoming home start, it's the 17 that will follow it that worry me. I want to stay here, playing all summer as a professional without interruption. Stepping out of the rotation onto the disabled list would either earn me a spot on the bench or a ticket home, neither of which I want any part of. A week ago, I planned for this to be my breakout season, turning heads and climbing ladders, but now my biggest goal is to make it to my next start—one start at a time—until this year is over and I can heal until next season. I don't even know what's wrong with me, but I know that I need something to help my arm feel better. Maybe it's an offseason of rest, maybe it's therapy, or maybe it's something I'm missing entirely. All I know is that I have to find some way to make my next start. That…is step one.

It's surreal reading that essay of mine—returning to that desperate place is not something I ever hoped to do. I did find a solution, a way to make my next start without speaking up: a palmful of Advil. I took over 1,000 ibuprofen pills that summer, something I did not want and would not recommend that others do. Though I never talked about it, my pitching coach eventually caught on to the fact that I was hurting.

"Hey Blew, how's the arm? Hurting ya, huh?"

"What?" I acted confused as I put my glove down on the right field line, getting ready to begin my sprinting routine. It was pregame, and Brooks was lingering, watching the pitchers throw.

"Look. You're not going anywhere, so you can tell me. I know your arm's hurting. You barely throw between starts anymore. Think I don't notice?" I rolled my eyes—of course he knew.

"I just have this horrible deadness, this aching spot between my biceps and triceps [I pointed]. It isn't sharp pain, it just feels awful most of the time, like hitting a bruise with a hammer. It gets better when I massage it and take a lot Ibuprofen; throwing less helps, too."

"How much of that stuff you taking?" He asked, raising an eyebrow.

"Twelve a day."

He grinned, then turned and started walking away. "Welcome to pro ball, kid!"

It felt like the wrong way out. I felt like a hypocrite telling kids to do precisely the opposite: *Never pitch through pain!* I'd say. *Covering it up covers up the root problem!* My situation was different, though—I had no alternative as I desperately tried to establish myself in pro baseball. Really, the only question was this: What would I have done if the Advil *hadn't* done the trick? I still don't have an answer. A dozen ibuprofen per day is a lot. Even then, it took just enough of the edge off to allow me to pitch, but I still pitched in misery. It dulled the pain just enough where it became grit-through-able. *Injured* means you can't physically play no matter how tough you are. *Hurt* means you can play if—and it's a big *if*—you can mentally will yourself to 100% performance with a less-than-100% body. Some guys choose to sit out when they're not 100%, or make excuses for themselves when their 80% body performs at 80%. I chose to play and knew the standard for me was still set firmly at 100%.

A few starts after I wrote that journal entry, I was sitting in the dugout at home, sipping water out of a small paper cup next to my catcher. Especially after an overnight bus ride, I'd get a lot of coffee in my system to ensure that I was alert on the mound. As we sat in the dugout he looked over at me, water cup in hand. His eyes got wide, and in his thick New York accent, said: "Bro! Your hand is shaking! You need to lay off the caffeine!" My hand *was* shaking—legitimately shaking like I had just been pulled out from an icy river with hypothermia. The water in my small paper cup was sloshing around as I tried to drink. It wasn't caffeine, though—*it was my arm.* I couldn't hold a six ounce water cup steady, but the combination of ibuprofen, caffeine and adrenaline allowed me to—every fifth day—throw a baseball 92 miles per hour 120 times. And that—in a nutshell—was *the grind* of pro baseball. One at a time, I pieced 19 starts together like that.

Yet, it was always what I wanted. I was living my dream and I did what was necessary to protect it and keep it alive. The sun shone on me as I played catch and ran sprints during pregame. The grass was always a deep emerald green and the mounds were beautifully maintained. Little kids asked for my autograph, even though the Sharpie was more valuable. The pain was worth it. Just five more minutes. In college, I sat the bench as a freshman because I wasn't good enough to play over other guys. But here, I was penciled-in for innings. I earned them on Friday nights in college when I was at home doing rehab and working on my mechanics in the mirror. They were *my* innings.

Two years later, I made my first All-Star game. It would have been a big, triumphant moment...except I sat through it, awaiting my second Tommy John surgery. That felt the way you think it'd feel. I was the leading vote-getter in the Frontier League in 2012, which meant I would have been the starting pitcher for my division. The kicker was that the game was held in my new hometown of Normal, Illinois. The prospect of me being the All-Star game starter in my hometown—with my baseball academy clients and friends in attendance—it sounded so great but didn't happen. Instead, I merely acknowledged the crowd as they called out my name, introduced as a reserve player. They got a forced smile and a half-hearted wave.

I didn't let that All-Star bid become my last. Three years later, I got off to a great start with Camden in the Atlantic League. The problem was—like most years—I wasn't healthy. My workload suddenly jumped from normal to high in the span of a week, compensating for the few pitchers who went down with injuries. Being relied on is great —it's what you always hope for as a pitcher. I was our setup man and we were in lots of tight games, which meant I often got the call. But after a stretch where I threw five out of seven days, my elbow wasn't ready for it and flared up. A few weeks later as I continued to pitch through it, one of my bullpen mates beckoned to me in batting practice.

"Blew! Come here." BP was always our time to gossip. I walked over, wondered what he had for me.

"Dude how's your elbow?"

"Not great, but the Doc said it's just tendinitis. It hurts kinda bad in the bullpen but it's usually fine in the game. I'm getting through it." He wasn't satisfied with that answer.

"Look, why don't you take a cycle of HgH? Just take one—it will heal you up so fast and you'll be done with all this. You could do Winstrol, too (an anabolic steroid taken commonly by sprinters) either one would be good. You'd be back throwing *hard* bro." I was a little shocked.

"Nah. I can't do that." I replied.

"Why not? One quick cycle—they never test, anyway. You'd be back off in a month and you'd be good to go."

"Yeah, but two things: One—I'm afraid of what that stuff does to your body. And two—if I got popped it would ruin everything I've ever done. *Everything*. No one would know—or care—if the truth was that I just did it for one single month. Two surgeries, two comebacks, man—it wouldn't matter. I'd be a steroid user—the only reason I came back would be because of the steroids. I just can't do that."

"Okay. I get it," he said, backing off as I drew my line in the outfield grass. I just couldn't devalue what I'd been through. If the doctor prescribed it, I'd take it. If I could buy it with 100% certainty it was legal, I'd consider it. But even then, I stuck mostly with food and didn't bother so much with supplements. None of those crazy pre-workout powders that contained *God knows what*, none of those sinister energy drinks beyond a Monster or Redbull every once in a while. Protein, fish oil and coffee were pretty much it for me, and I was content. The stakes were too high for a guy like me who had a backstory.

By late June of that year, I was leading the bullpen in ERA and news came down that I made the Atlantic League All-Star team for our division. I was hitting my stride and my selection positioned me to get in front of a lot of scouts. I vowed that I would pitch in the game no matter what. If I could physically throw a ball toward the plate, I was going to do it. My parents planned on making the drive to Bridgeport, Connecticut where the game was held. But with pain getting increasingly strong—about as bad as I'd ever pitched with—I needed relief. Our team doctor gave me an exam and thought he could help.

"Toradol will get you through the All-Star game. It lasts for a few weeks; it's what they give to NFL players with major injuries who need to still play on Sunday. It'll basically wipe out any inflammation that's in there at the time, and hopefully you heal up before it wears off. It's a corticosteroid pack; you take a few pills each day for seven straight days, then it keeps working for the next few weeks."

I nodded. "Can I pick up the prescription today?"

I felt a little bit important, a little bit like a celebrity—I was getting the same stuff a linebacker would get on Super Bowl Sunday. No more Costco brand Naproxen or Wal-Mart Ibuprofen. I *did* pitch in that second All-Star game—with my parents in attendance—to the tune of a 1-2-3 inning that went *punchout, flyout, punchout*. It was a quick, strong inning in front of a dozen Major League teams. Maybe I'd get a phone call, the Toradol would wear off and I'd find myself pitching healthy on a Major League team's Triple-A squad. But the call never came, though the Toradol did wear off. Still, I tried my best to smile and be present in the big moments. My parents took the train up to watch the All-Star game and looked on as I held my own as one of the best of the best. It was a memorable, proud evening—one that elbow pain and uncertainty could never take from me.

You moved away when I was 12 or 13, and no other kid was able to step in and replace what we had. I was so disappointed when I got the news that your Dad got a new job, that I never forgot his new company's name. I looked them up on the internet, maybe subconsciously trying to find a way to undo his hiring. I didn't want to lose my baseball buddy. A year or two later, I was past the age of backyard baseball and moved into the phase of life where baseball was always organized, always purposeful and profoundly less fun.

In college in my apartment, my roommates and I blew a fuse after connecting too many things to one outlet. I went downstairs to our fuse box, swung open the metal door and there it was, staring me in the face: the logo of Square D, the company that hired your Dad away to Tennessee. They made fuse boxes and other electrical products. Even then—eight or ten years later—I still felt a little twinge of anger as I flipped the offending breaker, closed the battleship-grey fuse panel and went back upstairs. In middle school, I hated that company for what they did; we had so many hours of baseball that went unplayed. Yet, it was those good times in the backyard as kids where I developed enough love for the game to push through all the heaviness I'd later face. Even at 30 years old, nothing had changed—I still just wanted five more minutes.

Dear Zack, There's more there.

In 2016, as a mere 16-year-old, you wrote me this email. It was your weekly update about how your season had been going. You were excited for one of your first varsity starts, but it didn't go as planned:

Well, that went poorly. I only went 2 and 2/3 and gave up 10 runs with eight free baserunners. I don't even know how many hits I gave up. If you can name it, it went wrong. I only gave up one run in the first. That runner got on base by a leadoff walk. There really are no excuses. I walked seven hitters and hit one. I also made errors. The primary problem is I could not locate my fastball. The secondary problem was that I took for granted my ability to manage runners and field my position.

My coach was pissed at me and called me out in front of the whole crowd and the rest of the team, rightfully so. I let my team down and really hurt our ability to compete. In the third inning, I completely lost it.

I could make excuses—like my teammates making errors or the pitches being close—but when it comes down to it, all of it leads back to my performance. I know from firsthand experience how tough it is as a position player to stay focused with a pitcher struggling the way I did today. I also should have made adjustments to the umpire's zone from the start. Today was tough, but it cannot be the end.

I loved this email. It told me a lot about who you were and why everything I believed about your future was correct. I learned that same lesson the hard way—when you're expected to perform, you perform. Nothing else matters—sick, hurt, or exhausted, you still do your job and do it well. There are people in all walks of life who hold this same mentality in their profession, no matter how important or how trivial it might be. And there's something to be said for always believing you're capable of your best, even when logic, reason and circumstance might objectively show that you're not. For young pitchers like yourself, it can be tough to develop this state of mind. Our modern American culture appears to have shifted away from personal responsibility—there's always someone or some thing that we can turn to in a pinch to deflect a negative spotlight. But growth as both a person and as a ballplayer demands culpability—we have to own our failures and force ourselves to walk the plank once in a while, to jump into the ring and fight with whatever might be in our pockets. During my second season, the point was driven to the core of me.

On May 1, 2012, I was on the interstate heading south in my green, 2002 Honda Civic. I had to report to Evansville on May 3 for my physical, so I made some calls to pass the time during my five hours on the road. I called my friend Fred to catch up on the previous season in full detail. He'd only heard bits and pieces of it and had recently texted me to wish me well as I departed to play for my newest team, the Evansville Otters. Fred and I played baseball together for the Yankee Rebels, a summer team in the Metro League of Baltimore. Though he's Italian, Fred doesn't live up to the hot-blooded stereotype—far from it, in fact. He is one of the most level-headed, sensible and diplomatic people I know. Yet, we hadn't been talking as much of late, my relocation to Illinois and his full-time job as an engineer drawing us apart.

As I tried to explain to him how my 2011 season had gone, it became clear that I could not adequately describe how crazy my short time with Lake County had been. There was just too much insanity packed into that short, seven-week span. To call it a debacle would be an insult to debacles.

"How much time do you have?' I asked, holding the phone to my ear as I drove.

"I'm just sitting at home—I've got all day, man."

"Okay. Well this story is going to be long, so stay with me."

"10-4," Fred replied.

The Lake County Fielders—the team I was traded to after my rookie season with Normal—was to start their inaugural season in an expansive conglomerate of leagues called the North American League. A few teams were peeling off from a few other independent leagues— the American Association, the Northern League, the Golden League and the Frontier League. In the early off-season, four teams from the Chicago area committed, as did a cluster in Texas, one from California, a few from Canada, and even a squad in the Mexican border town of Yuma, Arizona. In the end, though, the other Chicago teams pulled out and went to other leagues, leaving the Fielders with no opponent within 20 hours drive time. Public money had been committed to building a ballpark, one that wouldn't be completed until about eight weeks deep into the season. We players were assured that the makeup of the league wouldn't be an issue.

"So first off, spring training was not normal for indy ball. I drove up to Zion, Illinois and it was super cold and rainy there. I mean, it's near Wisconsin and it was early May, so I guess that's what you get up there."

"Cold and rainy is *not* baseball weather." Fred replied.

"Well here's the thing, we get up there and then they told us that we'd be flying to Yuma to have spring training, and scrimmage against José Canseco's team. No independent teams have the budget to do that, so I was skeptical but it ended up actually happening. I was only in Zion for like three or four days before we headed back out. But the thing was, we were starting the season on the road right from there, so we had to pack *everything*. And we only got one baseball bag and one personal suitcase, which had to last us for seven weeks on the road."

"Jesus. Did you leave a lot of stuff behind?"

"Well actually, no—I packed pretty light and just assumed I could re-wear street clothes and get the clubbie to wash them at the ballpark. So I packed light and left everything else in my car and in my host family's house."

"How was your host family? The family you stayed with in Normal was great, right?"

"Yeah, my first host family was awesome. But Dude. This one... *terrible*. I was so happy to get out of there. It was this big house in a nice neighborhood, just a single mom and her son. And, her son was gifted—he was maybe six or seven and crazy smart. But the mom was a legitimate hoarder—there was no way I was going to stay there. I was plotting how to get out of it from the minute I stepped foot in there."

"Like, trash everywhere? What do you mean 'hoarder'?" He asked.

"She was really nice and her kid was awesome, but the entire house was covered in trash. Imagine if every time you took off a piece of clothing, used a dish or made food…you never put it away, washed or threw it in the trash—you just left it there, exactly where you used it. That was how it was. It was unbelievable. I had to high-step over garbage, clothes and old cereal boxes to get through to the kitchen. Then I'd have to try to clear space on the countertop to make a sandwich by pushing old food out of the way. I felt so bad for her son growing up in all of that. I've never seen anything like it."

"Well at least you didn't have to go back."

"Yeah, I lucked out. As soon as we ended up getting back I just grabbed my stuff, said goodbye and was gone. There was no way I could have managed it. It made me appreciate Denny and Dory even more. They were great people."

Our schedule involved an initial span of nearly forty games on the road, against opponents in Maui, Yuma, Chico (California), Edmonton and Calgary, Canada. The long distance between cities meant we would fly to each series. The massive expense of flying a team of 24 ballplayers, coaches, athletic trainer and broadcast staff left the team no choice but to play longer series against each team. And to get there, they booked cheap "red-eye" flights, breaking the team up on multiple planes. The first red-eye brought us to spring training, touching down in hot, dry, Phoenix, where we then took a four-hour bus ride to Yuma. We stayed in a motel—two guys to a room—and I was paired up with one of the pitchers from Normal who had come over in the same trade.

"Did you like your roommate?" Fred asked.

"Yeah—he was a good dude…while it lasted."

"What do you mean?"

"Well, his name was Ricky. He and I were both slated to be starters in the rotation, but he was more of the fifth guy fighting for that last spot. There were three veteran pitchers and then me as the number four starter. I threw pretty well early and they told me that I was the main guy in the trade, so I felt pretty safe. But then a few days in, I woke up and he had freakin' vanished."

"What do you mean vanished!? Was he abducted by a cartel and taken across the border?"

"That would have made more sense. But here's what happened: he had one start left to basically earn that last spot in the rotation. Our manager, TJ, liked him a lot; it really didn't matter how well he threw, he was probably the fifth guy no matter what. So he and I walk to the field like we did everyday—we were bored at the hotel and it gave us something extra to do. We get to the ballpark and everything is normal. He had this snarky, dry sense of humor and made jokes the whole way there."

"Okay so what—he just split from the ballpark?"

"No," I replied. "He pitched *terrible* that night—shelled for like seven runs or something in maybe two innings of work. And then the weird thing was, we walked home and he was...*normal*. If it was me, I'd have said not one word on that walk home. However, he was his normal self the whole way back. As far as I could tell, he was just handling it in a more mature way. His calm approach was what made it so weird when I woke up in the morning and all his stuff was gone."

"So he just left in the middle of the night?"

"Yeah. I didn't realize it at first, but then it dawned on me that all of his stuff was missing and his bed was made. I would *never* have made my hotel bed if I was quitting the team."

"Yeah, seems like a waste," Fred said.

"So then I go to the hotel lobby—it's maybe noon at this point—and I see Rex, our shortstop. I ask him if he saw Ricky at all; he had. He said, 'yeah, he was in the lobby at 3 a.m. with his bags packed, waiting for a bus.' *What?!* I texted Ricky, asking where he was. He replied that he was in Milwaukee waiting for his next flight."

"What do you think his reasoning was for leaving, if he wasn't upset about the game?" Fred asked.

"He just said he didn't want to be there anymore, and didn't elaborate. That was it. Just ended his baseball career right there. Made no sense to me."

I loved traveling, seeing new ballparks and new cities, playing in new climates and facing new competition. I had never been to any of the states that were on our schedule, and I'd also get to see two major cities in Canada. I just couldn't relate to Ricky quitting the team. Sure, I didn't have any context on why he quit—maybe something big happened at home; I didn't know. But the excitement I felt to explore the country, see new places and experience new challenges...it overwhelmed any possible negatives. Little did I know, there were about to be a *lot* of challenges, a *lot* of negatives and a *lot* of new experiences.

After spring training in Yuma concluded, we hopped on the bus to LAX to fly from Los Angeles to the Hawaiian island of Maui. Our first day there was an off-day, which would be followed by seven games on the island; it was incredible. We stayed in a hotel on the poor side of Maui, which allowed us to see the "real" parts and mingle with locals, rather than just rich tourists. A few of us pitchers split a rental car, enabling us to drive around and take in the whole island. We got to see the touristy parts, the sort-of touristy parts like the Zagat-rated dive restaurants, and the very un-touristy parts like the nude beach called *Little Beach*, which was off-the-beaten-path for a reason. I saw naked bodies on that beach that still haunt me.

The team started off hot, beginning the season 10-2. It was clear that we had a good squad and a strong, team-wide swagger. When we lost, it was a shock. Games we lost were usually by a mere run and only because we squandered opportunities. It was tough to beat us and if a team did, they limped out with a win. There were very, very few times when we couldn't have won a game with one extra hit. Players and coaches alike meshed well, which was a big part of our success. Tim Johnson, our manager who went by TJ, and Pete LaCock, our hitting coach, were both former Major Leaguers. Chris Thompson, our player/pitching coach, had played at a high level in the minors. All three gave us free reign to be who we wanted to be while helping us learn the game. In return, the coaches were rewarded with scrappy, hard-nosed play. They didn't have to implore us to play hard or teach us what baseball was about. For the younger guys like myself, we learned on the fly. And for the older guys who had been around, they led by example and enjoyed being in a loose environment where all we had to do was show up on time and play hard. On the field, the game felt simple; the game felt easy.

After we departed Maui, however, travel, sleep-deprivation and jet lag quickly started to take their collective toll. Time zone changes, red-eye flights and caffeine were eroding my circadian rhythm. The second series of the year took place in Yuma, Arizona, and I was slated to pitch the first game, which followed a nightmarish travel day.

"Fred, the travel was so bad. I'd never been so tired in my life."

"Really? I figured flying instead of bussing it everywhere would have been a good change of pace."

"You'd think. But because of the flights they booked, it turned out to be way worse. And I had to pitch the travel game on that series and each of the next two. Listen to this travel situation: we played our last game in Maui and had to be in Yuma again for a four-game series starting the next day. Do you realize how far that is? It was *crazy*—we left Maui at 10 p.m. for a seven-hour flight across three time zones. We landed in Phoenix around 8 a.m., which was essentially 6 a.m. because of the time zone difference. I didn't sleep at all on the flight, so I was exhausted. We hung around the airport until 10 a.m., finally bussing four hours to Yuma, where we arrived at 2 p.m. The window curtains didn't do anything and the sun just poured in, so I couldn't sleep on that bus, either. Once we were in Yuma, I got to sleep for about three hours—from 2 p.m. to 5 p.m. When I woke up, I drank a Monster and caught the shuttle to the ballpark for our *show-and-go*."

This *show-and-go* is baseball lingo for a game in which a team takes no pre-game—you show up and go play. These were reserved for days the team needed a reprieve, typically day games following night games, stretches of swelteringly hot days in July and August and travel days when a trip was especially long. Taking pre-game was and is a sacred ritual even if it's filled with lots of extra, somewhat wasted time. Players need their routines to stay focused and productive over a long season, so deviating from the normal pre-game schedule is rare.

Back in the car, closing in on the Indiana border, I tried to convey to Fred just how tired I was for that game.

"Dude. I was just destroyed from not sleeping the previous night—you know how your body just feels kind of tingly when you completely miss a night's sleep, like it's inflamed all over? That was how I felt and my lids just wanted to shut. But I had to start that night —I didn't know what I was supposed to do to get through it."

"The Monster didn't pick you up?" Fred asked.

"The first one, no. The second one within the hour—which I did *not* want to drink—*did*. And then I had a cup of coffee at the ballpark, too. I felt more alert after that one, but I was a little nervous getting that much caffeine at once…"

"Yeah, that's almost a whole gram of caffeine. You know they measure that in milligrams, right?" We both laughed. I did have a high tolerance for caffeine…but still.

"I dunno, man. It was just what I had to do. I actually ended up throwing pretty well. I went seven good innings and we won, I think

5-1 or something. José Canseco got a hit off me, but I kept him in the ballpark. That dude still has insane bat speed…and he's enormous."

"What's his deal?" he asked.

"He's the player-manager of the Yuma Scorpions. I guess he's trying to still stay in baseball and people still come out to watch. He's in as good of shape as anyone in the league, though he doesn't really run anymore."

Sleeping after that game was all but impossible. A hideous combination of the caffeine still in my blood, time zone changes, the excitement that pitching caused (I never slept overly well after a start), and the light that entered my room at 5 a.m.—all those factors made sleep but a pipe dream. I slept from 5 a.m. to 7 a.m., before finding myself in an odd state of bug-eyed exhaustion; I desperately wanted to sleep but sleep would not come. Zero hours the previous night, a three-hour nap before the game and two hours after the game meant I was running the last 72 hours or so on five total hours of sleep. For a guy who was used to eight solid hours every night, this was *not* shaping up well. Insomnia became the new standard.

We went on to sweep that six-game series in Yuma. I got unlucky in the rotation draw and was slated to again pitch the travel game of each of the next two series. The cycle continued—I didn't sleep on the final night of a series, traveling all night and day. I'd then get hopped up on caffeine to muster the energy to make my start. Then, I'd lay awake that night until three or four in the morning, just to fall briefly asleep and wake back up around seven. The next day, exhausted, I'd naturally need more caffeine. It became an unbreakable cycle because having energy was a job requirement, and caffeine was the only way of summoning it. Sleep was elusive, and yet the cycle churned on:

Travel Day: We'd leave for the airport after the game, then spend the next 16-21 hours traveling, for which I'd often get zero to two hours of sleep. Most flights had two or three connections, getting us from City A to City B as cheaply as possible. Our club saved money by booking the longest, most highly connected flights, which is why travel took extra long. The majority of minor league baseball teams traveled by bus, so at first I thought air travel was exciting. Trying to get my usual block of sleep in three different airports, however, was not.

Day After Travel Day: This was the day that really got me. I'd be so very tired for the game on our travel day that I had to have at least one caffeine pill and two cups of coffee or a big energy drink. I was chomping through caffeine. The result was that I wouldn't sleep this night, either. So, I'd get up to two hours of sleep on travel day, then usually two to four hours on the day after.

The Rest of the Days Until The Next Series: Since my blood was comprised mostly of caffeine and we traveled to a new city every fifth day or so, my body never found its way back to baseline. I couldn't sleep on buses, in planes or chairs, so unless I found a bed or comfortable couch, I'd come away with nothing. Whether I fell asleep at 1 a.m. or 6 a.m, my body was done sleeping by seven or eight. After three weeks of it, I was still pitching well enough and hadn't yet fallen flat on my face (though I didn't really understand how).

The low point came during our second trip to Maui. After starts in Edmonton and then Calgary, we were scheduled to fly back to Hawaii with no travel day. No travel day meant that we had our last game in Calgary one night, then had to be playing in Hawaii the next. One might rightfully ask, "How—in God's name—did you make it there in time?" Well, the answer is that we didn't and that it's barely possible. We finished up our game at 10:00 p.m. and had to spend a solid 10 hours in the air, plus downtime in the airport between connections. Our flight out of Calgary was at 6 a.m., so if one did the math…it was a stretch just to make it there by first pitch at 7 p.m., even counting the five hours we would make up due to time zone differences. Here's how the situation broke down:

Our last game in Calgary started at 7 p.m. and ended at 10 p.m., which left us about three hours to sleep in the hotel after we showered and ate. The team bus left at 2 a.m. to catch our 6 a.m. flight. Some guys had two connections and others had four. I was lucky and only had two. The first group of players arrived in Maui three hours before game time. I was in the second group, which arrived a mere hour before game time. The third group did not make it in time for the first pitch, even after they delayed the start time by an hour. We started the game with no coaches and without five or six players, including our starting centerfielder and second baseman. A pitcher carried the lineup card to the umpire meeting. We players had actually created the lineup, writing in the starting nine we assumed TJ would have chosen if he was there. It was a weird feeling as four of us pitchers sat around and planned out the lineup, scratching it through all three carbon copies before heading out to the dugout.

The final flight groups, comprised of our coaches and the last few players, arrived starting in the second inning. By the fifth inning we had our whole team, but the game went 15 innings—it was a nightmare. The first pitch was at 8 p.m. with the last around 12:30 a.m. This was, of course, in a time zone five hours behind that of Calgary...so it felt like 5:30 a.m. to us. We won, 3-2.

We had a daytime doubleheader the next day, starting at 11 a.m. Naturally, I had to pitch that first game of the doubleheader. Lucky me. In every start prior, caffeine, adrenaline and a little self-talk got me amped up enough to feel normal when I got on the mound. This time, however, none of that worked. While taking a momentary break during my pregame bullpen, I found myself almost nodding off to sleep. My shoulders drooped, my eyes drifted and my body was going limp—my brain was physically trying to shut me down, to send me off to the sandman. There was no *go* left in me. I tried to psyche myself up: *I'm gonna throw the crap out of this next fastball! Let's do this! It's gametime! Rahhh!* I flared my nostrils, furrowed my eyebrows, drew in an angry breath and let it fly. This time, it just didn't work—nothing seemed to. I could not shake the bone-deep fatigue that had accumulated. It felt like a victory to simply not fall over.

I coasted through the first couple innings on a 77 degree, typically breezy Maui day. The Maui club wasn't very good, which was lucky because I was barely engaged in what I was doing. It was the most zombie-like I'd ever been in a real baseball game. Finally, an hour in, I got a little head of steam. I felt a bit more awake in the third inning and hit my stride in the fourth. I stitched good fourth and fifth innings together and walked off the mound feeling like myself, excited to go back out for the sixth. As I walked back toward the dugout, Pete was first in the high-five line that awaited. He was acting manager that day because TJ had a family situation he had to deal with back at the hotel. I expected a hand-slap from everyone and nothing more. Then, Pete stopped me.

"Hey Blew, that's it."

I was taken aback—I had just found myself out there. "What? Are you serious?" I said, throwing him a confused and defiant look.

Pete's eyes got wide, as he defended his decision: "Yeah! You're done!"

I got caught up in the moment. No one else knew the victory I had just won over exhaustion. I was excited to go back out but in my excitement, I screwed up badly. It was a cardinal sin to talk back to a coach or question their decisions. As I sat down on the bench, disappointed in myself and a little anxious about the possible consequences, one of the veteran starting pitchers, Zac Cline, came over. Zac was a soft-spoken lefty with a Cali vibe to him. He laughed easily and was a calming influence on all of us. But this time, he came with a warning: "Blewett. Bro. You can't say that. You need to go apologize to Pete." I had been thinking the same thing and didn't need much convincing, so I got up and found Pete.

"Hey Pete. I want to apologize—I'm sorry I showed you up just now. I shouldn't have second-guessed you. I know you're doing what's best for the team. I was excited about my previous inning and just let it get the best of me. It won't happen again."

"It's alright, Blew. I know you just got caught up. We're all competitive, but thanks for apologizing."

I walked back to my corner of the dugout to finally relax; my job was done for another four days. I had another long game to sit through, but after that I'd finally have a warm bed in my future. Yet, I was worried that TJ—our salty, old-school manager—would hear about it. Sure enough, he would come to find me later that night…

Living in a world without excuses was hard and it forced me to grow up fast. Brooks chewed me out about my blistered finger and my sleepless outings in Lake County solidified my views on excuses. I wasn't expected to *try*, I was expected to *do*. All of us could have made myriad excuses to explain away bad performances. We were tired. Travel was brutal. The game schedule was ridiculous. We could have just phoned it in and others would have understood. But it's not the way to do it, especially if you're playing the long game, trying to become great someday. Even at your young age, Zack, you've proven to me that success is waiting for you. Being held to a high standard is a blessing—it extracts our best and initiates a search within for strength we've always possessed but didn't know was there.

Dear Morgan, It was worth it.

From the first day you set foot in my academy, you lingered. It's a unifying quality, really—all of the best athletes linger. Five more minutes. Until it's dark. Dad, pick me up a little later. The story would change but it was always the same.

You were a skinny noodle at the time, but that changed in a hurry. Today, it's hard to imagine you that way as you throw 350lbs on the bar and squat it with ease. Just like anything, though, it didn't happen overnight. The lingering, the sponge-like absorption of our methods and madness—you took all that and ran with it, getting farther down the road than I think any of us would have guessed.

You didn't linger, though, solely for the next training tip. You'd sit, in no hurry whatsoever, waiting for my stories to run dry for the day. I always hoped I'd have Big League tales to tell, but I appreciated you listening anyway. Those days have passed and you're out traveling the country, coaching and creating your own memories. When I thought of who would most enjoy this story of knuckleballs, red-eyes and mutiny, there was no other choice—it had to be you. My time in Lake County and the way it came to an end—it summed up so much about what baseball, at it's best, can be. Precisely because it was such a hot mess, it became the thing of legend.

Pete LaCock, our fearless hitting coach for the Lake County Fielders, was a former Chicago Cub back in the 1970s. With light-brown, slightly curly hair and a tanned complexion, he reminded me of Julius Caesar. He was very much the mortar holding the team together, as Tim Johnson was a hands-off, low-energy type of manager, lurking in the shadows and keeping his interactions with players somewhat minimal. If something needed to get done, Pete took care of it. He was the liaison between the front office and the team, distributing paychecks, meal money, plane tickets, hotel keys, and itineraries. Pete's work made the team work.

As early as spring training, we started to experience irregularities with our paychecks and meal money. It's sad but customary that players aren't paid during spring training. Though this rule is ridiculous and probably breaks labor laws, it's par for the course. Despite grumbling and poor labor practices, all a player expects in camp is meal money and free breakfast. Typically, though, the team will provide lunch as well if morning workouts yield to an afternoon session. But as soon as workouts are done for the day, a player is on his own to spend the $15-20 per diem as he sees fit. For a grown athlete in his 20s, $18 in meal money doesn't go very far. It spreads even shorter when one is stiffed a few days' worth.

In spring training, we were shorted a few days' worth of meal money, getting seven days' worth of cash for the 11-day camp. I was unmarried and untethered with no rent to pay back home (I had moved out) and no wife or children to feed. I was frugal and stable with money, so being shorted $60 or so didn't cause me much concern. But for other guys with mouths to feed back home, it mattered. Pete explained that the front office was going to soon get us the meal money we were owed. He also explained that if someone was in a major pinch for cash, he could lend a few dollars.

Pete kept his word as the financial situation began to degrade. The rest of the meal money didn't show up and by the time we were owed more, heading to Maui for opening day, the team again sent only enough for about half the week ahead. Our salaries started on the first travel day of the season, so we all had to go another two weeks before seeing our first paycheck.

Hawaii was a bad place to be low on cash. When you wanted to save money, the best thing to do was eat a few extra PB&Js in the hotel and try to crush the spread of food at the ballpark. A guy could normally pick up all the necessary provisions to make a dozen PB&Js for a mere six bucks: two bucks each bought a jar of peanut butter and jelly, and a dollar or two for a loaf of bread completed the meal kit. You'd then scrounge for plastic silverware in the grocery store hot foods section or the hotel breakfast area, rather than buying a two-dollar box of plasticware. Put it all together and you had something unspectacular, yet adequate, to fill your belly with when money ran low.

On the island of Maui, however, a jar of peanut butter was six or seven dollars, depending on the brand. Jelly was the same and a loaf of bread cost four bucks. A gallon of milk cost eight dollars—it was insanity! There was no reprieve for the starving minor leaguer, especially not on an island in the middle of the ocean. Maybe it was the Baseball Gods making us pay the toll for experiencing such a beautiful vacation destination, when most players played in tiny rural towns with hardly a White Castle to walk to. I ended up finding cheap, filling food at the most unlikely of locations—Whole Foods Market— the wonderful antithesis of a cheap grocery store. After perusing its aisles extensively for the best bang for my buck, I went with an unsliced loaf of crusty old-world bread and a pound of $9.99 pulled barbecue pork. I got a handful of meals out of that loaf and pulled pork, then went back each day to replenish. I still revel in the irony that Whole Foods—of all places—was my value shopping location of choice. Economies of scale, I suppose.

As players fell deeper into the hole in Hawaii, Pete was forced into the awkward position of regularly announcing that the team didn't wire enough money to fully pay everyone. Between all the coaches, players, and traveling front office members (including a trainer and radio guy), meal money was a costly team expense—between $3,000 and $4,000 dollars per week—even at the paltry, inadequate rate of $18 per day. Nonetheless, we'd gather in the hotel lobby as Pete explained the situation.

"Guys, I'm sorry but they only wired $1,500 this week, which works out to $62 a player. If you need more, let me know, but this is all we've got to work with right now. You were supposed to get $126 this week, and I'm keeping a tally for everyone on what they've been paid and what they're owed. I'm sorry, guys—you deserve better, especially the way you've been playing."

We'd all then wait in line for our handful of 20s and singles, a few guys sticking around to take him up on his offer of additional cash. No one felt good about it, but the likelihood that Pete would be reimbursed, we felt, was greater than any of us. The further the team fell behind on payments to us, the more our optimism waned. The hole was getting awfully deep and if they couldn't pay us now, what would change?

Our salaries were paid on the first and fifteenth of each month, which meant that our first paycheck was to come when we returned to Yuma for our second series. Paychecks were overnighted to us and

Pete distributed them to each of us in the hotel lobby. Aside from the overdue meal money, it seemed that things were looking up. Bank of America was right next to our Yuma motel, so I walked over and deposited it in one of their miraculously high-tech ATMs; I got a nice receipt saying that my check appeared to cash and all was well. Others, however, were not so lucky. A big group of guys went to Wal-Mart to cash their checks and were embarrassed to get turned away: "sorry guys, but these checks have insufficient funds." They were livid. Others went straight to a bank like I had, but were also turned away with bouncing checks. We came to realize that there was maybe four or five thousands dollars in the team's account, not enough to cover every paycheck. The first 10-15 guys who cashed or deposited their checks saw them clear; all the rest turned to rubber. It was at this point that we were knocking on the door of a labor crisis. We had been away from home for the better part of a month and some guys had been paid only a couple hundred bucks in meal money. It was an understatement to say that there was unrest—guys were *pissed.* At our next lobby meeting, Pete calmly fielded their complaints.

"The team said the rest of the paychecks will clear and they'll be sending new ones. Guys, I'm really sorry. This has been an absolute joke, I know. I wish I could do more for you guys, but I've only got the same as last week—I have meal money, but we're short a few days' worth."

The half of the team whose paychecks bounced erupted.

"Are you kidding me? How are we supposed to make this work without getting paid? We've got bills to pay. This is ridiculous!"

"I know, guys, I know." Pete sighed. He didn't deserve any heat, but he took it anyway.

"I'll do what I can, and just know that I'm not any happier—TJ and I haven't been getting paid either. We hope you guys do before we do. We know what it's like; we know what you guys make."

He dipped deeper into his own pocket, offering to hand out a few hundred bucks to each player whose paycheck bounced, helping them get by until the situation was hopefully resolved. The stack of cash he removed from his pocket—freshly pulled from the ATM—was truly impressive. It was about four solid inches of twenties and fifties; Big-League money, we presumed.

I admired Pete. My paycheck had cashed, so I didn't have too much to complain about. I was having a ton of fun playing baseball, I went to bed with food in my stomach, and I still had a few thousand dollars in my bank account along with a crappy but paid off Honda and a credit card that had no balance. I was good with money, didn't buy much and didn't drink much. The only real expense I had was food and a cell phone bill, so I kept my focus on pitching.

Above all, Pete was patient—especially in the face of a front office that was lying to him about the money situation and players who were increasingly passing along their frustrations. He had to manage both ends of it, trying to calm down irate players who began making legitimate threats.

"Pete, I hear you but if we don't get paid soon I'm not gonna take the field. I'm not out here playing for free." That sentiment began popping up with increasing regularity.

A few of us knew better—we players had zero rights; refusing to take the field would yield only further problems. Cash wouldn't magically appear and we had flaming hoops that we had to jump through to claim free agency for non-payment. A player had to go unpaid for two weeks before he could file a grievance and petition the league to become a free agent. After he filed petition papers, the team would have at least seven days to resolve the issue and pay the player in full; if they failed to make good in that period, then the player would be granted free agency. It was a long road and refusing to play would merely result in suspension; we had no union and no leverage.

As our road trip wore on, it became a mad dash to the bank. If you got there too late, your paycheck transformed before your eyes into a worthless piece of paper. Things got so bad with a week left on the road that it became a very real possibility that the team would refuse to play. We had survived a horrendous travel schedule, jetsetting from Maui to Yuma to Edmonton, then on to Calgary, back to Yuma and finally Chico. After our four games in Chico we were mercifully scheduled to fly back home. Our seven weeks on the road began winding down as we continued to win games. Player-only meetings were held as if we were a union, the main idea being that—at some point—we had to make a stand. I didn't disagree, but I also had no idea where that would lead us. With a week left before flying back home and numerous pay periods without paychecks, we brought our consensus to TJ and Pete. They deliberated for a brief moment before addressing us. TJ spoke first.

"What do you guys think is going to happen if you refuse to play? That you'll win this battle? No. The commissioner will come down and suspend every last one of you; you'll be stuck. You won't get paid and it won't be the big *screw you* to the ownership that you want. YOU will be the ones getting screwed. Get your heads out of your asses." He then walked out of the room, sealing his mic-drop moment. That was TJ—blunt and unapologetic.

Well. So much for that idea. Dejected, I put down my sword, pulled off my eyepatch and threw my skull and crossbones bandana on the ground. Our skipper didn't share our vision for justice and the reaction from our side was understandably...*bad*. After he delivered his dissent and hastily left the room, Pete swooped in to offer a conciliatory opinion. It wasn't to undermine TJ, but rather to placate everyone—we had just received another collective slap in the face.

"Look, guys. I realize that wasn't what you wanted to hear, but it was the truth. You don't have any rights in this situation and it's going to get ugly if you refuse to play. I'm as tired of dealing with these people as you are—the lies get fed to me every day. But, we need to be smart about this and pick our battles. Let's wait 'til we get home to Lake County. They've told me that when we get home, the fans coming through the gates will free up a lot of money and everyone will be paid what they're owed. Can we do that?"

The group grumbled, rolled eyes, then begrudgingly agreed. I just wanted to play ball, so I glanced around eagerly hoping my teammates would accept it and move on. If I wasn't taking the field, I wasn't going *anywhere* in baseball. I needed them to play alongside me.

"Please, just do it for me," Pete pleaded. "If we get home and nothing changes, then I'll be with you guys 100%. We'll refuse to play if that's the group's decision."

Though there were a few holdouts, we agreed to wait until we got home while being crystal clear with Pete that we'd wait not one moment longer if we weren't paid at home. "I'll walk out the door right behind you guys," he said.

Our squad finished the seven week road stand at 20-10, a fantastic record considering the horrendous travel schedule filled with jet lag, sleepless nights and financial unrest. Off-field issues often caused a degradation of the on-field product. You'd see it when a guy was fighting with his wife, broke up with a girlfriend, or got sad news from back home—he wouldn't be the same player when the lights came on. To keep one's mind right and focus sharp amidst personal turmoil is a lot to ask. But despite it all, we were the best team in the league as we flew back to Gurnee, Illinois. A mildly sweet smell of optimism filled the cabin in that final plane ride home. We were about to take a turn for the better and play our final 70 games well-rested in front of an eager crowd that had been tracking our play from afar. We'd hopefully finish the summer with a championship ring and beer showers to redeem our struggle. Little did we know, our craziest days were still ahead of us.

I earned the nickname "Red-ass" from TJ. My main nickname was "Blew" and it was first coined in college. It was such an obvious nickname that I wasn't sure why I didn't grow up with it. Red-ass, though, only lasted for that half-summer as a member of the Lake County fielders, and it was noteworthy because it described me in a way that wasn't congruent with who I really was. At that time, though, who I was…was rapidly changing.

The Lake County situation was weird. The league's geographic expanse, the financial debacle, the visiting team destinations, the National League rules that were employed—nothing was as it should be compared to typical Minor League baseball. I guess in a sense, it was fitting that the league required pitchers to hit. What possible reason they could have had for this, we didn't know. Were they grooming us to get signed by National League teams, so we could jump right into the Majors and hold our own with the bat? It didn't add up. Really, it just seemed like a ploy to make the league stand out from others. As fun as it sounds, and as much as pitchers long to prove they have power and could do the job of a position player, I didn't really want to hit. I hadn't swung a bat since high school, when the average pitcher threw 75 miles per hour. Nearly a decade later, I was poised to get thrown into the fire, facing pitchers throwing 88-90mph on average. I wasn't optimistic about anything fun happening at the plate.

The starting pitchers made a pool: $10 per base went to the pitcher who got the first single, double, triple and homerun of the year. So, if you were the first pitcher to hit a triple (good luck), you'd collect $30 from each pitcher in the rotation for a total purse of $120; not bad for one lucky at-bat. I was fourth in the rotation and when my first start of the year came up, no pitcher had yet gotten a hit. We were all on short pitch counts in Maui, as was customary to allow our arms to gradually build up to a full workload. The goal of start number one was to make it through five innings; this meant that two, maybe three at-bats was all we'd get. In the second inning of my start, my team rallied, pushing across a few runs. Hitting ninth, I watched the 6-hole hitter get on base, then the 7-hole, allowing the 8-hole to hit with less than two outs. I anxiously took my practice swings as I walked to the on-deck circle. I knew that to actually get the chance to swing, I had to come up to the plate either with two outs, or with less than two and the bases clear; in most other situations I'd be asked to bunt.

The Maui ballpark featured dark, nearly black dirt because of its volcanic origin. It was a unique setting, an older municipal ballpark with the outfield wall giving way to palm trees. I learned that starting pitchers took their BP the day prior—not the day of—so that they wouldn't wear themselves out on the day they pitched. In my first round I did…just okay; I sprayed line drives and routine fly balls to all fields. I had chosen the biggest piece of lumber I could find from the team bat bag, a T141 model, 34 inches in length weighing 32 ounces. It was a big, top-heavy maple bat with a long, 2 5/8" barrel. I wanted whatever most closely resembled those plastic red whiffle bats with the enormous barrels, the ones we all swung in backyard pickup games. My idea was that if I was going to hit it, I might as well hit it hard. And if I was going to strike out and generate a breeze, it might as well cool off the entire dugout.

As I walked toward the batter's box with no batting gloves on, hands sticky with pine tar, I felt like a traitor—like I shouldn't be hitting against a fellow pitcher. We were certainly not on the same team, but it felt a little like I was in a civil war against my own countryman. Before stepping into the box, I looked down for my sign at third base. Pete, standing in the grass behind the bag wearing his black skullcap helmet, gave me a *what the hell are you looking over for?* kinda look before smiling and giving me a sarcastic "swing away" gesture. I refocused on the pitcher, a right-hander who was a little taller than me but thinner. I'm sure he was terrified as I dug in with no batting gloves and a huge bat, struggling to hold back a smile. I was, however, focused on winning that pitchers' pool. As he started his windup I instinctually started to recoil into whatever remained of my high school batting stance. He kicked his leg up and down, then without warning a white streak was hurtling toward me.

Someone swung. It must have been me, because the ball connected with my bat with a loud *THOCK!* and sent a one-hopper back at him, hitting the ground at the base of the mound and taking a topspin hop that collided hard with his left thigh. It *might* have qualified as a line-drive, but I wasn't sure on the official ruling. I dropped my bat and ran clumsily down the line as the ball trickled into the infield grass. I was always the first to admit that I wasn't the most graceful mover. Here I was, displaying my "Terminator" sprint in full view of my teammates and the screaming fans. The stunned pitcher scrambled to collect the ball as it rolled toward first base, but it was too late. I beat his underhand flip to first base by a step, and with it earned my first professional hit. A single on my first at-bat—on the first pitch, no less—had won me a tidy $40 plus bragging rights for the rest of the season. I grinned uncontrollably on first base as our dugout erupted in laughter and cheers. I quickly shut it down, replacing my smile with a more stern expression. I realized I was showing up the pitcher, who didn't find any of it funny. I thought to myself, *Oh Crap. He might drill me next time.*

A few innings later, I was back in the box against the same starting pitcher, only this time there were runners on base and I was tasked with laying down a sacrifice bunt. I was worried he might throw at me in retribution for the childish laughter the previous inning, so I wasn't keen on getting my face near the plate. I begrudgingly squared around early, displaying my intention to bunt as I simultaneously prepared to protect myself.

Maybe I was right and he was actually mad. Or, maybe it was just an unhappy coincidence. Regardless, he kicked and delivered, sending that same white streak roaring toward me. About a third of the way into its flight, my fears were realized: it was coming right at my face. I quickly snapped out of my bunting stance, as I turned and ducked out of the way. In a reaction that surprised even me, I got *pissed*. I held my bat in at my side, stared right at him and took a step toward the mound. The umpire walked out in front of me and shoved me back in a nonchalant way as he threw a new ball back to the pitcher. The dugout roared and I overheard TJ's belly laugh as he pointed at me with his right hand while holding his stomach with his left.

"Look at Blewett! Kid's about to go out there and fight the pitcher! What a red-ass! I love it!"

On the next pitch, the pitcher piped a fastball and I successfully bunted it down the first base line. Somehow, I was two-for-two in quality at-bats without having any idea what I was doing. I jogged back into the dugout and was greeted with smiles, high-fives and jeers about my near mound-charge. TJ was strutting up and down the dugout, still laughing and shouting about my newly minted status as a red-ass, a term with which I was not familiar. Four innings later, I reached my pitch count and was removed from the game. In between innings, I asked our skipper to clarify the term.

"Hey Skip. What does that nickname even mean? I don't get it." He laughed.

"You know, like George Brett—George Brett was a red-ass. A guy who gets red in the face, gets really angry really quick. He put his hands on his head in disbelief: "You stared right at him and took a step toward the mound on a fellow pitcher! Oh man, that made my day!" I sighed. TJ loved this too much to let it go. I was forever going to be known as Red-ass.

The thing about it was that I wasn't really that type of person. Sure, I was competitive and I played the game hard. I'd love to lie and act like I'm this brawling, take-no-prisoners kind of guy...but I'm really not. I'm a calm, deliberate person who never screams in the dugout or throws his glove after a bad outing. I was more of a robot on the mound than anything, the silent assassin who did his job and didn't show much emotion about it. But I had been changing and noticed it for the first time in the previous season. It was an ordinary day and I had just taken an ordinary shower at my host family's house after my late-morning workout. I looked in the mirror. Despite having looked in it the previous day, I distinctly remember tilting my head, confused at who was looking back. My jaw looked different. My eyes looked different. My five o'clock shadow had crept farther up my cheekbones than I'd ever seen it. Despite looking into a mirror on a daily basis, I was different. I was 24 and I didn't look, nor feel, like a kid anymore. Even when I had risen to a leadership role in college, I hadn't felt like a leader. Yet on that day in that mirror, it was the first day I felt a grown man was looking back at me.

Maybe it was being away from home, maybe it was being in the viciously cruel world of pro sports; I didn't know. I hadn't lacked confidence as a younger man, but I'd say that I possessed more of a neutral affect. I knew I could accomplish big things and I worked toward them in a very pragmatic way. As far as actually taking the bull by the horns when it charged? I just didn't have much experience in that. Before college, I had always just magically been one of the best players. And in college, though it was a struggle to get better and earn playing time, I was never subjected to the life or death, pitch well or be gone pressure that I was met with in pro ball. The pressure was forging me, providing little clues as to my new shape each year.

When Pete pulled me out of my fatigued start in Maui, two and a half weeks later, the red-ass in me showed up again. Snapping at a coach and showing him up in front of the whole team? It was not me at all, yet I did it. After the incident, just as I suspected he would, TJ came to find me. I was in a teammates' room sitting on the bed, sharing in a conversation as a few guys played cards. I wasn't much of a card player, but I knew I'd be up til the wee hours of the morning, so I hung out and observed. With the door open, TJ suddenly slipped in like a whisper. He silently surveyed the room and then locked his eyes on me. I gulped.

"Blewett." The name rumbled slowly and lowly out of his throat. "Pete told me what happened out there today." TJ always talked slow and low—he was often hard to hear unless you sat close. My heart sank, knowing that he knew. He continued.

"You know, you're lucky. If you had done that to me, you'd have never played another inning. Anywhere. You'd be done. Do you believe that?"

My neck sunk like a scared turtle as I nodded.

"Good. Pete loves ya." Then, TJ chuckled. "What a red-ass! Love ya, kid! See ya out there tomorrow. Good job today. Good win today, boys."

That was it. Just like that, his switch flipped back to being my biggest fan. Skip's brief address was ominous, reminiscent of how a gangster would warn his minions to stay in line. The idea that he could blacklist me from all of baseball was odd and certainly an exaggeration, but I got the point. I screwed up and even though good-natured Pete forgave me, the final word needed to come from the top.

That was a microcosm of who Tim Johnson was—a quiet, mysterious, but easygoing former Major League manager. We had a roster of 24 and played National League rules, which I learned took a lot more managing than American League rules. He had to carefully monitor his pitchers so he could pinch-hit for them with the right player at the right time without leaving bullets leftover in the chamber. Double-switches were common, yet I hadn't seen one in my rookie season and they were rare in college. But playing National League rules, tie games in the late innings had major implications. Most of the bench players would get used up—pinch-hitting for pitchers—which escalated as short relievers came and went. Often, the outcome would still be uncertain as our last position player left the bench, putting us an injury away from a pitcher going in to hit or play the field. Major

League rosters have 25 players, so TJ was playing the same game but short-handed by one player. And with one less guy and no one to call up from the minors, his moves had to be precise. When a player would get banged up, his options thinned. Can't burn the backup catcher to pinch hit—what happens if the starter goes down? Can't pinch hit too early if the game might go into extras. It was a juggling act with a lot of questions and I was impressed by how well he made the pieces fit.

A month later, we finally arrived back in Illinois to play our first home series. The team owed us a good amount of money and we had all agreed to give them one series at home—five games against José Canseco's Yuma Scorpions—to reconcile our paychecks and meal money. Each starting pitcher would get one more turn before our deadline expired. I was anxious about it because I really wanted to get paid and keep going. I loved the team and wanted us to stay together, so I was hopeful we'd avoid further drama.

My final start for Lake County was my best of the year. I pitched the third game of the series, with three thousand fans packing what amounted to a traveling carnival ballpark. The bleachers were all temporary with chair-back seats that folded completely down for easy removal. Windscreen was draped on the outside to make it look more like a ballpark and less like a high school football stadium. The grass was slightly more yellow than green, as irrigation hadn't been installed to automatically water the field. The grounds crew hosed it down prior, but they used an ordinary garden hose that was woefully inadequate in dampening the rock-hard infield. Nonetheless, it felt good to be home and to be supported by fans that had been tracking us as we killed it on the road. Returning from a 30-game road trip with a 20-10 record was, without a doubt, *killing it*.

One of my personal training clients, a man in his late 40s named Gerry, had made the trip from Naperville to watch me turn in a 4-1, complete game victory with eight strikeouts. The Scorpions had three former Major Leaguers in the lineup—José Canseco, Joey Gathright, and Willy Aybar, so I felt accomplished navigating through all that terror in just my second pro season. In the ninth inning I was still throwing hard—touching 93 on my 120th pitch—as I wrapped the game up in a nice bow, ending it with a 6-4-3 double play. As we went through the handshake line, the high fives felt just a touch like goodbyes. It was my second career complete game, but the unknowns that lurked beneath took away some of the sweetness. I wasn't going to pitch again before our deadline and had no idea what was coming next for the team. If we broke up, this game would be rendered meaningless. I hadn't pitched all that well in my previous two outings, so I wanted this gem to contribute to the bigger picture. There was a pit in my empty stomach, as the last thing I could control was now complete. I was just along for the ride until our deadline for mutiny hit, hopeful it would all work out.

The next day, paychecks still weren't there when our left-handed starter, Zac, was set to take the mound. Zac pitched well and we again won in easy fashion. After the game we huddled in our "clubhouse," a portable classroom in the parking lot adjacent the left field bleachers. It contained 25 metal lockers so thin that a wallet turned edgewise almost scraped the sides. The space was maybe 40 x 20, and all 25 lockers fit on just one of the long edges with room in each corner. Rather than get in each others' way trying to use them, we spread out and stored our gear in piles on the floor, our chairs leaning against the beige walls. TJ had asked us to gather because he had something he wanted to tell us. Many of us half-naked, we turned to listen to our skipper speak.

"Guys, you've made me incredibly proud. Being a part of this group of dirtbags has been a privilege and a hell of a lot of fun. Despite everything we've been through—the horrible travel schedule, the lies about paychecks, playing on no sleep and here in a fake clubhouse with no lockers and no shower, you've done incredible. We're in first place and it's because you guys truly are the definition of *dirtbags*— guys who will win no matter the circumstances." We cheered. The captain of our Jolly Roger told it like it was.

"But I can't tolerate the front office anymore—what they're doing to us, to you guys. They've lied over and over and here we are again—we gave them a deadline and yet I've got no paychecks to give you. I don't need the money and me and Pete are both thousands of dollars into our own pockets. But for you guys, I have to make a stand. So, as of tonight I'm resigning as manager." My heart sank—it was really happening. We would not be able to recover from this. TJ continued.

"Pete has agreed to finish the next game as manager, after which he will resign as well, along with Chris. I love you all and I'm sorry it had to end this way." And just like that, Tim Johnson, our mysterious, brilliant skipper, was *out*.

The whole experience—paycheck or no paycheck—had been incredible. We bonded deeply as a team, played with hustle and grit on no sleep, slept in airports and won games in some of the most exotic places ever by a humble, underpaid group of ballplayers. It was unlikely we'd ever get paid but very well might be held hostage, forced to play for a team with new leadership that could never live up. With TJ gone from the room, Pete, letting out a sigh so big that he deflated about 20 pounds, asked for our opinion on what we'd like to do. Our response was instant and I projected my deep voice into the mix. All of us wanted to be heard.

"We're not playing without you and TJ. So if he's gone, then we're done." Pete nodded.

"Okay. I told you guys before that we'd wait until we got home and here we are—they lied to us again and are telling us there's no money. With TJ gone, I'll do whatever you guys want; this is a group decision. But, we have to play one more game; if you don't play, they'll suspend you and then you'll be stuck. No one wants to be stuck here, so let's just go out there one more time. What do you guys think?"

"Let's just call it! Screw this—we don't need to play!"

"Yeah! They can't suspend us all."

"Why do we keep waiting? Let's just end this."

Then, someone shouted an answer that made a bunch of us mutineers stop in our tracks.

"What if pitchers hit, and position players pitched?" We all looked at each other. Smirks, then smiles began to crack on faces throughout the room.

In our final game, we decided, pitchers would play the field and position players would pitch. If we were forced to play, we'd make a mockery of the game. We finished changing into our street clothes and went home to our host families and hotels, preparing for our final day as Fielders.

The next day, about an hour before game time, just after batting practice, we were in the clubhouse pulling on our baseball costumes when José Canseco walked in. He turned left into the coaches' office and emerged a few minutes later. He heard through the grapevine what we were going to do and stopped in to chat with Pete about it. After their brief talk, he explained on his way out that his squad would do the same out of respect for us. Thanks to him, we had a full-blown beer league game on our hands. And, as the cherry on top...José—throwing knuckleballs, no less—would be the starting pitcher. Holy crap.

Even in his forties, José Canseco was still a gigantic, intimidating human being. He was still every bit of the 6'4," 240lbs he was listed at during his incredible Major League career. MLB glory long in his rearview mirror, he was in the other dugout as player-manager for the Yuma Scorpions. When we decided that the paycheck situation required desperate action, he took the high road. Rather than throw out his normal lineup and slaughter us, he chose to play along and field the same inverted lineup that we did.

Our ship had been taking on water for some time, but we were just now tightening up our life jackets, preparing for a cold swim. We had no illusions. Though we all got a little giddy about playing out of position, it still felt...*off*. I was penciled into the lineup as the DH since I had just thrown a complete game two days prior. I also didn't have much desire to run around in the outfield, nor did I have the skills to play infield. All I really wanted to do was take José deep and jog around the bases. I didn't want to run the bases and expose that I'd forgotten many instinctual baseball skills, having been a pitcher-only for so long. Canseco would be throwing knuckleballs, after all—how hard could they be to square up?

I remember the first time I pitched against him. He had an aura that followed him wherever he went—and he knew it. José approached the plate with a fearless swagger, staring right at you without breaking his gaze. He wore a military-grade arm guard that was strictly necessary, as he'd promptly wipe out the inside line of the batters' box and plant his back foot nearly on the point of the plate. I swear I'd never seen another hitter—before or after—crowd the plate as tightly as he did. It was an aggressive, albeit superficial tactic—he clearly wanted to scare pitchers into throwing him away. Why? So he could extend his massive arms and take you deep. You'd never risk hitting the 6-time MLB All-star and 1988 AL MVP...would you? What sane pitcher would dare damage and incur the wrath of a 4-time Silver Slugger Award Winner?

At 25, I was just coming into what I would call my "consciousness" as a pitcher. I'd been pitching since the age of 10 or so, but the higher stakes of professional baseball drove me to think more than I ever had on the mound. I had brief moments of this beginning in college during my sophomore year. In my rookie season at age 24, my job was on the line in a very real way, and intelligent pitching helped maximize my chances of staying in the game. I'd say that by the time José stepped in, I was operating at 25% of my maximum baseball brainpower—I knew a few things about pitching, but nowhere close to what I'd come to know in the years that followed.

Twenty-five percent was enough to know that pitching José inside was the right approach. Not just inside here or there, but pretty much *exclusively* inside. If I hit him? Well, I hit him—and he'd either walk to first or bring his bat to the mound to end my miserable, brutish life. Either way, I knew just enough to know that any fastball away would be virtually the same as throwing it down the middle to a hitter with a regular batting stance. I had seen the way he whipped his bat through the zone—he did so with terrifying speed, like the bat was made of hollow plastic. No one I played with or against, before or after, swung the bat like he did. I couldn't have imagined pitching to him in his prime. Nonetheless, I stuck to my plan and during exhibition games in spring training, I pitched José inside. During my first start in Yuma in the second series of the year, I pitched José inside. As the at-bats piled up, it became our script—I'd pitch him inside and when I missed, I'd hope to God he either didn't send it right back at me or into orbit where it might injure some hapless astronaut. Seven at-bats in, however, all he had managed was one measly single; the plan was working.

At home in Lake County, just a few days before the end, he was batting cleanup. As he dug in, for yet another meeting between us, I got ahead with a curveball and a few fastballs. With the count at 1-2, I chose to go hard inside just under his hands, which would ultimately set up another curveball if he didn't bite and put it in play. I took the sign, shook in acceptance and started my windup. My catcher crept underneath his mammoth elbow guard as I began to stride toward the plate. From the moment it left my fingertips, I knew it was headed high of our intended target. My fastball started hunting him, climbing and riding in higher and tighter. As the white streak reached the halfway point in its flight, he must have realized it was time to bail. José raised his bionic arm to shield himself as he turned and leaned, hoping in vain to get out of the way. It was well above his elbow, so he had to protect himself or risk wearing a 93mph fastball in the eye socket. At the last moment, bracing for impact, he raised his elbow up like a chicken wing, catching my speeding fastball flush as he crashed down to the dirt below. Everyone in the crowd gasped.

Down. Goes. José.

He milked it. As he laid flat on his chest in the batters' box, taking a second or two to gather himself, he cocked his head my way and stared me in the eyes for what felt like an eternity. I had no real fear of reprisal, because at his core, no matter the current flavor of theatrics, he was a *baseball guy.* He'd been pitched inside before and he'd also been hit before, so this wasn't the first nor would it be the last. He knew exactly what he was doing in choosing his batting stance, his elbow guard, and his approach at the plate. He knew that sooner or later, one of those countless inside fastballs would get loose. That was why he wore the guard in the first place, because his hit-by-pitch risk was through the roof. Sure enough, the stare down waned and he dusted off his maroon jersey before walking slowly to first. He walked so slowly, in fact, that I feared fans would start packing up to beat the traffic before he got there.

After the game, as I walked to our portable trailer that they called a "clubhouse," I was stopped by a reporter eager to hear my thoughts on the stand-off with the mighty former MLB All-Star.

"Hey Dan! Do You have a second?"

"Sure." The man got out his portable audio recorder.

"Tell me about the at-bat with Canseco."

"Well, he really looms over the plate, so it's been my approach to pitch him inside. If I let him extend his arms, I'd be in trouble."

"Was hitting him intentional?"

"Of course not. I had him 1-2 and it was a close game. I wanted the out."

"When you hit him, it appeared as if there was a stare-down. Can you speak on that? Did you think he was going to charge the mound?"

"No. He's been around the game a long time and the way I've been pitching him hasn't changed. That one just got away from me as we set up inside. It happens."

Though Mr. Canseco perhaps had a negative reputation in the baseball world after the release of his book in 2006, from all of my interactions with him he seemed to be a pretty decent guy. He treated everyone on my team—myself included—with respect and the few players from Yuma I had spoken with also had positive things to say. He was the real deal as a Major Leaguer and yet didn't act above any of us lowly Indy players. I wasn't sure his motivation for continuing to play at age 47, but there was no glory to be had and so I assumed it was because he still enjoyed competing and being in the dugout.

Two days after our last "real" at-bat, I found myself swinging my burgundy-lacquered log in the on-deck circle, watching him float knucklers in from 60'6" away. The lights were bright, my hands yet again sticky with pine tar. I was about to get my first at-bat as a DH in the farce that we were apparently calling a professional baseball game. José was throwing some pretty decent knuckleballs as reported by my teammates following their first at-bats. I was excited for my chance to become famous, which would surely be the case once I went big-fly against him. I had been getting more comfortable at the plate, so it was less the exciting rarity that hitting usually was for a pitcher. Typically just once a season, a pitcher would be forced to hit because of a double-switch, a depleted bench, a coaching error or injury. When that happened, everyone watched from the top step to see how hilariously ugly the anticipated strikeout would be. If the Baseball Gods smiled on a pitcher, maybe he'd squeak a 19-hopper through the hole and become the hero of the day. Anything above and beyond a bloop or a seeing-eye single—such as a legitimate line drive or (dare I say it) an extra-base hit—was unheard of, the stuff of legend.

As I walked from the on-deck circle toward the batter's box in my cream-colored uniform, I couldn't help but notice the absurdity of the situation. There were *a lot* of fans not only watching, but actively cheering us on. I raised an eyebrow as they clapped as intently for me as they would any normal batter. I asked myself, *Do they not know? Do they not realize what's going on? They shouldn't be clapping for me. I shouldn't be hitting*. Those fans should have been irate that the team running out to the field—the team they paid to watch—was not the real act they came to see.

Regardless, my walkout song—*Heartbreaker* by Led Zeppelin—blared its deep guitar riff, signaling my turn on stage. I took my warm up hacks as I walked into the dirt circle then stepped into the box, not sure what to expect. I stared at the giant on the mound, unsure of what I was looking for. Was there a special way to approach a knuckleballer? I hadn't a clue. But the bat began, and quickly the first knuckleball fluttered in. The umpire stayed silent; it was ball one. Seemed like an OK knuckleball to me, nothing noteworthy. I had played catch with guys who threw knuckleballs before, but never tried my luck hitting one.

José again kicked and dealt, his long arms and legs looking very out of place as he towered over us on the mound. The second knuckleball flew in nice and straight as I tracked it with my eyes, which promptly got big—like those of a lion watching a stray gazelle walk closer and closer. Suddenly, just as I had prepared to smash it into a dented ball of white cowhide, it took an exactly left turn in midair. Good. God. It was ball two as it zagged out of the strike zone. I had never seen a baseball move that way. It was like it hit a jet of air, just shot sideways in what could have only been explained as the work of the devil. Now I understood why a handful of men made their living in the Major Leagues throwing those dancing, floating things. There was no way someone could hit a knuckleball like the one I had just watched—it defied physics and the laws of all that was holy and good. The count, however was in my favor: it was 2-0.

Before my at-bat, I had been watching the at-bats of my teammates. I picked up on José's pattern—he'd start with knuckleballs and would catch up in the count with fastballs if he fell behind. 2-0 or 3-1 counts had earned an automatic fastball and here I was, sitting in a heater count. I licked my chops and prepared to demolish the 75mph get-me-over fastball that I assumed was on its way. He started his wind up and as the pitch left his hand, I quickly realized that it was flying harder and straighter than the others—I had guessed right! I started my home run swing. As the pitch approached, tracking for the inner-third of the plate, my long pitcher's swing and heavy bat dragged through the zone. I made contact.

My hands stung as the bat vibrated, the ball colliding just near the trademark. After seeing two 55mph knuckleballs, the speed change wrecked me. I bounced a weak, jam-job grounder to third base. Disgusted with myself, I jogged slowly to first. After a good throw across the diamond, I was out. Sigh.

A few innings later, my next at-bat went down largely the same way—José fell behind in the count and I rolled over a fastball in the middle of the plate, bouncing it to the shortstop. On my second obligatory run through first base, I jogged even slower, which resulted in something that caught me by surprise—I was *booed*. I looked over my shoulder, flashing a confused glance at the crowd as if to say, "Do you guys still not know who I am and what's going on?" It was clear now that they didn't. I was a pitcher, after all, and had no interest in running hard, hitting a single, or playing baseball the way a real position player should. I was there to hit a bomb and that was about it—it was more like beer-league softball or a driving range. When I failed in this task, I didn't want to run it out. In fact, I didn't want to stand on first base one bit. If I did make it to first, then I'd be on the hook to run to second, then third, maybe even home! Running around the bases meant I might have to slide, something I hadn't done in eight years. No, thank you.

In the National League, pitchers pretty much crawl to first base and the crowd *gets it.* They know that their favorite pitcher makes his money on the mound. The pitcher's job is pretty much just to bunt a guy over if that's the situation, or swing away without injuring himself and hope for the occasional lucky bounce. The crowd doesn't need a Major League pitcher to try very hard at the plate. The issue of real hitters running routine ground balls out, however, is a little more heated and very misunderstood. Fans get *angry.* They say that players are lazy, that they've lost passion for the game, that money has changed them, that they don't play the game the "right" way, the way it's supposed to be played. The problem is that fans aren't privy to what's really going on behind the scenes or just how hard it is to take the field every single day in professional baseball. If a fan was given the chance to be down in the dugout of Dodger Stadium, he or she would undoubtedly give 100% effort on every ball they put into play. It's without a doubt a privilege to play baseball, but there's a little more to it.

I came to learn that every player has some combination of daily aches, pains, and nagging injuries that they play through; I dealt with my own share of them. Pre-game is also really long, the longest of any sport. By August, the heat starts to get to players and wears their bodies down significantly. So, hitters at the highest levels tend to run hard when it counts and conserve energy when it doesn't. Injured players who still take the field are often directed by the training staff to take it easy on runs to first and jog back in between innings. If a player has a nagging injury, all the little things can either make it worse or help it heal. Because longevity is every player's goal, eliminating unnecessary wear and tear is paramount. When a player is out 99 times out of 100 on a routine ground ball, sprinting at 100% could definitely be considered wasted effort. Would the Baseball Gods approve of this logic? Would the great Jackie Robinson side with this view? I'm not sure, but the issue of hustling out routine ground balls that aren't double plays is a foggy one at best. I steadfastly believe in the value of hustle, but admit that there is merit on both sides of the argument.

I, however, deserved to be booed. There was no physical reason I couldn't run hard to first base and none of the above reasons applied to me—I simply didn't want to run. But regardless, the situation was ridiculous—here we were, playing a "professional" baseball game in which the talent level on each side of the ball was no higher than high school. Sure, we were all professionals, but good high school players hit better than I did and good high school pitchers pitched better than our position players. Yet, we had over three thousand fans cheering, ooo-ing, ahh-ing, and booing. In the end, it seemed like they still had a great time. I think I had assumed that the crowd would stream out early in disgust, realizing what was going on. I was wrong.

In college, my classes on the philosophy of sports taught me that I probably should have known better. Sports carry people away from their troubles, giving them something to latch onto that provides excitement, entertainment and shared glory. At the core of it, we athletes are entertainers. The idea of statistics, wins and losses, championships, the underdog athlete and the hometown team gives fans a deeper level on which to compare the players and teams to one another. Sure, fans wanted to see their hometown team, the Lake County Fielders, beat the Yuma Scorpions. They rooted for *us*, even though we were playing out of position. They were still invested in my laughable efforts at the plate and were disappointed when my level of passion proved incongruent with theirs. They wanted to beat Yuma and my heart didn't appear to be in the same place.

We ended up falling short and my contribution was a pathetic 0 for 3 effort—two groundouts and a pop-up. One of the Yuma pitchers hit a homerun in the later innings and they beat us handily. When the game ended, we gave each other hugs in the dugout as Pete thanked us for a memorable night. As we approached our portable clubhouse, we found a nasty note from the owner taped to the door, basically telling us how immature we were and how we didn't respect the game. Right.

In the clubhouse, we all said our goodbyes and sat at our skinny lockers, unsure of what we were doing next. Some of us had things brewing but mostly we were unsure, feeling gut-punched by the realization that this journey with our scrappy, resilient team was now ending. We didn't know what our contract obligations would be, but with Pete also resigning, our team as we knew it was officially dead. I said goodbye to the ridiculous portable shower, located just a long enough walk across from the clubhouse that fans could see us in our towels from the parking lot. It was an *only in Lake County* experience that we wouldn't miss (though it did have exceptional water pressure).

The sad fact was that we loved that team and felt loved by the fans, despite being utterly neglected by the ownership. The fans followed us as we navigated islands and red-eye flights, filling up the win column under impossible circumstances. More drama and experiences were packed into that seven-week stretch on the road than in a typical 22-

week season. Despite the uncertainty and drama, I know that I wasn't alone in feeling privileged to have been a part of it, to have sailed on our own little pinstriped version of the *Titanic*. I was crushed to have to pack up and leave, yet knew I'd proudly tell my grandkids one day that I went down with the USS Lake County.

Dear JD, I just didn't understand.

"What do I do? What if they hold me hostage and try to keep me here? It'll ruin my entire season."

"Danny, I know this has been a rough go here. But remember, you guys are only making a thousand bucks a month. If we can just get another team to sign you, you can go. You think a team having financial trouble is going to sue you—and the other team—for breach of contract if you leave? We'll get this sorted out. Call the commissioner if you can and I'll do the same."

As I hung up with Goose, I felt better about the situation. I was terrified that I was going to be stuck playing for a new manager on a dead-end team that didn't pay their bills. Now that Pete and TJ had left, all of us needed a fresh start. But, the owner of the Fielders was holding our futures over our heads, trying to force us to stay. We were a winning team that would put butts in the seats, after all.

"Mr. Blewett. What's the latest?"

"Hey Duff. Eh. They're still trying to act like they can keep us here, but we've filed the paperwork for non-payment of our salaries and meal money, so they really can't...I think."

"Okay, good. Well try to relax about it. I know you're in limbo right now, but I've got good news. I called my old team—Fargo—and they need a starter. I told Josh, the GM, about you and they're interested."

"Really!? That's great! I'm still not sure if I can legally sign yet, but I'm in. Tell them I'm in."

"Alright. I'll text him back now and you'll hear from me. Talk to ya."

Coping well with unknowns is perhaps one of my superpowers; it takes a lot to get me visibly stressed. When Lake County disbanded, however, I'd have imagined it was clear to everyone that I was... basically freaking out. All of us players were stuck in limbo over what would become of our contract rights with Lake County. I had spoken with a senior executive in the league, with our own front office, with Goose, Duff and anyone else who even smelled like advice. It was a struggle to keep my head on straight while I pondered the very real possibility that I'd be forced to stay in a Lake County uniform. My career needed to continue forward, and being stuck there would bring it to a screeching halt.

After the third game at home in Lake County, I had called Brooks back in Normal, verbally agreeing that I'd return to my old team, the Cornbelters, if and when the Fielders fell apart. After hanging up with Brooks, however, Duff came through and I spoke with the Fargo-Moorhead RedHawks of the American Association, a league of older, more experienced players. I instead decided that I would sign with Fargo whenever I'd finally be granted free agency. It was a hard decision because in my panic earlier in the week, Brooks had assured me that I shouldn't worry and that they'd take me back. He was there, a safety net in uncertain times. But going back to Normal, Illinois was, well, a step back. I wanted to move forward, and to do that I knew that I had to sign with Fargo. I wanted to be challenged, though if I knew exactly how big a challenge awaited…I might have reconsidered.

On the last day of my time in Zion, Illinois, I was told to drive to the team's headquarters in the Gurnee mall. There they'd have paperwork for me to sign and I'd be free. It was a rough few days waiting under the threat that none of us were going to be let go. But since we had all filed valid petition papers, ultimately they had no choice. The RedHawks emailed me a contract which I promptly signed and faxed back. I was told to drive immediately to Sioux Falls, South Dakota, to meet the team, and if I kept receipts I'd be reimbursed for gas mileage and a per diem. I jumped in my junky Honda Civic and hit the road. It was already late in the afternoon, so the nine hours plus Chicago traffic turned me in around 2 a.m. I had a hotel room waiting for me; I walked in and face-planted into the cheap bed. All of it was finally over. In the morning I'd meet my new team, new league and new opponents.

Fargo-Moorhead was a perennial winner. When I joined the team they were below five hundred for the first time in as long as any of their fans could remember. The team was led by Doug "Simi" Simunic, who had a reputation for being a cutthroat, blunt, *tells it like it is* manager. He took no prisoners, wanted to win and did not accept losing. He was short, round and overweight—he waddled more than he walked and spoke with a deep, throaty voice. All managers wanted to win, but I'd come to learn that it was especially miserable to be in the Fargo clubhouse following a loss.

The Sioux Falls Pheasants (now the Canaries) played in a cramped little ballpark. Left and right field were each listed at a little over 300 feet—a generous appraisal—and the gaps couldn't have been deeper than 350. Center field was typically deep—listed at 410—but dead-center home runs weren't much of a concern. Rather, it was those pesky, deep-but-routine fly balls to the gap that seemed to go for home runs way too often in Sioux Falls. It turned every hitter into a potential power hitter. Line-drive homeruns? Absolutely! Broken-bat dingers? Why not?! The Pheasants had a few scary hitters in their lineup—the very tall Brandon Sing, who would go on to hit 24 jacks that season, as well as former Florida Marlin Reggie Abercrombie, who apparently dropped his leadoff-hitter mentality to swing for the fences on 100% of pitches thrown his way. Abercrombie hit 17 homers that year, which in a 100-game season is quite good. Sing, all of 6'5" and 220lbs, wore Oakley high-visibility glasses at the plate (those crazy yellow ones), which added to an already intimidating presence in the batters' box. Once a highly-touted Cubs prospect, this much was certain: I hadn't faced hitters of this caliber before.

I was slated to pitch the second game in the Sioux Falls series. It was nice to be on the bench for the first day to just get acclimated and evaluate my opponents and teammates a bit. We wore grey pinstriped pants and traveled with black and red tops. The first day, we wore black and on my day, I'd pitch in our red jersey, black hat and grey pins. It was also the first time I'd had my name on the back of a jersey since I was a kid—they stitched BLEWETT across the back in gently arching letters; Fargo did things right.

The next day, it was mostly business as usual. I really wanted to get off to a good start and impress my new team. I'd never joined a new club mid-season and doing so came with the pressure of proving your worth to them. Any new player was a replacement of someone who had either gotten hurt or been released. I wanted to come in and prove that I was valuable, that I made the team better. Unfortunately, I wasn't able to prove that in my Fargo debut. It wasn't a train wreck, but I didn't make it out of the fourth inning—a lot of hits, few strikeouts and little execution.

Because of the schedule and an off day, I got the ball again six days later. It went a little worse, as I yielded four runs in just three innings of work. After my first two outings, my ERA was in double-digits and I had been depleting the bullpen as they came in to clean up my messy games. I tried to leave that in the past and turn my sights toward my third start, which would come in Gary, Indiana, an industrial town on the east side of Chicago. My parents, eager to hear about my exciting new team way out in the middle of nowhere, called me to catch up. I was not a beacon of positive energy.

"Hi honey! Dad is on the phone here with me. Tell us about Fargo! How is it?"

"Eh, it's okay. I mean, they've treated me really well so far—they paid for my travel to meet the team, the uniforms are awesome and all of it feels a lot more professional than in the past. It's clearly a well-run organization. I even have my name on the back of my jerseys."

"Wow! It sounds like they care a lot about their players," my mom replied.

"Yeah, they do. The little things are important."

"Well, how about your teammates? Do you like them?"

"Uh, I don't really know. Honestly, I haven't spoken much of a word to anyone. It's hard—I'm trying to just keep to myself until I prove I belong here. I don't want to come across as feeling too comfortable until I'm actually a contributor."

"Honey, just open up. I'm sure they know you're trying your best."

"Yeah. I do know one guy—Jake Laber and I played together on the T-Bolts. It was pretty weird that he played in the D.C. area, being a North Dakota native. Pretty much everyone else was from Maryland or D.C., and yet there was Jake from Fargo. Duff made the connection; he's one of the best pitchers out here. Really small world that he and I are teammates again, so I at least have him to talk to."

"Well I'm sure you'll get more comfortable there soon and make more friends."

"Yeah. I just need a win under my belt. My next start will be in Gary, Indiana, which is near Chicago, so it'll be nice to hopefully have some of my clients from Normal come out to watch. Maybe that will help me break through."

A week before my scheduled start in Gary against the Railcats, I had emailed my clients and friends in Normal. Many of the young pitchers I worked with were interested in making the drive to watch their instructor do his thing, since Gary was only 2.5 hours from Bloomington-Normal. They'd get to see that I practiced what I preached...or so I thought.

Gary's ballpark was stunning. It had a huge clubhouse, gorgeous, neatly trimmed grass, padded outfield walls and a playing field that was sunken deep beneath the stadium bowl. I liked feeling small in ballparks and Gary's U.S. Steelyard Park delivered. On my scheduled bullpen day, I jogged out to begin my pregame stretching and looked around for my pitching coach and catcher. After I found them both, I asked when I could throw my bullpen. I was greeted with an awkward "ummm" from pitching coach Steve Montgomery, aka "Mongo."

"We've decided to skip you this start and you'll be in the bullpen for this series. That's not to say that you won't go back into the rotation—because you might—but we're going with a four-man rotation this time through and then we'll re-evaluate. Okay?"

"Okay," I said.

I jogged into the outfield, feeling unsure of what I should do now. As I looked around at teammates I barely knew, I tried to figure out what my pregame would consist of; I hadn't been a reliever in years. I wasn't about to walk up to one of my teammates and be like, "hey man, so they just yanked me out of the rotation and I have no idea what relievers do in pregame; can you help me?" I felt stupid enough.

My cleats sunk deeper into the outfield grass when I realized I now had to email and call everyone who was planning on coming to my start. I had to explain that I'd been demoted and wouldn't know when I'd pitch. After frowning for another minute or two, I re-focused on figuring out what the hell a reliever did in pregame. The last time I came out of the bullpen was my freshman year in college some six years ago, and back then I hadn't the slightest idea of what a pregame routine even was. Now, I knew I needed one but didn't know what it looked like. I stretched, ran some poles and decided not to play catch, since I didn't know who would play catch with me. Then I spent the rest of my energy trying to act like I wasn't really, really disappointed. I probably didn't do a great job.

Later that night, I walked out in my team-issued jacket and sat on the bullpen bench. I figured I would only get in the game if we were way up or way down, as was customary when breaking in a new reliever. I hadn't been pitching well so it wasn't as if I'd be trusted to close a game. Our closer at the time, Donnie Smith, touched 98mph some nights and had been pitching exceptionally well. Everyone in the bullpen was tired, though, in part due to starters not going deep into games (guilty). My odds of pitching in that first game, I assumed, were low. The score was back and forth and as the navy blue sky gave way to solid black, it was close. After the final out of the bottom of the eighth, we had tied it up 6-6. A lot of the usual suspects had gone in after the starter departed, and I assumed the stream of seasoned relievers entering the tight game would continue. I was wrong.

Get Blewett up. He's in the game if we don't score.

Me!? I threw off my jacket and furiously started waving my arms in circles; I was going in to pitch the bottom of the ninth. As I started to throw, I could feel the eyes on me much more intensely than normal. When a pitcher warms up for a start, many fans arrive at or after game time, meaning there aren't a million people watching you warm up. But that night, with a Friday crowd of 4,517 and eight guys in the bullpen next to me, it was different. We failed to score in the top of the 9th, and so I handed off my jacket, took a last deep breath and sip of water, then jogged between the lines. My adrenaline was high as my gameface slid down like a welder's mask. How would this go, my first relief outing in pro baseball?

I walked off the mound just a few minutes later; I had mowed down my three hitters in about 10 pitches. Two quick strikeouts and a pop out and the inning was over, the mitt sounding like a shotgun blast as it echoed off the tall outfield walls. Mongo met me at the steps, patted me on back, and enthusiastically said, "I wanna send you out for another. Feel good?" I nodded. Maybe this relief thing wasn't that hard.

In the tenth, the first batter lofted a lazy fly to right field for the first out. The next batter however, sent a double down the left field line, putting the winning run on second base. I fell behind in the count to the next hitter and allowed a single to right field. My heart sank as I ran to back up the plate; the game was probably over, but I had to back up anyway. With the winning run chugging around third, our right-fielder threw a missle, hovering about six feet off the ground. I tracked it and as I glanced back to reference the runner, realized that we might have a chance at him. A beautiful, long hop hit the catcher right in the glove. He applied the tag and wow! He was out by a step-and-a-half. I just needed one more out.

The hitter had moved up to second base on the throw home and I thanked the Baseball Gods for that miraculous game-saving throw. With a break in the action, Mongo came out for a visit. Their best hitter, a lefty named Brad Boyer, was walking up to the plate. He was 2 for 5 on the day and hitting .360 on the season, so I needed to be careful.

"You have a base open here and two outs, so let's be smart—nothing over the plate, try to get him to chase. Your changeup looks pretty good tonight—what do you think about starting him with a changeup?" I nodded. "Alright."

Satisfied, he walked back to the dugout and my catcher trotted back to the plate. Since he knew what I was throwing, my catcher didn't put down any signs. I kicked and delivered, missing for ball one. I glanced back at the runner on second, took a deep breath and fired again. Ball two. I didn't have a good feel for my curveball that night and had been throwing hard—91 to 93 on the stadium gun—so I decided the heater was the pitch of choice on 2-0.

I rammed one over the outer corner of the plate for a strike, moving the count to 2-1. Big exhale; 2-0 was a dangerous count. Because first base was open, a walk meant nothing; we went back to the changeup. I tried to bear down and focus up, but the pitch didn't quite "catch" as it left my hand. I tracked it as it stayed up, floating over the middle of the plate. Boyer swung and connected, swatting a medium line drive into the air down the left-field line. He sprinted out of the box as I prayed it would tail into foul ground, but as it peaked and began to fall, I realized it wasn't going foul. The winning run scored easily as the ball rolled into the corner. I turned my head back and started walking off just as his team flooded the field to congratulate him. I blew the game and was now 0-3 in three appearances for the RedHawks. We walked off a loser and silently streamed up the tunnel to the clubhouse, our cleats not making a sound in the rubber-matted stairwell.

The journey back to the clubhouse was not only figuratively long, but *actually* long. Nicer, newer ballparks like Gary's had large clubhouses, which meant they were tucked deep beneath the concourse where ceilings could be made higher. As we got near the top of the steps, the rubber runways ended, making the slow clacking of our cleats on the concrete floor the only audible sound. I turned left into the clubhouse, put my hat and glove in the top cubby of my locker, and sat down inside it. I stared at the ground for a while, wishing I had some sort of camouflage reflex that I could activate. My quest to prove my worth to my new teammates was *not* going well. I was that new guy who couldn't get anyone out. It was the most lonely I'd ever felt in a baseball uniform.

Simi and Mongo, the last ones out of the dugout, stormed through a couple minutes later, taking a beeline to the coaches' room. The door slammed closed. A few seconds later the silence was broken. It was Simi.

"YOU SAID HE WAS LIGHTS OUT! YOU SAID TO SEND HIM BACK OUT!
WELL, HE STINKS!! HE FUCKING STINKS!"

I'm not sure if the walls were actually thin, or if it was just really that loud. My manager's words pierced through the walls as if they were tissue paper, flooding the silent clubhouse and hitting me square in the chest. Everyone else, I'm sure, thanked God that they weren't the object of that brief tirade. I exhaled and kept staring at the ground, hoping somehow I would dissolve into it. I sat in my locker for what felt like an eternity before deciding that I didn't want to spend one more minute in that godforsaken room. I took a brief shower, made a peanut butter and jelly sandwich and walked out to get on the bus.

As I sat on the team bus, waiting another forty minutes for the rest of the squad so that we could depart, I tried to sort out how I'd gotten there. Just two weeks ago I had been having fun, throwing complete games as a valued member of a good team. How was I now the enemy of the state? Getting killed every time I took the mound, embarrassing myself? How did this happen? I was on a new team and now had a 10+ ERA, a manager who hated my guts and teammates who surely didn't think I belonged in pro baseball at all. I had never before thought about quitting a team—not once. But on that bus, I thought maybe I could beat Simi to it and ask to be released before he released me. After the longest wait of my life, that bus finally got rolling. A short drive later, I face-planted in my hotel bed. I curled up in the sheets and tried to fall asleep as fast as I could. I wanted that day to be over. I had never felt so alone, so far from home. I didn't want to play baseball anymore.

The next day, as I ran in the outfield during pregame, I decided that I had basically three choices: quit baseball, keep trying to figure out my struggles on my own, or ask for help. After the final game of the Gary series, we departed for Wichita, Kansas. I had plenty of time to think during the 11-hour bus ride and decided there was no way I could quit. I was not a quitter and even if I was a dead man walking, I had to let it run its course. That left only two options: I either had to figure things out on my own or swallow my pride and turn to the very coach who hated my guts. After a shortened, 110-degree pregame in Wichita on one of the hottest days I've ever experienced, I sheepishly nudged open the door to the coaches' office.

"Hey, Simi. Can I speak with you?" He and Mongo waved me in.

"I want to ask you both for help. Obviously, I'm not getting good results on the mound. I was successful before I came here and I'm honestly not sure what I need to do to fix things. I know I can do it, but I just feel overmatched and can't seem to get these hitters out. What do I need to do?"

Simi leaned back in his chair and crossed his arms. "The big problem is that you don't trust yourself. You have the *stuff*, but you go out there and don't throw strikes and you don't believe in your ability to get hitters out." I nodded. He continued.

"Don't think too much. We have a smart catcher and he knows how to call a really good game. Just throw what he puts down, don't think about it and be aggressive. You have the stuff, so let's make it simple. We're keeping you in the bullpen for this trip, but after that we may put you back in the rotation."

"Okay, I can do that" I said. "I just want to help the team and I want to pitch better. This isn't me, what's been happening." They shook their heads.

"Thank you," I said. I walked out.

I pitched in relief once during that series in Wichita and gave up four runs in two and two-thirds innings. Though nothing was better, I did exactly what I was told. We then departed to play Sioux Falls yet again, our last stop on the nine-day road trip. Simi kept his word and I started against the Pheasants. I turned in my best performance to that point—three runs in five and a third innings. It wasn't great, but it was certainly an improvement. When we got home, I was informed I'd continue in the rotation, pitching against Wichita as they made the trip to Fargo. With two days to go before that home start, I was in the bullpen throwing my final side session to Todd Jennings, the smart catcher who Simi and Mongo both loved. I felt good. I was coming off the first positive of the year and my bullpen session went really well with Mongo supervising. When I was done, we stopped for a minute to talk. Mongo, who hadn't said much of anything during my meeting in Wichita, went first:

"That bullpen right there was *good*. You have great stuff; if you were in big league camp, no one would question it; you'd fit right in with those guys. You throw hard and your curveball reminds me of how mine was—it's really sharp. But, that means that it can be pretty tough to throw for strikes. In the end, it's what Simi said—you need to trust yourself; that's the difference between you and the guys in big league camp. They throw the same as you, but they do it in the game." He pointed to the game mound. "They don't let anything get in their way of doing it out there."

I thanked him for watching my bullpen as he walked back down the left field line toward the dugout, leaving me with Todd. He had a slight build, a far cry from the prototypically thick catcher. He was 5'11 or so, probably 175 pounds—you'd have guessed he was a second baseman. Yet he had a gift—Todd knew how to catch the ball. In my starts with him behind the dish, he stuck the low pitch better than anyone I'd ever seen. I realized early on that he was getting me probably five extra strike calls compared to other catchers, framing borderline pitches with uncommon precision. I threw pitches that I *knew* were going to be balls when they left my hand, only to have Todd snap them back into the zone with his strong wrists and sneaky glove work. The art of deceiving the umpire was one at which Todd excelled. He was also exceptionally blunt.

"Blewett—you know he's right, don't you? You've got good stuff, man, but you pitch like a pansy; you don't believe in yourself at all. I was in big league camp with the Giants the last few years—everything Mongo said was spot on. Some of those guys definitely have better stuff than you, but a lot of them don't. Their belief in themselves is crazy. Any time they get hit, they laugh it off like it's a fluke. They're there because they compete harder than anyone else. You don't have any of that. You fall behind in the count, then get afraid and walk guys. That's gotta change."

Todd, a California native who was a high draft-pick out of Long Beach State, didn't waste time phrasing things gently. What he said to me stung. I didn't consider myself a weak, unconfident guy. But I also had no evidence to disprove him. He continued.

"If guys start hitting you, you gotta get mad back. Just say *screw it* and go back in there, show them that they don't get to take big swings on you. Your stuff is way too good to pitch the way you're pitching. You've got to have some confidence out there. Even if you don't know what to throw, just throw what I put down and let it eat!"

The upcoming home start against Wichita was important. I wanted to prove to the home crowd that I was a somebody, someone deserving of their adulation. I was picking up steam and seemed to have the coaching staff on my side along with a great catcher behind the plate. I was focused on being aggressive and executing pitches. I was *ready*. The fans—all 4,000 or so of them—piled in to see me pitch and redeem myself.

I started off strong wearing all-white pinstripes in front of a great crowd on a sunny North Dakota day game. We scored early and I entered the third inning with a 3-0 lead. Then, I started to falter. I gave up a string of hits, getting smacked around the yard, coughing the lead back up as Wichita hung a five-spot on the scoreboard to put us down 5-3. They tacked on a sixth run in the fourth and after I started the fifth with back-to-back singles, Simi came sauntering out to get me. A right-hander jogged in from our bullpen and my day was done—six runs already in and two more potentially on the bases. Those two *did* come around to score. My final line for the day was four innings, ten hits, eight earned runs, no walks and four strikeouts. I did prove something to the home fans: that my ERA, now swollen to 10.80, was an accurate representation of me. Exhausted by the ups and downs, I sat on the bench waiting to incur Simi's wrath when he returned from the mound. Thankfully, there was nothing. Both he and I refocused on the game, watching from the dugout rail. I tried my best to be supportive of everyone else, just like Coach J had taught me back in college. Sulking wouldn't help anything.

The hitters rallied and we ended up winning 10-8 in a slugfest; I was off the hook. Maybe the victory boosted Simi's spirit—I couldn't say for sure. But when the game ended, following the hand-slap line on the field, Simi stopped me. I was still nervous I would hear *something* about my awful day on the mound. But to my surprise, he put his arm around me, and said, "You're gonna get there, I really believe it." I was stunned.

As August showed it's face, signaling the last month of the season, I continued to be up and down. Physically I was fine but mentally, I was basically broken. What needed fixing wasn't about to be fixed overnight—not with rah-rah talks, positive thinking or a catcher calling the game. I needed to overhaul my mindset, and leave this shell of myself behind. I had never experienced public shame like I had in Fargo. Failing in front of large crowds was a lot different than failing in college in front of a hundred or so parents and girlfriends. At UMBC, I was too strictly focused on the future to worry about the ERA of five or six that I posted each year. In pro baseball, however, the pressure to perform *now* was immense—I didn't have next year to look forward to unless I pitched well this year. It was the first time I was pitching poorly enough to potentially lose my job. Mentally, I was completely unprepared for it.

As I reflected on the fact that I still had a jersey in Fargo despite consistently awful performances, I tried to make sense of the about-face I witnessed in my manager. I realized that the gruff, cutthroat Simi probably wasn't used to viewing players as people, but more a means to an end: *winning*. When they didn't win, they were of no use to him; he'd cut ties and was well-known for getting rid of poor performers in a hurry. A friend of mine told me a story about how a former Fargo player got released in the dugout tunnel after a game. Typically, a manager would wait to use the guillotine in the coaches' office. Not him. And so I wondered—*Why am I still here? Why does he continue to keep me around with an ERA above 10? Why the arm around my shoulder? Why not another blow-up like in Gary?*

When I was a kid I was always pretty good and thought I would just cruise on up to the Major Leagues. When I arrived in college—with a roster spot secured but no scholarship money—I realized something had changed, that I was no longer on the fast-track. I worked hard to keep climbing the ladder and asked for help if I was unsure what to do next. And above all, I wanted the respect of my teammates and coaches, both for how I performed and how I conducted myself. When I asked Simi and Mongo for help, it was that same young kid in me wanting to be good, help the team and earn respect. I wanted baseball to be fun not just for myself, but those around me that I affected. As a starting pitcher, you have a huge effect on the game. I wanted all of us to celebrate after games with laughs and loud music, not sullen silence.

I think that when I turned to Simi for help, he saw me as a person for the first time. I had arrived as just another jersey, and he'd managed hundreds if not thousands of those in his long managerial career. But when I summoned the courage and humility to stand before him and ask for guidance, everything changed. I can't imagine that any player he'd ever managed got more chances than I did with such a sky-high ERA. I deserved to get released. The conversation in Wichita was probably the only reason I stuck with Fargo for the rest of that losing season.

When I tell the story of that awful day in Gary, Indiana, I do so not in the sense of hero and villain. Simi was *not* the villain. On that night in the clubhouse, tempers and emotions ran high in all of us—it was the sixth or seventh straight loss for the team. In a dugout full of fierce competitors, it's impossible to go 100+ games without many of us showing our teeth. I snapped at the kind-hearted Pete when he pulled me from a game earlier that summer. Like everything else, it was about the response, not the situation itself. Though I draw gasps from a crowd when I recount that moment in speaking engagements, it became a positive, defining moment, setting in motion mindset changes I had to make sooner or later. Simi emerged as yet another guide, a mentor who treated me fairly and helped me grow as a player. When I look back on my time in Fargo, I still get a pit in my stomach because it was in knots the whole time. Yet, it was two of the most important months of my career. I did eventually get to know my teammates, and all of them rallied with advice to try and help me find my footing. Advice, though, wasn't enough. I never wanted baseball to be that hard again, so I started searching for a solution. Like always, I quickly found a man with a lantern. His name was Alan.

The RedHawks released me the following off-season, just before spring training would have begun. The Evansville Otters scooped me up as soon as I hit the market, explaining that they hoped I could fill the number one spot in their starting rotation. Up to that summer in Fargo, I had focused solely on getting physically better as a pitcher. I was an animal in the weight room, as lifting, running and performing arm care exercises consumed my life. Everything was physical, measurable and tangible. I had seen my velocity climb from the low-80s to the low-90s, so naturally it wasn't hard to want to do more and more of what clearly worked. But there I was, at an impasse because of my lack of mental strength. Everyone was right: I needed to find a way to believe in myself or I was *done.*

Alan Jaeger has been selling J-Bands since the 1990s. His bands were the first of their kind, helping pitchers both strengthen their arms and avoid injury. Shoulder exercises didn't exist before Dr. Jobe introduced the *Throwers' Ten,* a series of exercises to strengthen the rotator cuff. Alan followed the research, bringing to market a set of latex bands with a program of exercises specifically for pitchers. Over time, they became a ubiquitous item in the baseball bags of players everywhere. Alan was a *guy* in the baseball industry—well connected, successful and universally liked. In 2010, I woke up to find a short message from Alan in my email inbox. I had been blogging for about two years on baseball and strength training, and apparently Alan had read some of my work.

> Way to go Dan...someone who gets it. Keep putting
> out great information that's helping kids realize their
> dreams by being healthy. Best wishes, Alan Jaeger

I felt privileged to exchange emails with him over the years, and slowly we developed a rapport. Near the end of the season with Fargo, I started looking for help on the web, some kind of program or person to follow. Alan popped into my head and I remembered that he had written a book. I looked it up and sure enough, it was all about mental training for baseball players. I cranked out an email:

> Hey Alan,
>
> I really struggled with confidence on the mound
> this season, stemming from a team change midseason

in which I put a lot of pressure on myself to live up to expectations. Knowing that this is one of your areas of expertise, would you mind if I gave you a call sometime in the next week or two?

I've come to a point in my career where I could have a physically perfect off-season, perfecting my pitches and location and physical conditioning, but still not get any better on the mound in a game. I've been asking a lot of people and doing some reading on forming my mental training program for the offseason; I really need to get it right—it's probably the only thing left holding me back from getting into affiliated ball and subsequently the very elite levels of professional baseball. I've realized this year that I am physically good enough to pitch in the big leagues. But, I'm just holding myself back with negative thoughts and doubt.

So, if you have time, I'd really appreciate just a few minutes on the phone, or if not, maybe I could shoot you a more detailed email about my ideas for a mental training plan. Thanks, Dan

Alan responded with an invitation to speak on the phone, along with links to his book, some articles and lectures. Reading his book was the first priority. Once I finished it, we spoke on the phone and he suggested I travel to Los Angeles to spend a few days with him learning about mindset and meditation. I had about $3,000 in my bank account. Airfare, hotel, transportation and meals would cost me a little more than a third of it—it was not a great financial move. I knew I needed it, though, and believed the financial investment would force me to follow through and institute what I learned as part of my routine. Regular meditation would be the keystone of my routine and I had to make time for it. I had felt the hurt, seen the consequences and didn't want to end up down that same, lonely road.

Fifteen or so pro players attended Alan's mental training camp. We sat in a martial arts studio each morning doing yoga, sharing our experiences, and meditating. There were some high profile young players in attendance, names that I didn't know much about at the time, but came to hear more about in the coming years. Lucas Giolito and Max Fried, two top high school prospects in Southern California, would both later become first-round draft picks and pitch in the Major Leagues. Mike Montgomery, another pitcher at the camp, went on to record the final out in the Chicago Cubs' 2016 World Series victory. All of us shared similar testimony of how our minds often held us back in high-pressure situations. I felt liberated knowing that I wasn't the only one and that even million-dollar arms went through tough times.

The real challenge, however, was when I flew back home after the trip. I had to settle into a routine and force myself to do the work. I was living alone at that point in a big apartment, so I had an oddly large amount of space with not nearly enough furniture. The first day of meditation on my own was awful. I was sitting on a pillow in my living room with my phone on silent on the floor next to me, timer set to 30 minutes. My goal each day was to meditate for 20, and if I felt like I wanted to "stay in it" longer, I could. Alan explained that it was important to set aside more than enough time so that one didn't feel rushed.

I hated every second of it. I felt anxious as I sat cross-legged, leaning gently against the wall behind me. Even with my challenges from the prior season, I've never been an anxious person. But as I sat there, my mind was furiously busy. I was thinking about anything and everything—my task list for the day, my workout that I'd complete later, conversations with friends and family and tons of random things. About five minutes in, I wanted to quit. *I can't do this,* I told myself. My brain was too busy and too active to be quiet. *Maybe I'm just different and this won't work for me.* I'd never reach the level of calm and clarity that Alan explained could be in my future.

I sucked it up. I completed that first session and forced myself to sit down and meditate every single day. Over time, it got better. One of Alan's analogies was that of television.

"Dan, imagine it this way. You're sitting at home watching TV. You take out some athletic tape and tear off two strips and make a big, white X on the front of the TV. Chances are, you can still watch TV just fine even with it there. But if you're trying to focus on that X, it's going to be hard because there's so much going on around it—so much noise."

I imagined the TV in my head as he continued.

"But what happens if we turn the TV off? All the stuff in the background turns to black, and the white X pops up, clear as day.

That's what we're trying to do when we meditate—tone down the background noise so we can more clearly see what we want to see. The X for you will be the catchers' mitt—you'll visualize each pitch as it follows a tunnel on the way to the mitt. Visualize yourself executing big pitches in big situations all while in a calm state of mind."

The reason human beings, as a species, are so accomplished is because we can think. The main problem with human beings, however, is also that we think. Pitchers, especially, have an incredible amount of time to dwell in their own heads. And what do we tend to do with it? We ruminate on the past, future, consequences and implications of our actions. It ruins us; it ruined me.

If I miss my spot and he hits a double, the bases will clear and my ERA will skyrocket.

If I throw this 3-1 changeup and miss, I'll walk in a run.

If I don't throw well while this scout is watching me, I'll miss out on my opportunity to get promoted.

I've had two bad outings in a row. If I don't pitch well today I might get released.

All these consequential thoughts paralyze a player, making him unable to act with the freedom and fluidity that he otherwise possesses. I lived through this paralysis during my time in Fargo. I failed so much and so spectacularly that I basically just expected it to keep happening. I expected to pitch poorly. I expected to miss my spots and expected to get hit. A player's potential is revealed in practice, as his movements are never impeded by these consequences, stakes, and doubt. And thus the goal is to play exactly as well as one is capable of practicing. Athletes accomplish this by slowing the game down mentally by calming the mind and by creating a mechanism to return to that calm place. One of the centerpieces of meditation is a focus on the belly breath. The belly breath forces the stomach to go out and in like a bellows. Many people breathe up and down which anecdotally causes stress to be stored in their shoulders. Infants breath out and in with their bellies, using the diaphragm more than the shoulders to the fill their lungs with air.

My task was simple: meditate every day while breathing from my belly, so that I could teach my mind to slow down and become clear. Then, over time—as my mind became less cluttered with thoughts, conversations, worries and distractions—I could visualize myself on the baseball diamond. Then, I could observe myself succeeding in stressful situations. When the season would arrive, I'd feel like I had already conquered those situations when they came up. If, in my meditation, I practiced pitching with the bases loaded in front of a packed house, it would be no big deal when I finally found myself in that same real-life situation. Alan gave me all the pieces to be successful and I was beginning to see how they fit together. The pile of jigsaw pieces would eventually reveal a picture of a new, better me. But first, I had to learn to sit still.

Just. Sit. Still.

The proverb is right: A journey of a thousand miles starts with a single step. A week later, things were improving and I became deeply relaxed within the first five minutes. After about ten minutes, I could barely feel my arms and legs as they melted into the carpet. I was drastically less anxious and began enjoying the time to myself. I was still deep in thought much of the time, however, and I worried that visualization—the part that I needed most—would remain out of reach. I tried imagining myself on the mound but the scenes I'd paint would quickly get fuzzy; I'd find myself back thinking and explaining things to fictional people in my head. My mental television was so loud that it was keeping the neighbors awake.

A month later, it finally happened: I spent about five whole minutes pitching baseballs in my head. I had come to enjoy meditating—it was like a nap for both my body and my mind. My daily practice rejuvenated me without sleeping and refreshed my mind in a way sleep never did. I became deeply relaxed after just a minute or two and the doubts and worries, thoughts and conversations abated...my television was turning off. I had made a change in my brain's circuitry and was on my way to practicing in my head, anytime I wanted. I was excited to have a secret practice facility all to myself, to work on exactly the issues that I couldn't work on in games. One can't just replicate game pressure—games are games, and everything else that isn't a game...is simply not a game. But in my head, sitting there in silence and stillness...I could put myself on the mound in front of the big crowd, against the big hitter, in the big situation that would make or break me. I would break no more.

As I sat, my body so relaxed that I wasn't sure it was still there, I felt a slight tingle, a minute contraction that flowed down my arm. I was *in it*, about to throw a 3-1 changeup to a lefty hitter with the winning run on third base and no one out. The tingle was fear. It was the flawed connection, my brain trying to keep my arm from screwing it up. After another few months of meditation, though, I'd thrown that 3-1 changeup hundreds of times. Without any more tingling, tension or tightness, I calmly executed the pitch. Then, I struck him out on the next pitch, a 3-2 fastball on the inside black of the plate, freezing him as he looked in vain at the umpire, hoping for a generous call. The real question, though, was this: *Would it translate?* Would this new version of myself show up on the mound the following season? I didn't know for sure.

The following year with the Evansville Otters, it became clear the mental work did the trick. In 2011, I finished my time in Fargo with an ugly 7.69 ERA. After my winter of meditation and visualization, I put up a 1.06 ERA in 42 innings with Evansville. I was clear and confident and didn't look back. Alan checked in on me once in a while as he continued to beat the pavement, educating kids on just how important the mental side of baseball was. The old version of me died that winter; the new one kept his eyes on the horizon.

JD, we've had a tough decade as brothers. And maybe not until this moment have I taken the time to reflect on whether I've ever viewed the world through your lens. I'd never been anxious, worried or felt like I had a standard I couldn't live up to. I could handle pressure. That is, until the summer in Fargo. I spent every day worrying, nervous about keeping my job and getting embarrassed on the mound. I set an impossible standard for myself. I get it now.

As I wrote out this story, I initially wasn't sure how it connected to you. We grew up together and didn't understand each other as kids. We reconciled as young adults only to drift apart again on what seemed like irreconcilable differences. I didn't understand how you saw the world and often still don't. Writing the conclusion to this story about the two most miserable months of my life, however, I think I understand. When I walked out between the lines expecting to fail, it was not just hard to succeed, but impossible. No one had the antidote and there was no easy solution. Few of my teammates could empathize and their advice often wasn't realistic, though they had good intentions. It could not be hugged out, faked, gritted through or fixed overnight. It was a process, just like everything else. When you struggled, I often wondered why you couldn't just grit through it, fake it or fix it. We hugged it out to just wind up in the same place a month or year later.

I mishandled our relationship over the years, in part because I was so quick to put to death the old me who wilted under pressure in the

Dakotas. I worked hard to build confidence that constantly teeters on arrogance—it's in many respects a suit of armor an athlete needs to survive. Bad games are flukes. Naysayers and hecklers don't know what they're talking about. Those who say "you can't!" are wrong. Confidence keeps a ballplayer going through all that sludge.

This story is *my* story—a defining moment in who I later became. But in rewriting it, it's become even more than that. It's not just about rebuilding and then forgetting who I was that summer. Rather, it's about remembering. Simi saw me for what I was at the time—weak and struggling—and gave me the time and opportunities to try and work it out. Alan gave me a plan and I ultimately moved forward. I think the armor, at times, makes me forgetful and less sympathetic to something I myself felt. If this chapter in my life taught me anything, it needs to be that I can't forget how hard it is to feel powerless. Life is easy when confidence boils over. But it can't and won't be like that forever, and so I need to remember—for both our sake.

Dear Baseball Gods, The rotten planks were a gift.

One of my favorite thought experiments is the ship of Theseus. King Theseus was a naval war hero in Greek mythology and had his ship preserved in memorial. Over time, the wooden boards of the ship rotted and were replaced with new ones. The ship lived on, but was no longer comprised completely of the original planks. It's a problem of identity and the question posed is this: as boards are replaced, when does Theseus' ship become a *new* ship? After the first board? 10 boards? If 51% of the original ship is still intact is it still the original?

My career clock ticked daily in my head, reminding me that if I didn't evolve and get better today, tomorrow I'd be two days behind. The standard rose each year and it became necessary to replace planks *before* they rotted. By the time a pitcher realizes he needs to change, its often too late. When I entered pro baseball in 2010, I was one of only a handful of starters in my league who could throw every fastball in a game above 90. As a reliever I average 92, a measure considered much too slow by today's standards. I underwent a second Tommy John surgery and beat the odds by restoring 100% of my previous velocity. Yet, restoring a two-year old version is still…a version that's two years outdated. We have to change and change *now*. The herd of younger players thunders on with or without us.

I received a gracilis tendon allograft in my first Tommy John surgery. An allograft is tissue donated by another person. My tendon came from a deceased man and they gave me the option of writing his family an anonymous letter. I declined. I wanted to, but I wasn't sure what I'd say or how I'd say it. I just couldn't find the words. I regret not penning that letter and thought about my elbow a lot after that surgery. With four years of philosophy under my belt, Theseus's ship immediately jumped into my mind. Was I the same person? Was I still me? Was this man living through my elbow?

In January of 2018, I spoke at the American Sports Medicine Institute's 36th Annual Injuries in Baseball Course. The seminar is organized each year by renowned surgeon Dr. James Andrews and his institute. I received a rare invitation to speak from a non-medical perspective; I jumped at the chance. In front of a sea of doctors, trainers and physical therapists, I spoke about what the surgery meant to me, how there was a gap in the rehab process and how important the emotional side of the recovery was. Afterward, a group of doctors and physical therapists shook my hand and chatted with me. I revealed in my speech how I received an allograft. With raised eyebrows, the first question they asked was "who did your surgery?" I confirmed their suspicions, as my doctor was known for using allografts. One of them told me I almost certainly had a case to sue for malpractice. The use of a cadaver graft in a first Tommy John procedure was so uncommon that it was almost certainly the reason it had failed. My leaking, busted plank was replaced with another equally rotten one.

I immediately dismissed the idea of a lawsuit. In baseball, all of us see politics at work. We all notice when the son of a scout, pro player or manager gets drafted despite a .210 batting average or 86mph fastball and a 5.50 ERA. I never envied those people and spent as little time as I could being bitter about it. I've always wanted to earn the money in my wallet and the trophies on my wall. I didn't want to dig up old ghosts in court and wag my finger about the pain and suffering my doctor caused me, even if I was righteous in doing so. I don't feel wronged and couldn't make a straight-faced argument that undue pain and suffering came my way because of that allograft. I know my career path might have been completely different. But it wasn't. When a plank needed to be replaced, I pulled out my hammer and nail. Blaming the ocean would only allow more water to flow into the hull.

It's impossible to always come back better after an injury; sometimes, a restoration is about as good as it gets. Though I couldn't trend physically upward every year, mentally I could. What I found most valuable was the way I changed. A new, stronger man regularly replaced the old one in the mirror. The surgeries didn't hinder that—they helped it. The year after leaving Fargo, I saw hard work pay off. I watched myself rise to the challenge Fargo imposed upon me. I realized that Simi's outburst had forced me to replace an entire section of my boat. Because of it, the sailing was smoother and faster than ever. Mentally I *never* stayed the same—to stay the same meant being left behind. In my return to Evansville, I grew up faster and taller than any year prior.

In 2012, Simi called to release me from my contract in Fargo just a week before spring training was slated to begin. He had a backup option for me.

"Andy from Evansville really wants you to pitch for him. They think you can be their #1 guy. I know the American Association was tough on you, so give it some thought. I can trade you there if you want and we won't have to officially release you. It's your call."

I asked to be released, assuming the step down, back into the younger Frontier League would be bad for my career. I'd hold out for another American Association team to call. A short time later the phone rang—it was not who I expected.

"Hello?"

"Blew how are ya, kid? I heard you're back on the market." It was Brooks.

"Hey Brooks. Yeah, I guess I am."

"There's a few things you don't know. First, I'm no longer with Normal because I took the pitching coach job in Evansville. Andy McCauley is a good man. He's the manager here. He and I both want you to come pitch for us. I want you to be our ace. You can do that job, I know you can."

I resisted, but so did Brooks, continuing to explain that Andy was a fair, honest, good manager. I should play for him, he said. I'd get plenty of chances to redeem myself. After a few hours of deliberation, I decided being a second-year holdout wasn't good. I hadn't earned enough in the game to be holding out for anything. I had an opportunity to pitch and to be a #1 at that. I dialed Andy's number, which both Simi and Brooks had sent me.

"Hey Dan. Glad to hear from you. My guess is that Brooksy filled you in on the situation? What do you say? I think it'd be a great fit for you here. The owner, Bill Bussing, really loves the team and takes good care of the players here."

"Let's do it."

"Fantastic! I'll fax over the contract. Is a thousand bucks okay?"

"That's the most I've made thus far. Sure. Thank you."

"You got it. Look forward to seeing you here soon."

* * *

In baseball your statistics, known in the lingo as "your numbers," become your résumé. My ERA in Fargo, the most important number in a pitcher's résumé, was an abysmal 7.69. Anything above 4.50 is grounds to get released, so I didn't have the luxury of being choosy. Really, I was lucky to get another chance at all. I thought back to that day in the Chicago hotel. If I hadn't called Brooks before leaving for Fargo...would he have called me? The answer had to have been no. Andy had been in the league, managing for Evansville, when I played for Normal. Yet, I was a year removed and though Andy and Simi were friends, there wasn't much good in my 2011 season. Brooks had to have been the driving force. He really didn't owe me anything for that phone call, but he kept his word nonetheless.

A month and a half later, I was sitting beneath the scoreboard in my sweat-soaked pregame shirt and shorts. The sun was beating down as I sat cross-legged beyond the centerfield wall. Still new to my meditation practice, I tried to find secluded places where I could sit in silence, away from judgmental eyes. With the exception of Garrett Bullock, a Wake Forest grad and left-handed pitcher, I didn't know any other players who meditated. Those who played with Gare-Bear would corroborate that he was both a genius and an unabashed nerd. What I loved about him was how he completely owned his dorkiness —he found ways to one-up himself until the last day of the season. "Dude! Are you reading a textbook on the toilet?!" He'd just cackle with laughter. When I later needed an escort to and from Cincinnati for surgery, Garrett volunteered. He drove me both ways and played nurse for a day. Today he is a Doctor of Physical Therapy and is completing a PhD in Epidemiology and Biostats at the University of Oxford. There, he says, "everyone is a super-dork like me."

Because I couldn't own my dorkiness like Gare-Bear could, I went out of my way to find new hiding spots. The scoreboard was secluded, but there was a reason I would never choose that gravely location again. As the first few ants crawled up my arms and legs, I snapped my eyes open to brush them off me. I only had 20 more minutes before I had to start getting ready, so I was committed to my spot.

Will you die? Will the ants kill you?

No, I replied to the voice.

Then sit still. Isn't being comfortable with discomfort...kind of the point?

I closed my eyes and tried to relax. As a few more tiny black ants crawled up my arms, legs, back and chest, I stayed still. I kept my lids shut as I traced out their path in my mind. Ordinarily, I'd focus on my breath and repeat words of confidence in my head, reminding myself of who I was and who I wanted to be. I visualized my next start and how I'd attack hitters, watching each pitch stream toward the mitt with a visible tail like that of tracer round shot from a machine gun. The ants were just a new challenge, a new distraction to block out. They were tiny little hecklers and would only steal my clarity if I let them. Twenty minutes later, I opened my eyes, stood up and shook them all off like a wet dog. I was hungry—I needed a peanut butter and jelly.

I had rolled into town with mixed feelings that quickly faded. I loved Bosse Field and immediately bonded with my starting pitcher brethren. Evansville hadn't been a winning team in a few years, despite enjoying a championship in 2006. In his 40s, tall and tan from days in the hot Southern Indiana sun, Andy took the reigns in 2010, the same year I first entered the league. He had been managing for a dozen years prior, with notably long stops in Schaumburg and Kansas City where, in 2008, he won his first championship. In a 2016 article for the Evansville Courier & Press, he shared his desire to wear an Otters jersey until the end: "I will be ending my career here whether it's retirement, death or firing." After countless winning seasons and a 2016 championship, he's probably in the captains chair for a good while longer. He gives his players respect, freedom and more chances than most to turn around a slump. Good will emanated from his coaches' office in Bosse Field.

Pitchers in pro baseball don't interact with their manager nearly as often as amateur players do. During batting practice, the manager typically hangs out behind the backstop—known as *the turtle*—as position players take their daily three or four rounds of BP. The hitters interact with him between rounds, whereas pitchers are relegated to the outfield, shagging batted balls and generally being bored. At all other times, pitchers are elsewhere doing pitcher things that simply don't concern the manager. Once on-field activities are done for the day, the manager will then go into hiding as he confers with his coaching staff, writes the lineup and plans out the minutia of the game. Throughout my career, my manager was somewhat of a work acquaintance, to whom I'd say hello but not stop and speak with in the hallways.

Our relationship evolved beyond those typically sterile interactions. The turning point came in the season in June, when after a few go-rounds of the starting rotation, I had been consistently leaving with a lead. We bussed up north to Traverse City, Michigan for a three-game road series. By the time my start rolled around on the third day, we were in the throngs of a four-game losing streak. Our squad got blown out in games one and two of the series and we needed to stop the bleeding. When you're the ace of the staff, it's your job to plug that wound.

It was the seventh inning and we had just pushed across a run to take a 2-1 lead. The Traverse City Beach Bums had a curiously designed ballpark. Most stadiums are all brick and mortar, rising high above the playing surface. The shell of Wuerfel Park, by contrast, was clad in white siding, grey pitched roofs with square-paned windows that belonged in a bedroom. The entire shell resembled a long row of two-story beach townhouses. Inside the park, the suites were the same— they looked like beachfront homes on the tall stilts that protect against storm surges. White Adirondack chairs lined the concourse areas. It was a unique ballpark unlike any I had seen.

With one out, I gave up a double that put the tying run on second. After a strikeout, Brooks came out to talk to me. I could hear Eric Massingham, our closer, warming up.

"Mass is over there." He motioned toward our bullpen in the right-field corner. "He's about ready. I can bring him in now. Unless…" I gave him a disapproving look out of the corner of my eye. Brooks was clearly trying to bait me into saying something, and doing so with no subtlety whatsoever. He prattled on a bit longer, not being the least bit clever in disguising what he was doing. He wanted to hear me say, *I got this! Leave me in, Brooks!* So I did.

I looked him in the eye and calmly explained that the next hitter couldn't hit a curveball, and that I had the best one in the league. It would be most wise to leave me in. Brooks smiled and said "that's all I wanted to hear!" He departed back down the mound toward the dugout, walking his lopsided walk. I made good on my promise, striking out the final hitter of the inning to end the threat.

I returned to the dugout after that inning to a few extra few pats on the butt and a big "Heck of a job, Blew!" from Andy. A perpetually even-keeled guy, I felt good drawing some excitement out of him. I wanted to help him win games because managers needed to keep their jobs just like we players did. He had given me a fresh start in Evansville and so we were in it together. Mass came into the tight ballgame in the eighth for a two-inning save, though we tacked on a few runs in the ninth to give him some breathing room. We hit the road with a much-needed 5-1 victory, ending our losing-streak.

It was one of the first times in my career when I truly felt like a leader. I thought back to my conversation with Dr. Templeton. Maybe I was finally growing toward the canopy of the forest as my experiences in baseball deepened my roots. Maybe I *could* lead, not just by example off the field but in action—when the lights were on. In my upper-class years in college I know that I helped show the young players what hard work looked like. Yet, my performances were never good enough —I simply couldn't put it all together on the field, even as I earned the #1 pitcher label of that meager staff. Competing for my job was bringing out the best in me. I was slowly learning how to put a team on my back and rise up. On that night in Michigan, *I* was the guy. Hard work was paying off, I thought. If I kept it up, maybe I'd soon get a chance with an MLB team.

Players police themselves at high levels and thus many aspects of dugout life are subject to unwritten rules, enforced by whoever decides to enforce them. One of my friends in the starting rotation was a guy named Matt, who got the short end of the stick by our offense. He was 0-6 after six starts despite an ERA that was in the mid-4.00s. A 4.50 ERA is about average—it's not good, but it's also not terrible. It will get you released sometimes, but pitchers also make it whole seasons pitching to a 4.50. This time, because of his pathetic win-loss record, Matt was on the chopping block. Brooks had told me in confidence that Matt needed to pitch well in his next start or the ownership was going to get rid of him. He couldn't control his losing record, but it would be the death of him nonetheless.

As Matt made his next start at home, he opposed a good starting pitcher who threw harder than average with a very good curveball. This fellow mowed down our hitters for the first few innings on nothing but high fastballs and knee-high curveballs. As I watched, nervous that we needed to start hitting him, I felt exceedingly frustrated that our hitters weren't adjusting. Our opponent was pitching with a very predictable pattern—curveballs for strikes and high fastballs above the strike zone. A hitter had to do one of two things to adjust: sit on the curveball that he tossed over the plate or ignore the high fastball. Either would force him to bring his fastball down into the zone, where hitters would have an advantage. Rather, we continued to swing and strike out on pitches that were out of the zone. We also continued to stare at curveballs right down the middle. It was ugly and Matt deserved better.

The hitters' jobs weren't on the line but Matt's was—he was pitching for his life. Later in the game, one of our hitters took a big, aggressive cut at a first-pitch high fastball and drove it to the wall. A knee-jerk reaction to my frustration, I blurted out "Great! Looks like at least *one* of our hitters is trying!" This did not sit well with the two hitters hanging on the dugout rail next to me. Both backed off the rail as they turned toward me, brows furrowed in anger as they asked in explicit terms what I was implying.

I thought for a moment: would I retract it and apologize? I felt the scared college kid in me tug on my shirt. Then, I smacked his hand away. *No. I meant it. Matt deserves better.*

"What I mean is that my teammate is out there on the mound battling, and you hitters keep striking out the exact same way. Someone needs to make an adjustment."

This did not go over well.

They got in my face and I wagged my finger right back as the shouting match nearly exploded into a brawl at the top of our steep, concrete dugout steps. Andy ran over from his post.

"Break it up! You're teammates!"

We backed off into separate corners, slumping onto our stools as the rest of the team nervously wondered if the bell would ring again. I spit into the bucket and scowled across the ring. Eventually, we all took off our boxing gloves and got back to the game.

The next day, Andy grabbed me while we pitchers were out doing pitcher things.

"Hey Blew, so listen—what you said wasn't wrong, but I can't have the team tearing itself apart from the inside." I nodded.

The hitters needed to do a better job of making adjustments, he explained, as I apologized to him. What I did wasn't productive—no one would have responded well to how I said what I said. It stuck in my mind though as either a turning point or a sign that I'd already turned. Snapping at Pete in Lake County and now nearly brawling in the dugout? I was just...changing.

In college, some of our team rules and policies made me feel like a child, unable to explore my limits. At times I felt like little more than a bonsai tree, being pruned into a handsome, albeit limited shape. I got most of the opportunities I needed, but looking back I see now why I didn't come to understand who I was as a pitcher until much later. Pro baseball didn't just provide freedom, it *was* freedom. I was out exploring the country, playing the game I loved while growing into myself. I could get drunk all night if I chose and as long as I showed up and played well, no one would say a thing. Though I didn't choose that, the knowledge that my decisions and consequences were purely my own, all of it allowed me to become who I really was—to grow tall or not—as Dr. Templeton had alluded.

Despite another tally in Matt's loss column, he stuck around. Having battled back from injuries and a terrible season prior in Fargo, I felt a strong sense of ownership in that team. I wanted to repay Andy, Brooks and the ownership for not only taking a chance on me after a bad season, but putting faith in me. I hadn't earned the #1 role, they just believed I could rise up to meet it. I wanted to prove that I was worthy. Maybe that had something to do with the shouting match in the dugout.

A few weeks later, I made what would become my last start of the season for Evansville. I walked off the mound yet again escorted by the umpire and my coach, the same walk I had done years earlier in college. I got the news that my elbow was again torn and required Tommy John surgery. I deflated completely. A few weeks later I received the good news that I was voted a member of our division's All-Star team. It was held in Normal that season—my adopted hometown—and thus I had been greatly anticipating that vote. Until the news of my elbow, it felt like a dream to start the All-Star game in front of all the young kids I trained. They'd get to see their coach in action. Sadly, all I could do was wave as I readied boards and nails for my upcoming surgery.

When I returned from the game, the only thing I could do was wait for my surgery date and so I became, more or less, a member of the coaching staff. I spent more time with Brooks and Andy and existed in a strange in-between where I was no longer an active player but wasn't a coach, either. It was tough carrying on the same as I did before, knowing that I wouldn't step onto the field again for at least another 18 months. I tried to be a good teammate and not bring anyone else down with me. My 2012 season was over and 2013 was done before it even began. I knew well what a long, tedious journey I had in front of me, but I committed to it that day in Rockford when I suited up. I was having too much fun finding out how good I could be and how tall I might grow. I would not fade quietly into civilian life like so many others had.

I was scheduled for surgery in Cincinnati by the Reds' team physician, Dr. Tim Kremchek. As a "revision" patient, I needed a world-class doctor who could clean up the mess from a previously-repaired elbow ligament. As the August 7 date approached, Andy assured me that he'd make calls for me when I was ready. Once you're out, getting back in is not easy—the game waits for no man. Duff got me to Simi. Simi gave me chances I didn't deserve. When Fargo released me, Brooks kept his word and handed me off to Andy.

"Blew. When you're ready, you call me." I nodded, but it wouldn't be the same me that showed up on his caller ID in a year or two. I was rotting already, time and age accelerating the process. If I merely revived my old self, I'd never get back in. I had learned better than to wait for change. The old me would not return. Those rotten planks were a gift.

Dear Doc, I needed you to know.

I had already made up my mind—the ballplayer in me would *not* die. I wasn't like the other 150 Tommy John patients that would stream through your office that year. Based on the exam, that fact was obvious —I was there for a "revision," a repair of my now torn first UCL reconstruction that I underwent in college in 2008. Revisions were rare and I was sent to you because the team doctor who read my MRI had never seen one, much less repaired one. He named three doctors in the world who were the right men for the job and you in Cincinnati were the one.

I knew the success rate of a second Tommy John surgery was less than 50%, but I wasn't deterred. As I sat on the faux leather training table in your exam room, I scanned the signed photos of Cincinnati Reds players that covered the wall. I wasn't important enough to be on that wall, but still firmly believed I was a somebody. The only thing I really needed from you in that moment was for you to, well, *know.*

My last day on the mound was the worst. I had about 40 innings under my belt in my seventh start of the still-young season. Entering the game, my ERA was 0.90 and I was starting to get excited that my time might come, that someone in the stands with a radar gun might sign me away to better places. I was an Independent League player, pitching for the Evansville Otters. The previous year, I'd had an abysmal season in Fargo. I found redemption in Evansville and knew that if I pitched well enough, a scout would buy out my contract and give me a chance in an MLB organization. Leading the league in most pitching categories, I was on the right track to finally get my big break, the break I'd been pushing to create since I was a kid.

As I warmed up in the visitors' bullpen in Southern Illinois, I reveled in the feeling of smallness the ballpark provided. Rent One Park was an immaculate facility with towering concrete retaining walls and a concourse that majestically enveloped the field below; it was *Big League* among Minor League fields. A few fans hung over the railing 20 or so feet up, watching as my final few warmup pitches punched the catchers mitt with an amplified, ringing *CRACK!* The cortisone shot I had gotten in my elbow a month earlier was wearing off, and I apparently hadn't hid it well enough. As I retrieved the ball following my final warmup pitch, I gave my catcher a fist-bump and took one last chug of water. Brooksy handed me my jacket for our 380-foot walk across the turf field to the dugout. We usually didn't talk much on that final walk. We were both men who didn't waste words. When it was *go time,* there was little to say. Yet this night, Brooks had a suspicion.

"It's really hurting you isn't it, Blew?"

I glanced at him out of the corner of my eye; my look served as the reply. I was pitching today so what the hell did it matter how my elbow felt? I was a little surprised he even asked.

"How did you know?" I asked.

He shrugged. "I can just tell. Give me a sign if I need to come get you later."

I nodded and ended the conversation. I never received a medal for hiding elbow pain, but one was probably in the mail. I learned what *not* to do from a young age: don't flex it, straighten it, make a fist, fan your fingers, shake it, and definitely don't look at it. If you want to stay on that mound, you act like you don't have an elbow. If you pull thick enough wool over their eyes, you'll get to pitch until you physically can't. Baseball keeps a man from growing up. And young people classically make the mistake of acting as if they're immortal. I was a ballplayer, and so the feeling of immortality never wore off. I wondered what I did to tip Brooks off, but it didn't matter much—it was time to do my job.

It was a great night to pitch. I always loved pitching against the Miners in their top-shelf ballpark with their big crowds and perennially good teams; it brought out the best in me and all my teammates. That night, I noticed a scout in a Royals hat sitting directly behind the plate. As I warmed up I stole glances of him, radar gun fixed on each fastball that hissed toward the plate. I assumed it was just a matter of time—as well as I'd pitched, sooner or later scouts would come to see what the fuss was about. I was four years removed from my first surgery and my velocity had been in the 92-94 range.

And, I was one who historically held that velocity deep into the late innings. But I'd had elbow problems that spring, and a preseason cortisone shot kept me on the field. The assumption was my pre-season pain wasn't serious, and that cortisone would allow me to keep pitching while it calmed down. It *did* mask my pain, but it became clear early on that something was lurking beneath. I pitched seven scoreless innings on opening day. It was a special moment, but the optimism quickly faded. My "stuff" declined with each subsequent start—my velocity faded earlier into each outing as my command became downright shaky. I was turning in superb outing after superb outing, so I grinned and doubled down.

As I fired off my final warmup pitches, I was hopeful the pain would subside. Sometimes it just needed to get warmed up before calming down. Sometimes, the adrenaline of the first hitter would polish it off. But as the leadoff hitter strolled into the batter's box…it hadn't. A few hitters later, *I knew*. Every pitch had that familiar stabbing sensation and many had the nauseating feeling of the bones in my elbow spreading oh-so-slightly apart. The "gapping" in one's elbow is something you don't forget—it's a distinct feeling of looseness that leads you to believe if you throw too hard, your hand and forearm might fly off. My body started to retract and revolt when the gapping started, holding back to protect itself even as I tried to hit the gas.

I got through the first inning, sat on the bench with my jacket on and rubbed my elbow. Brooks already knew, so I just wanted to massage some blood into it in hopes it would improve. I went back out for the second and got through that one as well, despite intensifying pain. But with two outs in the third inning, the pain was too severe to ignore; I felt the gapping on every pitch. I had to get off that mound without the scout knowing it was because of a potential elbow injury…but how?

Earlier, I had hatched a plan—I'd start picking at my finger between pitches in a very obvious way, making it appear that a blister was bugging me. I'd ignore my elbow and dig at my finger so if the time came, I could call out Brooks like he asked and remove myself without the scout knowing. Despite the pain, I never imagined my surgically-repaired elbow could be blown again. I'd only known one other player who had gotten Tommy John a second time, and my first doctor had explicitly told me in 2008 that I'd never need it again. "It's stronger than the day you were born!" He exclaimed as I awoke in the recovery room of the hospital.

Rather, I assumed I had bone spurs or severe tendinitis, two very plausible outcomes that afflicted lots of pitchers. Countless abnormal things went on in the body after the scalpel and drill first entered, so I wasn't yet jumping to the worst possible conclusion. Tendinitis could be incredibly painful and I'd heard the same about spurs, so my pain didn't necessarily mean another Tommy John surgery. If I could just escape the mound without pointing to my elbow—the way I had in college in front of 15 or more scouts—maybe I could still get a chance with the Royals. No team wanted to sign a guy who had injury problems, and so it was imperative that I stay off the disabled list if at all possible. Assuming it was something small, I'd get it taken care of and be back in action in a few weeks.

I was close to getting out of the third inning, but every pitch I threw sailed high. I tried with every fiber of my being to pull the ball down into the strike zone, but couldn't do it. Finally, a big lefty hitter sat back and ambushed a high fastball. It was hit hard but a little too low to sneak out...or so I thought. I rubbernecked as my left fielder went back-back-back to the warning track. He made a valiant leap, coming up just short as the ball squeaked over the yellow fence line for a two-run homer. At that point, I concluded it was time to end my night. I had no clue where each pitch would end up and I was shaking off both my changeup and curveball because they hurt too much. I wasn't helping the team and was likely destroying my arm.

I waved to the umpire and to Brooks, beckoning them to walk out and examine my middle finger. Little did they know, my finger was always stained with dried blood beneath a thick callous, so it did look blistered despite being completely normal.

"What's the problem, guys?" The umpire asked. Brooks jumped in for me.

"Well, he told me in pregame that he had a little blister forming. Is it bothering you, Blew?"

I nodded, offering up my middle finger for inspection. Brooks was smart—he had picked up on my ploy without us even discussing it.

"Yeah, there's some blood pooling beneath my finger and it's starting to affect me. I don't want it to rip open; I've had problems with it before (this was actually true)."

"Alright, so you're coming out of the game?" The umpire asked.

I *was* disappointed, so it didn't take much acting to tell him that yes, I needed to come out. I walked off as Brooks walked out to the bullpen to sort through the issue of who was replacing me on the mound. I didn't know it then, but it was the last pitch I'd throw for nearly two years. It was *not* bone spurs, nor was it tendinitis; it was indeed the worst-case scenario.

A few weeks later the MRI results rolled in and I rolled up to your office in Beacon Orthopedics in Cincinnati. You noted in the post-op report that my surgery took you twice as long as normal because of all the scar-tissue, suture removal and general messiness. After you completed your work, I awoke from anesthesia feeling drunk on a cocktail of drugs and disappointment. I knew it would take the better part of 700 days to return—I had no illusions about a 2013 comeback. I dug in for the long haul of boredom and hard work, with a little uncertainty mixed in about how I'd get around. I wrote a volume of *You're My Boy, Blew* to fill everyone in, which included a photo of my MRI. It was titled *Workplace Injury.*

Workplace Injury

So I made it up to Dr. Kremchek finally, and they confirmed that it was torn at the proximal insertion (the end closer to my body). The spot I circled shows the tear, I think. I meant to ask about the MRI, out of curiosity, but I forgot. It was sitting there on the computer as I waited so I was checking it out, and I think the circled spot should be one solid color, not all frayed with grey and white. I'm no radiologist and there's an 86% chance that everything I just said was 100% wrong. Anyway, I thought it was interesting. Worker's comp has approved my surgery and everything is on the house. Huzzah.

Manual Transmissions Are Now My Biggest Enemy.

I just realized that I'm going to be shifting my stick-shift car left-handed, while simultaneously steering with the same left hand. I'm going to be in a brace with limited elbow extension for 4 weeks...so I'm screwed. If I manage to not die in a car crash, I think my recovery chances are good! I'm going to see if worker's comp will buy me an Escalade...automatic transmission, of course.

* * *

Two Weeks Of Purgatory To Go

I've been pretty bored. Last week I missed a six-day roadtrip because of my pre-op appointment and I have very little to do at the field. I've been doing lots of writing, have resumed weight lifting and a little bit of running. I need to get back in shape before surgery, and I'm revamping my diet in a big way. I'm starting to get some motivation back and have ordered some fun tools for the gym that will help all of us when I return.

That's about it! Updates will start via my website once surgery goes down, as I'll be doing videos weekly about my progress and training. My doc will be filming the surgery and taking pictures, which I'm excited to see. Maybe we will have a movie night at the gym...

After the first operation, my first pitch back in action was a called strike thrown in Evansville, Indiana. My parents were there. My best friend, Andrew, called me that night with an inflection of pride in his voice as he congratulated me on a good first start. I earned my paycheck. Conspicuously absent though, were any feelings of kinship toward the man who performed that first surgery.

I'm confident that my first surgeon never knew my name. I was an athlete he repaired and no more—he might as well have been a veterinarian. At the time, I didn't need more—I merely wanted the best available doctor to fix me because I knew I'd handle the rest. I didn't need to chit-chat about my feelings, though a little more procedural advice would have been appreciated. My typical visit with him lasted about 90 seconds, with half of that devoted to him examining—in silence—my MRI and files. After he'd decided what I needed he glanced up just long enough to explain it in as few words as possible, briefly confirming that he *was* capable of eye contact before walking out. His rehab team then came in to actually speak with me. I wasn't his average patient—I worked hard and appreciated what he did for me. I kicked down doors to get into pro baseball with my repaired elbow. We didn't need to be best buds, but I was *not* human surgical patient #96139212. I worked awfully hard for people in the bleachers to open up their program and dig for information on #13. I didn't have a Big League uniform for his wall, but the name on the back of my jersey was worth knowing.

Nevertheless, I persevered through that first recovery that was really more tedious than anything. It jabs at you every time you try to do normal, everyday things that just don't work with your arm in a sling. Staring down at the bruised, black-stitched scar, a feeling lingered: *how did I ever end up here?* The things you used to be able to do are such a distant memory as you begin therapy with the strength of a toddler, unable to perform even the basics. I remember squeezing a balled up sock on the second day after surgery—it was *hard.* I remember moving my arm manually as I tried to regain range of motion—it was *hard.* I remember trying in vain to wash my back in the shower, my arm taped inside a Cramer plastic ice bag—it was *hard.* All of it nags and mocks you. You pick up a fork with your throwing hand, just to set it back down and pick it back up with your glove hand. Then, you remind yourself that it's a mere 699 days more until you're back to normal. It's liberating, but more so annoying when major milestones are merely the return of normal functions:

Hooray, I can shower without a bag on my arm!
Hooray, I can turn a doorknob!
Hooray, I can start jogging!
Hooray, I can do a bicep curl with a 6lb pink dumbbell!

Despite my cynicism, the milestones *do* keep you going. Like anything, it's one step at a time. It just mentally breaks an athlete down as he checks off milestones that are so far removed from the amazing things he used to be able to do with that arm. It makes you question if it will ever return…

When will my arm stop hurting?
When can I start throwing?
When can I participate in practice like a normal player?
When will I be myself again?

Sixteen months after my first operation, in the early winter of 2009, my elbow continued to hurt. The pain had initially subsided as I eclipsed the 90mph mark in month 10. It was a huge milestone, but pain resurfaced afterward, coming and going as it pleased. Well past the year mark, pain continued lingering and no matter what I did…it hurt. More time off? Hurt. More rehab? Hurt. Anti-inflammatories? Still hurt. It just would not stop hurting and I was well past the point where I should have still had pain—sixteen months was way, way past my due date. I finally got tired of babying it, tired of worrying about it, and tired of feeling like I was in a purgatory where I wasn't hurt but wasn't healthy. I saw a barbell and said *screw it.*

I started deadlifting the bar. I was alone in the weight room of a rock climbing gym where I had a day pass and had just been doing some light bouldering as an out-of-the-box workout to help regain finger strength. I put two plates on the barbell and deadlifted it for eight reps. Then, three plates. Eight reps. Three plates and a twenty-five. Eight reps. Four plates. Five reps. The wide, rubber bumper plates took up most of the bar sleeve until there were only a handful of plates left that would fit. I piled them on, one at a time, as I moved to single-rep sets, hoping my arm would just tear off and stay on the ground with the bar. I was *over* it—tired of the daily pain and the constant worrying. Well over 400lbs, the weight wasn't quite heavy enough to deter me from pulling it off the floor. I was angry, ripping that bar off the ground as furiously as I could. I added little plates until I ran out. Finally missing a rep, I quit and went home. I was so tired of all of it. I just wanted to pitch.

Funny thing was, my new elbow didn't break. Rather, it miraculously stopped hurting. Maybe the weight popped some scar tissue loose, or maybe snapping mentally was the variable of interest; I didn't know. But the grind of rehab, pain and the sadness of being away from the game started to give way after that moment in that little gym. I otherwise was never reckless with my arm—I did my rehab exactly as written and added exercises that I felt would be compatible and safe. I did a million variations of finger-strengthening exercises and scoured YouTube for any secret that a guitarist, rock climber or powerlifter might have for forearm health and strength. At the time, everyone knew that the forearms protected the elbow but there was a strange dearth of training methods beyond the very basics. If strong fingers and forearms were my elbow's bodyguards, I wanted to give them all the weapons possible to keep it safe.

I was never a healthy pitcher, dating back to high school when I first partially tore my UCL in a varsity game; my elbow bugged me from that point on. Pitching in pain was more normal than not, so I paid that toll as part of the highway to the mound each day. Until I reached college, I had no guidance on how to care for my arm or how to prevent pain and injury. It was a different time then compared to now, where there's an outpouring of good training information in every corner of the internet. As 2009 gave way to 2010, I continued to follow my rehab, make (mostly) sensible decisions in the weight room and tried to think outside the box for little things that could help me ward off future injury.

The hardest part is the mental side of the recovery; it attacks a player from so many different fronts. Early on, it's boredom—you can't do anything active, fun or challenging. Squeezing a balled-up sock is a pitcher's daily excitement in the early-going. Then, as you gain your strength back, it's the constant itch that *you're close*. Your brain constantly reminds you that *you're close* to doing fun things again like throwing, lifting weights, running and jumping. It's like a kid resisting the urge to run down and spoil Christmas before the morning arrives. Every day as strength returns, there's constant pulling of the reigns to make sure you don't jump the gun and hurt yourself, because you feel good enough to do things you shouldn't.

It gets even more complex once throwing begins. Throwing again is great but no matter how hard you throw today, you want to throw *harder*. Its almost unbearable holding back and trusting that it's a long-game you're playing. As speeds do start to increase, your arm starts to react and pain comes back. When pain comes back during throwing... the doubts flood in.

Did I do too much?

Is this normal?

Did I re-tear it?

Do I need surgery again?

DO I NEED SURGERY AGAIN?

Getting this voice to shut its mouth is unbelievably difficult. With pain and setbacks, it becomes a terrible waltz of two steps forward, one step back until at some point all steps move forward. Once most of you is heading in the right direction, another issue crops up—the question of *am I ready?* This one is perhaps the final—and hardest—voice to respond to, because the answer is one that you only know when it's happening. You're ready when you're out doing it and realize that you're finally ready. Before that point, you just don't know.

It was a week or so before the draft in June of 2009 when I heard the Kansas City Royals were hosting a local pre-draft workout; I desperately wanted to do it. The tryout date was around 10 months post-op and my fastball had reached 90mph again at the 8.5 month mark. In 2009, throwing 90 was still a very good milestone and I felt that if my curveball showed up, I'd show well. Tim, my pitching coach who ordinarily oozed optimism, talked through it with me.

"Well, what are the pros for you going to this tryout? Are you ready to pitch if they want to sign you?"

"Probably not," I replied. "But I'm throwing hard, so maybe it's a good thing?"

"You are! Your velocity is returning really fast. But it's also still fluctuating, and you'll have to throw all your stuff for strikes with scouts watching. That's a very different task than just throwing the ball as hard as possible with no regard for location."

I nodded. It was true that my ability to locate the ball was still returning.

"I used to scout. What scouts would often say is, *I've seen him.* Once these guys see you once, they'll write a report and that will be that. If you don't show your best, you may be written off forever. Then, if two months go by and you're throwing even harder...*I've seen him* will probably be what they say when you ask for another shot. Scouts are busy people and they can't waste time looking at the same players over and over."

I understood. It was good, objective advice not meant to discourage me, but rather to have realistic expectations. Tim was right—scouts didn't have time to come watch every player who cried wolf. If I went to this scouting combine, it might be my only shot with them. I knew also that I would most likely just be *touching* 90, not sitting it. My velocity range would probably be 87-90, which was far less impressive than 90-92, for example. I pondered it for a few days, talking some more with Tim and my parents. Finally, I decided to just go for it. I knew it probably wasn't my time, but I wanted to see anyway. It was only one team, so it wasn't like it would close all 30 Major League doors if it didn't go well.

The question of *when am I ready?* is one of the hardest to answer. In Independent Baseball, there are no farm teams and there are no rehab assignments. If they sign you, you're volunteering to do the job anytime they ask. In college and high school baseball—as well as the affiliated Minor Leagues—there is more leeway because teams want to see their investments come to fruition. But Independent ball is solely a business, the same way the Major Leagues are. Putting up good numbers, helping the team win and thus getting fans in the stands is the only goal. I knew I'd most likely have to go through independent ball first, so being truly *ready* was of the utmost importance. If I got signed too soon and couldn't do the job, I might get released with bad statistics and be written off by every team...*forever*. It was a legitimate fear that required careful consideration.

During my six years in pro ball I saw lots of rookies get their first chance just like I did, only to play terribly and get released just a few days or weeks later. Sometimes, players got released that same night as if they kept the taxicab waiting outside the ballpark. When they'd get released on bad statistical terms, it was like carrying a job resume' that showed you were fired at your only previous job. Many of those guys never got another chance.

Beyond the contract implications, it's just plain hard to pitch well coming back from a major surgery. Velocity is the first indicator that a pitcher is "ready" again, but it's not a good predictor. It took me well into my rookie season—nearly two years post op—to start feeling like myself again on the mound, locating all my pitches and adjusting to the pace of the game. Time was all it took, but taking more time drove me crazy.

I still remember that Royals' tryout. I was nervous both because I was scared my arm would blow up, and because important people were watching. Tim was right—my velocity was only about 86-88 that day. I threw a lot of strikes in my 15 or so pitches in front of the radar guns, and threw some decent curveballs to boot. The low velocity surely got me written off, but I didn't care. It was another little milestone, another little challenge that I had to rise up and face in my eventual return to form.

The last challenge—and one that the tryout helped me with—was *letting go*. It's natural to hold back and try to do the job at less than 100%, because 100% is fast, scary and dangerous. Pitchers injure their arms throwing as hard as they can; they don't get injured at 95%. So when injury befalls not just a pitcher but any athlete, the natural reaction is to be less aggressive, take the safe road, hold back and stay healthy. But athletes only succeed by playing at their full potential—at 100%. One of my friends in college got Tommy John the same year I did and never truly recovered. When it was time to rise up, he held back. He was constantly bogged down with pain and worry. He couldn't perform when he got his chances and faded quietly into the real world. I refused to go out like that—I'd either blow it out again or go down swinging. It would take another 11 months after that tryout, but I *did* eventually get there, making my debut in pro ball. And when I did, I hit the ground running. I refused to hold back or pitch in fear of re-injury.

Four years after that first surgery, when I found myself crinkling the paper on your exam table, being told that I'd have to go through it yet again, I vowed the same things. I wouldn't hold back, I wouldn't pitch in fear. It would be harder than the first time, that I knew. I wasn't heading back to school to rehab in the comfort of a D-I training room with staff to attend to me on a daily basis. I wasn't heading to Florida or Arizona to rehab in the warm comfort of extended spring training. I had no pitching coach and only three months of paid physical therapy. After that, I would become my own pitching coach, my own strength coach, my own physical therapist, rehab coordinator, massage therapist, and mental skills coach. There would be no rehab starts, no waiting for me to get back into shape.

Yet, I didn't think much then about what I didn't have. Rather, I looked forward to doing things my way, in my baseball academy with my weights, my yoga mats, my baseballs and my batting cage. Despite not having human resources, I had plentiful physical resources—tons of strength training equipment and space to work. It was enough…it had to be.

When I returned, I knew I'd be thrown right into the fire, expected to perform at the same 100% as my healthy peers. In Independent Baseball, there is no farm system and no one patiently waiting for a player to develop. You show up and do the job or you're sent packing. I also was going to age out of the Frontier League while rehabbing and would have to get signed in a higher league when I returned. It was the equivalent of a Rookie-ball pitcher getting Tommy John then being assigned to rehab starts in Double-A. I had to be ready. I dug in for two long winters and built myself a plan. The statistics on revision patients didn't matter, nor did I need a rehab facility in Arizona. I was coming back.

First, though, I had to get a chance to do either. You and I met for the last time in the spring of 2013. I was doing well and unless I had issues, one final handshake was all I needed. A few more months passed. In August, a little over a year after that second surgery, I felt that my time had arrived. I called Andy.

Andy was friends with Brett Jodie, the manager of the Somerset Patriots. He sent players to Somerset when he felt they were ready for the jump in competition offered by the Atlantic League. The Atlantic League had no age limits and most players were formerly Double-A, Triple-A or Major League players who were looking for another chance at getting to the Majors. Somerset was perennially one of the best teams in the 8-team league.

"Hey Andy."

"Blew! I knew I'd hear from you sooner or later. How's the rehab? How's the arm?"

"Well, it was unexpected but I hit 94 the other day in my first time in a men's league game. I'm pretty excited about it, and I want to give it a shot before the 2013 season ends. I think I can do it."

"Say no more. If you say you're ready, I'll make the call."

A day later, he arranged a tryout for me in Somerset, New Jersey. It marked the end of my time as a patient. The rest of the village took over, bustling in the background to carry me the last few miles across the finish line. I'd be on a mound again soon.

Doc, I know you didn't really know who I was, and you were understandably too busy taking care of others to dig for information. I got the impression, though, that if you had a free moment, you would have patiently listened. At the time, I'm not sure I could have found the words to explain what I'd been through to end up in your office, and what I was planning to do when I left. Now that I'm moving on, I needed you to know that I did almost all of it. Your work held up. Thank you for giving me that third chance.

Dear Mike, You wrote me into existence.

The odds were stacked against me making the team as I rolled into 2014 spring training in Somerset. Maybe you knew this, and I suspect that's why you took a special interest in me—the longshot, unremarkable right-hander with a deep scar on his elbow. I didn't need validation and to this day, I get awkward and uncomfortable when praised. I do best when my work stands for itself and I can see from afar whether it had the desired impact, whether it can be objectively viewed as good.

I'll admit, however, that the longer I played, the more I wanted there to be some record of my existence. I cannot remember a single time my photo was used in a press release in college. Just one would have been enough to show that I was someone who contributed. Yet, I reasoned that if I didn't like it, I should pitch better. So I did.

As my career wore on, I earned an accolade or two and my picture was printed—I existed, I was here. Then, I met you—you weren't like the other reporters. For unknown reasons, you didn't just regurgitate my stats, quote my thoughts and recap a good game. I had good games and bad and there was nothing overly remarkable about any of them. Rather, you reported on *me*—why I was returning to baseball, what I'd been through and what my intentions were. Even when I signed with Camden—the local rival—we sat down yet again and another story went to the press. You took an interest in me and encouraged your readers to urge me onward. It meant a lot.

There was even more backstory to that spring training than you or anyone else knew. Coming back from a second Tommy John surgery? Interesting story for sure and I had been meticulously preparing for my return. That, however, wasn't the story. The story was the last 17 days.

* * *

I was finishing my rehab as the summer of 2013 was winding down. I had my sight set on that 2014 return to baseball. Everything from the date of that surgery was building to the day in early April when I'd drive back east for spring training. A short time after that, I'd triumphantly make the team and reclaim the seat in pro baseball that the Baseball Gods were keeping warm for me. I wasn't planning on rushing the process and so the 2014 season was a safe, prudent, realistic target.

In August of that year, however, I returned to my pre-surgery velocity and started thinking about catching on at the very end of the 2013 season. I called Andy. Andy called Brett Jodie, setting a date for me to throw a bullpen for Somerset in early September. If I was better than a guy they had, he explained, there would be a contract for me. I knew I would have to throw bullpens for multiple teams to get back on the inside. But a wave of optimism hit me and I told myself that I'd be one and done—I'd head to Somerset, throw lights-out and stick there. Comeback complete.

I called Goose to let him know about the date with Somerset and he insisted on chauffeuring me up and down I-95, to and from TD Bank Ballpark. As we drove, he filled me in on the local Delaware baseball scene and what some of the other Raiders were up to. As I sat listening in the passenger seat of his black Suburban, it marked the first time I had ever been *that* guy. Every year during the season, players get released or injured, spurring coaches to bring in new players to audition for their spot. Maybe they'll release someone if they really like the new guy. These potential players walk into the clubhouse with a big gear bag over their shoulders, and awkwardly look for a place to get changed while everyone sizes them up. They slink in, put their bags down in a corner, find the manager, change, then hustle out to the field before the collective stares of 24 players burns a hole through them. If the new guy is good, someone goes home either that day or the next. For a struggling catcher, it must be a bad feeling to see a new guy walk in with his catchers' bag. And on this day, I felt it—for the first time, I was the enemy. I put my stuff in an empty locker, grabbed the manager and asked for instructions. I could feel the stares, then tension and subdued but palpable animosity directed toward me; I got out of there as fast as I could. I had no remorse about it—I was dead set on sending one of those guys home—but it felt like I was a lone wasp invading a hornet's nest.

Out on the field it was hot and sunny, all the screens, mats and field protectors set up for batting practice. They had alerted the grounds crew that I'd throw to their guys just before BP, and I was slated to face eight or nine hitters. It was nice to feel the grass crunch beneath my cleats as I jogged out to right field in preparation for the outing. I'd run a few foul poles, stretch, perform some calisthenics and sprints, then finally play catch and get "hot" once a catcher appeared. I threw to the team's bullpen catcher, a guy paid a small stipend to do all of the catching before and during games in the bullpen, reducing wear and tear on the team's two rostered catchers. I got hot, felt good about what I had that day and walked my mildly lopsided walk toward the dugout as hitters began sauntering out, bats and helmets in hand.

Goose talked to Jodie as I warmed up on the game mound, attempting to boost my stock as much as he could, "selling" them on why I'd fit on their squad. As I warmed up in my white pants, black hat and black Warbird Academy t-shirt, he leaned against the dugout railing, sharing his legendary stories with the rest of the coaching staff. He knew just about everyone and if he didn't know someone personally, he knew at least five guys who played with or against him.

My first fastball sailed up and in, brushing the hitter back. Oh boy. Getting that first one out of the way was *big*. The last competitive pitch I had thrown resulted in surgery and fear of re-injury was still on my mind. Their hitters were big and they were not the least bit intimidated, even as I accidentally brushed them back. They were grown-ass men compared to the younger players of leagues past. However, most didn't swing much against me. The majority merely watched the ball in, seemingly studying every revolution of the ball's mid-flight spin. They took a hack or two then let another hitter jump in. Twenty minutes later, one of the coaches called out that they had seen enough. I walked off the mound and wasn't optimistic. As a pitcher, you know when you throw well and you know when you don't. I had thrown...just okay. I was throwing hard—the adrenaline certainly helped—but I didn't locate all that well and their hitters let a lot of high fastballs whistle by. This was typical of those early outings each season when I—along with every other pitcher— had to shake the rust off. The problem was, I was the only one with rust—everyone else was deep into the 2013 season. Jodie waved me over toward the dugout where he was standing.

"Hey Dan. I thought you threw well. Thanks for coming out, I know you traveled a long way."

This was not a good sign.

"I think with another six months, you might really have something. You've got a great fastball and that curveball of yours bites hard," he explained in his slightly southern draw.

"I don't have space for you today, but I can offer you a spring training contract for next year. How does that sound? You can come back and compete for a spot in in the spring."

I was disappointed, but agreed. He said he'd pay me $1400 a month, a 40% raise from my previous contract in Evansville. I thanked him and he explained that they'd be in touch after the new year.

As I drove back with Goose, I was sore and disappointed. I didn't want to admit it, but I was also a little relieved. I, too, had been questioning my own readiness—I wanted to be ready, but was I able to jump back into the demands of pro baseball that very day? Not so much. I couldn't pitch on back-to-back days, which is part of the job— you pitch when you're asked to pitch. I had planned on making my return as a reliever, and relievers have very unpredictable workloads.

"Danny, think of it this way: you may not have gotten what you wanted today, but you got what you needed, didn't you? You've got your foot back in that door—you've got an opportunity. You're in spring training next year with a chance to make the team. I think you got *exactly* what you came here for." He was right. Goose was always right. I went home, made a training plan just like I always had and stuck to it. Come March, I was in great shape and everything was shaping up like I'd hoped. Then, it happened.

In December of 2013, the owners of the facility that my academy shared a space with approached Lucas and I. They wanted to sell their business to us and wash their hands of it. It was odd hearing that the 14,000-square-foot Goliath wanted to sell to us, very much the David by comparison. Our 2,000-square-foot strength and conditioning space occupied just a fraction of the huge warehouse. We were faced with a tough decision because if we didn't buy them out, they intended to find someone who would. Would a new owner form a partnership with us in the same way they had? If the answer was no, we could potentially be forced out and onto the streets. There was both risk and opportunity in front of us, so we took time to deliberate and think through it.

A few months later, after numerous business plans and meetings with banks, advisors and investors, we had an answer: we would not buy them out. Uncertain who would, we decided that our best option was to flee and find our own space. We *did* need more square footage, but not 14,000 more. Becoming that big overnight would have completely changed the way we did business, and we knew if we made the wrong move it could bankrupt us.

Lucas and I rolled up our sleeves. It was March and I was set on departing on April 7 for Somerset. I had a spring training contract to redeem, destiny to reclaim. Leaving on April 7 would afford me a buffer week back home to throw to live hitters as final prep. I'd throw for my alma mater, the University of Maryland-Baltimore County, as well the high school team in Pennsylvania that Duff was coaching. I needed to face some live hitters so I'd be game-ready for spring training; indoor bullpens were not enough. Because spring training was short—just 20 days or so—I had to be sharp right out of the gate. I was driving east on April 7.

I rarely plan head farther than I can spit and don't stress about much. Rather, I accept the possible outcomes and do my best to achieve the one I want. We didn't know where we'd move our business, but I just assumed it would work out, just the same as things always did. Sure enough, the third place we looked at was justttttttttt right—three times the size, three times the rent, with a footprint that had a great potential configuration. We needed at least two batting cages (we got three), at least 3,000 square feet for our weightlifting area (we got 3,600), modest office space and a lounge area for parents and athletes to wait comfortably. It was all there.

On March 20, shiny brass keys were in our hands to what would become the new Warbird Academy. In the 17 days that followed, Lucas and I worked like dogs, 6 a.m. to midnight, converting what was a filthy old auto-body shop into our new academy. It would give hundreds of athletes a place to stretch their legs and reach for their dreams. Lucas, all 6'3" and 240lbs of him, supported me 100%. It sucked that I was leaving—there was no way around it. The way we approached it, though, was this: it must get done before April 7. But what if it doesn't? *It has to.* But what if it didn't? *It just...has to.* There was no plan B. We had 17 days.

I'm not sure why my memory of the early stages of my friendship with Lucas is so foggy—I have little recollection prior to the night we decided to become partners. Lucas had worked at the partner baseball academy, finishing his Master's degree in Sports Management from Illinois State University. In undergrad at the University of Illinois,

Lucas got all As and one single, solitary B, a B that still haunts him. A creature of routine and discipline, he's the guy you want on your team when you've got a deadline.

Our partnership over the years has been a lot like a marriage, though probably a lot more harmonious than most. Probably the most bizarre detail is our shared birthday. My memory is fuzzy, but I'm pretty sure we found out one night in early December as we were shooting the breeze near the front desk.

"So what are you up to this weekend, Lucas?"

"Eh, not too much. I'm laying low this weekend since my birthday is coming up the following week."

"Oh really? Mine too. What day is yours?"

"December 15." My eyes got wide.

"Shut up. That is *not* your birthday."

"Yeah it is—why?"

"My birthday is December 15. Are you kidding me? We have the same birthday!?"

It's still insane and still feels weird. Our podcast is aptly named *Twinsies* because we share the same birthday, though I'm three years older. Most years, we were too swamped with lessons and strength classes to even bother celebrating. The middle of December through the end of February was always crazy, often forcing us to work seven days a week. Saturdays that time of year usually consisted of churning out as many as 16 straight half-hour lessons. Teaching boys and girls how to play sports can be exhausting.

At least two different auto shops had occupied the new space in the last decade and it had sat vacant for over a year. The place was a spectacular mess and yet we couldn't just dive in all at once. We were subject to an order of operations, where some tasks had to be completed before we could tackle others. First, we had to clean the concrete floor so that the turf we ordered would adhere. Because our turf had a two-week lead-time, we ordered it immediately and got to work on the floor project. We spent the first two full days on our hands and knees, scraping the concrete floor with putty knives to remove every last chunk of hardened Bondo, engine sludge, tape, dirt, and grease. The facility felt extra roomy as we scraped and crawled on all fours with throbbing shins and bruised kneecaps. They apparently make knee pads for such jobs and as we hobbled around like old men for the next week, we cursed our ignorance to this fact. Twenty hours of work later, we were back on hands and knees yet again to fill cracks. Any crack wider than hairline had to be filled to prevent the turf from bubbling up. Countless heavy cars and trucks had come through the garage door, so the floor was lousy with cracks; it took another whole day to fill all of them, and we basically limped around the facility thereafter.

Our clients came to our rescue. They showed up every day to help paint our walls, install sheet rock, remove trash and clean floors, windows, bathrooms—you name it. We had probably 50 man-hours of help every day and without them, none of it would have been possible. The whole place was originally painted a repulsive baby-poop brown. We chose a medium grey and couldn't have fathomed how long all the painting would take. The work was monotonous and the space felt cavernous without equipment. Yet as the drywall came together and our new gray topcoat dried, things started to shape up.

Our new landlord had this old cherry-picker lift that held one person and went up to a maximum height of 30 feet. The lift wasn't one of those fancy, safe, self-powered models with a huge, plate-steel base and tractor tires for stability. Nope—instead, it was just a heavy base thrown in a garden-variety steel trailer, the same one you'd haul lawnmowers in. One had to lift up the hitch and push the two-wheeled trailer to the proper spot. Our roof pitched at 27 feet and I was tasked with ascending to the heavens in that rickety lift. We had to change out the old, 4-foot fluorescent light bulbs in about 10 bays. I have only a mild fear of heights and yet it proved to be one of the most terrifying experiences of my life. The lift extended like a typical boom pole—as one upright fully extended, the next one—slightly thinner and nested inside—would go up. As it got higher the arms got thinner, which made the basket wobble more and more with every foot it climbed. I was the smaller, lighter half of the business, so the job was mine. It was better to send my 6-foot, 200-pound self to the stratosphere rather than my monstrous counterpart. Lucas could easily be mistaken for an NFL linebacker and bears a strong likeness to Matt Holiday. He might have tipped that bad boy over reaching for the first bulb, so I reluctantly volunteered.

My routine was this: I'd pick up the lift and roll it into place. Then, I'd grab a new box of bulbs. After that, I'd close my eyes and pray for a quick death with minimal cleanup for those who would find me. Then, I'd climb into the basket. Slowly and methodically, I rose until I reached the top. I then extended both arms up to grab a bulb, my head just a few feet from the dusty silver insulation. I slowly twisted it until it snapped free of the retainer. Then—even more slowly—I'd bend over and swap the old one for new. With every movement, the basket bobbed like I was salsa dancing in a canoe. At 27 feet above a concrete floor, every subtle step, reach and bend sent a gob of adrenaline through my veins. The only thing I wanted out of life at that moment was to steady myself by putting at least one hand on the rail of the cherry picker. Alas, each bulb required a hand on both ends, leaving me wobbling for my life. I replaced all six bulbs in the bay, wiped my brow, exhaled deeply and headed back to reacquaint myself with the most wonderful concrete floor I'd ever known. Back on my beloved Mother Earth, I'd then repeat my process. It was a mentally exhausting day but I lived to type the tale. A week later in an act of sheer cruelty, we discovered that even with new bulbs, the old bays didn't produce enough lumens to safely light a baseball academy. Back up we went, this time in a scissor lift to replace all of the bays. Round two was only mildly better.

The low-point of the transformation came with about four days before my departure. Everything was painted, the floor was complete, lights were installed and our landlord had built out the interior walls. We were both utterly exhausted, the two weeks of consecutive 16-hour days taking their toll. But we were almost done and just had to power wash the entire 7,300-square-foot space before the turf installers arrived. I had power-washed a deck before and thought it might be fun, so I volunteered. We had to start at the end of our long day, though, so that the wet floors could dry overnight. When the clock struck midnight, we got in our pumpkin carriage and started blasting.

Because our building had only one garage door, all the water had to eventually make its way toward it. I started in the deepest, darkest corner and with a 10-foot tall plume of dust—a literal tsunami of allergens—the power washing began. I weaved my way around the edges for two hours, pushing all the dust and dirty water toward the center. As the water pooled, it was Lucas' job to squeegee it out the door like St. Patrick banishing a herd of wild cobras. Mercifully, at 2 a.m., the last wave of brown water went out our door. I walked outside and plopped down on the curb, gasping for air as I clung to life. I had forgotten about my childhood asthma.

As a kid I had reasonably bad asthma, and it limited me in pretty much any endeavor that required running. Like most pitchers, though, I hate running so I wasn't too sad to avoid it. My dad, though, has a heart as powerful as Secretariat and is a lifelong runner. He's stayed involved since retiring from racing, organizing the Bill Brown Cross-Country Series to give back to the community. Each year in elementary school, I'd optimistically try to run in one of the races honoring the late Bill Brown. 200 yards in, however, I'd start wheezing heavily as I watched the pack sprint on without me. I'd then find a nice spot to cry while I gasped for air—that was a typical race day for eight-year-old Daniel. I'd like to add, though, that my baseball coaches all corroborate that I never once cried on the baseball field. Anyway, no matter your age, it's a scary feeling when you can't pull enough air into your lungs to take a normal breath. Those with asthma know that panicking only makes it worse, accelerating the feeling of drowning in a sea of air. I outgrew my asthma in high school, however, and hadn't thought much of it since. But on this night, it was a rude greeting from an old friend.

Sitting on that curb in front of our now squeaky-clean facility, I wheezed like it was 1995. I sucked so much dust into my lungs that it took me the better part of an hour to compose myself. Lucas looked on, wondering if I would live, then asked if I wanted dinner.

"Yes," I wheezed.

A half hour later, he pulled back up with milkshakes and 7x7s from Steak 'n' Shake. The 7x7 is a huge secret-menu burger from Steak 'n' Shake that features seven patties and seven slices of cheese; it is both the fastest and most delicious way to send 3,000 calories back into an aching body. One of our hitters, a strong, thickly-built catcher named Nick, would bring us both a 7x7 every year on our collective birthday. Onlookers would marvel—some in awe, others in horror—as we'd demolish the greasy softball-sized burgers in three minutes flat, then go back to our lessons. Nick would smile and we'd tell the skinny gawkers to go put on some weight. Sometimes I wondered if he bought them just to feed us and watch the spectacle, in the same way a person feeds a live mouse to a python.

As the cold milkshake coated my dusty throat, consoling me after my asthma attack, it was the first time I felt the path ahead of us was downhill. All the major tasks were complete and we were mostly on track to open back up for business on—or very close to—my departure date. We committed ourselves to an extra two hours of sleep and set a 9 a.m. appointment to be back at the facility the next morning. Wake-up calls had been at six or seven, but since we worked almost 20 hours straight, we afforded ourselves an extended date with the sandman. At this point, you might be wondering any or all of the following:

How did I make time for workouts, sprints and conditioning?

When did I squeeze in shoulder and elbow rehab?

When did I play catch and throw bullpens?

Where did simulated games fit into the construction schedule?

How did I find time to prep for the most important spring training of my life?

It was the third of April when we finished those 7x7s. We were tired. The fatigue had set deep into our bones in a way neither of us had experienced. The answer was that, well, I hadn't made time for any of it—I hadn't lifted weights a single time since we got our keys. I squeezed in 15 minutes of shoulder exercises a few times each week. Once the floor was completely clean, we dragged one of our portable mounds onto the concrete floor. I played light catch a couple of times and threw a total of three bullpens on that mound at about 75% effort. I couldn't muster the energy to throw a ball at full speed and had never been so poorly prepared for a season in my entire life. What I didn't realize at that moment, however, was that being unprepared would prove to be a blessing.

Our real life was at stake and it was bigger than just my own needs. We could not let our business fail and so it was the undisputed #1 priority. I was too exhausted to do any more than I had done—I gave 98% to the business and had only 2% left to apply to those few games of catch and exhausted bullpens. I didn't care. The voice spoke up:

You've worked too hard for 18 months rehabbing and rebuilding to let these last three weeks change anything. Did you forget how to pitch?

No.

Did your arm lose all of its power in three weeks?

No.

Did you forget how to throw a curveball and changeup?

No.

Not one thing has changed. So what if you missed three weeks? You're going to make that team. You'll rise up. The velocity will be there. The stuff will be there. It has to be. You've been through too much.

After surgery in August of 2012, I spent three months going to formal physical therapy two or three days per week. For the other four days of the week I followed a plan I designed myself, taking into account everything I'd learned from my first surgery, from all my years as a strength coach, from Liz, the athletic trainer in Evansville and from Bryan, my amazingly thorough physical therapist. After the three months of formal rehab that worker's comp paid for, I was on my own. I'd drive to see Dr. Kremcheck every handful of months for a quick check-in, but back in Bloomington, all of it was on me. I found new ways to strengthen my hands, forearms and shoulders. I used creative exercises in the gym so I could train harder with no strain on my elbow. Instead of using distances in my throwing protocol to gradually increase throwing intensity, I used my Stalker radar gun and pieced together stepping stones from point A (hurt) to point B (healthy). It was a long road that I walked mostly myself, without the luxury of a team with which to rehab and stay accountable. It was too much work to let it go down the drain. If I mentally refused to be weak, I believed that my body would respond.

17 days. We had 17 days to turn the business around. There was no plan B—it had to get done. And now, as I drove off in my green Honda, I decided that I was making that team. Three weeks would not destroy 18 months of work. Again, there was no plan B. I'd go down swinging.

Enough work was done by the time I departed that Lucas finished it off with a little help from a few of our favorite baseball, softball and volleyball parents. The new Warbird was up and running just a few days after I split town. With business taken care of back home, I arrived at spring training with Somerset able to focus on the task at hand.

I've always taken great pride in my preparation, as a player's routine is crucial in creating consistent performances. Yet, one can easily become consumed with routines and training to the point where it becomes a crutch. I've seen many players who get frazzled when their routine gets disrupted and they don't play well unless everything is perfect. My routine was utterly destroyed, but *I* was not. My strength of will got me through it because, well, it had to. All I had left was my mindset. In being stripped of everything else, I learned that I could compete rain or shine, as long as I firmly believed in myself. I wasn't done pitching through pain and would be tested in each of the three seasons that followed. Though it took took nearly 700 days before I'd return to professional baseball, it took a mere 17 to prove that I was not fragile, that I was not easily broken.

Mike, there were so many people pulling for me to make that team, rooting for and following me—it almost made it harder, the pressure more intense. What would happen if I let them all down? What if I had to crawl back home, if I just couldn't do it? I didn't tell people I was setting off to try—I hate "trying." I was leaving the village and wouldn't be returning no matter what—that steadfast mindset comes with a self-imposed pressure of its own. So much of it was beyond my control, though, that I always needed and appreciated a renewed jolt of optimism. Your words gave me that. Players fade out of existence when they get hurt, many never to return. But not me—there was a comeback story brewing and you refused to keep it quiet.

Dear Tom, I'm coming home.

Kids in our academy have never really understood who you are or why you're the lone older man who trains, dripping sweat, beside them. They don't understand the grip that baseball has had on you, has had on me and will one day have on them. You're the same guy today that I met years ago when I moved to Illinois. I shook my head after the first time you interviewed me for your tiny, local baseball website. A baseball cap collection hundreds deep? Cubs fantasy camp every year? Custom-painted batting helmets for your teammates? Relentless devotion to over-40 league baseball? *That guy loves baseball more than I ever have or ever will.*

Nine years later, I think I finally understand why baseball's talons are so deeply embedded in you. Even after spinal fusion surgery, you refused to go on the shelf and hang up your cleats.

"What will the surgery mean for your career? Are you walking away from the old man league?"

"Nope," you said. "I'm gonna keep playing, and I need you and Lucas to get me ready again when the doctor says I can start training."

"We'll be waiting."

Though being around you makes me feel like an inadequate spouse to baseball, I do think we've been united in a common mindset. I approached my elbow surgeries in the same way you approached your spine. I just happened to get it stitched on my glove:

Go Down Swinging.

A lot of players get their names or a little proverb stitched on the thumb of their custom baseball glove. On this one, though, I had asked for something different: a reminder. Stitched into the thumb of my newest mitt was a mantra I intended on living by: *Go Down Swinging.* If I was going to cut an inroad back into baseball, it would only happen if I truly let go. I hadn't forgotten what it was like to jog out to the mound, uncertain if *that* was my last day as a baseball player. Coming back from surgery #2, I could only assume more of those days were lying in wait. I would not be bullied by fear and the weak voice in my head. If I were to go down, I'd go down swinging.

Some people naturally possess a killer instinct, this innate combination of focus and aggression that is so important in sports. I'm not sure I had this. Yet as my career wore on and I got older, wiser and more experienced, I worked hard to cultivate an aggressive side that prevented me from fleeing when challenged. You develop this trait when faced with situations in which you have two choices: yield or attack; fight or flee; rise or fall. We aren't animals, though, and in real life there's often a third choice—to reason and talk ourselves out of a situation. But in sports…an athlete's reaction is either one or the other. You show your teeth or yield to being eaten.

Giving in is the easier of the two. Maybe it's the predominant, natural response of humans—I'm not sure. Only when we're really backed into a corner on the field do we learn that fighting hard and using aggression to our advantage often improves our chances of winning. The problem is that when we give it our all we become vulnerable and face harder truths about failure: that perhaps our best just isn't good enough. When we yield to fear, we always leave something in the tank that can provide us with a comforting sense of, *it wasn't my best, so the fact that I failed doesn't reflect on me.* There was a distinct moment when I had to override all of my fear to get what I wanted. It was a big moment for me, so important that every detail is burned into my memory. One inning would make or break my comeback from surgery. I was deathly afraid of getting cut because at that point it could have meant the end.

I was on a charter bus with the Somerset Patriots en route to Camden, New Jersey. I was slated to pitch one inning in our final exhibition game. Each outing was better than the last and I had racked up a bunch of strikeouts against only a few hits. I held my own and was optimistic that I'd make Somerset's opening day roster.

In my first outing, two weeks earlier, I made an error on an easy comebacker and gave up an RBI single, the only run I'd allow during the three-ish week spring training camp. I was nervous in that first outing, which we call *sped-up* in baseball slang. It means your mind was working too fast for the situation, wherein everything felt out of control. Even as grown men, we baseball players still find ways to screw up things we've done literally thousands of times. I got a comebacker (my first ground ball in two years) and instantly got so nervous that when I tried to make a simple, short throw to first…I airmailed it into the stands. I was all sorts of sped up. I settled in, though, and struck out the side, surrendering just a single run.

As the bus hummed down I-295 toward Camden, I had one decisive outing to go. I was of the mind that if I threw poorly, I would probably get cut. If I threw well, however, I was certain that I'd make the team— I felt that I had shown too well to be let go. I did the mental math and assumed I was in contention with three other pitchers for the final spot in the bullpen. Much of it was based on who guys were and where they played before—many had Double-A, Triple-A and Big League time, and those pitchers weren't getting released no matter how many runs they gave up.

As I slumped against the window of my blue-upholstered bus seat, headphones in, I meditated and focused on words of confidence, something I had adopted as I grew into the practice I learned from Alan. I was nervous; as soon as my mind sat still, doubts and fear crept in. I saw myself walking everyone and giving up the runs that would doom my comeback to baseball. I worked too hard for that to happen. Sitting in that bus seat, I was at a crossroads. Fear and doubt were on one shoulder; confidence and the pitcher I wanted to be was on the other. The voice in my head was loud. I sipped my Monster energy drink and observed the conversation.

Don't you be a coward.

Don't you back down out there.

You throw every ball like it's your last.

ARE YOU LISTENING!?

…what if I get cut?

Sometimes, I wanted to be comfortable and safe. The voice wouldn't stand for that, wouldn't let me take the easy way out. He knew what I needed. I needed to show my teeth.

You're not getting cut. You're too good to get cut. These other guys around you on this bus? They're nothing compared to you. Today you prove that. You go out there and you PROVE IT.

Summoned was the side of me who lived deep inside, a man who held no quarter. That was who I needed to be that day.

You leave it all out there. You go down swinging or just get off this bus now. You can't go back home knowing you held back.

Yes sir.

I sat on that bus and inhaled while saying the word *confident*, then exhaled and said *dominant*. Those were my words of confidence and that was my process—two simple words that I repeated with every inhale and exhale. I focused on them instead of merely observing the *whoosh* of my breath. On that bus with those words streaming ear to ear, I slid the familiar mask down, covering up my doubts. This moment was bigger than moments prior. For nearly everyone else on that bus, it was merely another meaningless spring training game. For me, though, everything rested on the one inning I'd pitch. I was not ready to be done with baseball, in the words of Squints from *The Sandlot*, "for-ev-er." The problem was also that it wasn't business as usual—I was attempting to make a comeback into a league that was much higher than my previous. One third of the team was comprised of former Big Leaguers, as was Camden, the opposing team. I had to up my game in a hurry.

I warmed up to pitch in the sixth inning, a typically unremarkable, low-pressure portion of a game. As I got the call that my inning was indeed next, I tensed my lips, puffed out my jaw and pulled hard breaths through my nose. This ritual made me both look and feel angry, helping me pump adrenaline into my veins. I needed this, because nothing but doubt and fear entered my mind when I prepared to enter games—it was how I always was as a pitcher, despite always being a mostly successful hurler. When it was almost my turn, I would silently hope that the game would change and they'd call someone else in to pitch. I loved pitching—don't get me wrong—but that was my personal version of stage fright. I couldn't explain it; it was my unique struggle before every single outing. As soon as I crossed the white line, though, I'd pull the mask just a little tighter until it fused with my skin. Once I made it between the lines, the game face became my real face.

It was a beautifully sunny afternoon with the mighty, blue Ben Franklin Bridge looming in the background. Camden's Campbell's Field, named after the famous local canned-soup company, sat a hundred yards from the waterfront of the Delaware River. A thousand-meter swim later and you'd be toweling yourself off in Philadelphia. I warmed up on the mound like I always had—four fastballs, two curveballs and a single changeup before signaling for the catcher to toss the next one down to second base. I'd then fire off my eighth warm-up pitch—one last, hard fastball—before pacing around the grass as my infielders tossed the ball to each other, warming up their arms one last time. As the leadoff hitter grabbed his bat by the barrel and pounded the knob on the ground, releasing the white bat weight with a loud *CLINK!* on the on-deck circle mat, it was time. I watched him walk slowly to the plate as *the voice* chimed in one last time.

You're throwing every pitch as hard as you can.

You will hold nothing back.

Today might be your last day.

You go down swinging.

DO YOU HEAR ME!?

I pulled more air through my nose as I bugged my eyes out. That was a *yes*.

With the smooth, cream-colored baseball in my hand, I punched the pocket of my black and red glove as I took my place on the pitching rubber, straddling it before digging my right toe in, then moving my left further out to complete my pre-pitch stance. I kept my brow furrowed as I scowled in for my sign. The first hitter—a righty who would later become my teammate—walked into the box. I nodded, accepting the "one" my catcher put down. It was time.

Sssssss POP! My fastball smashed the mitt right on target on the outer-half of the plate. Strike one. I quickly reset.

Sssssss POP! Strike two crushed the mitt on the outer corner. He was down 0-2. There was no time to waste.

Sssssss TICK! He feebly nicked the next pitch foul, keeping his pathetic at-bat alive a little longer.

Sssssss POP! My fourth fastball again caught flush the pocket of the black catcher's mitt.

I had drilled the inside third of the plate, freezing him for strike three. I pulled in more air through my nose as the infielders threw the ball around. Two more to go.

Those were perhaps the four angriest pitches I'd ever thrown to that point in my life. I remember reading Ty Cobb's autobiography when I was a kid. Ty *never* backed down, and that little boy who liked reading baseball books...he needed me. I could not flee; I had to fight for him—*he* was not done. I loved baseball too much to cower in the corner now that the game was pushing back. It was going to push back sooner or later. I paced back up my mound and re-focused on the mitt. I quickly got ahead, then induced a ground out on a sinking changeup. One out to go. I retrieved the ball, looked for the exact spot where my right cleat belonged, sank it precisely into the bluish-grey, slightly tacky mound clay, then peered in and accepted my sign.

POP!

POP!

POP!

I punched out the third hitter on three pitches and walked off the mound with pitching fist clenched inconspicuously at my side. It was a dominant, extremely well-executed inning, one that still sticks out despite thousands of others. I had uncovered a new switch and flipped it. The guy who feared contact, who feared baserunners, who feared making a mistake a few years ago in Fargo…he was nowhere to be seen.

As I doled out fist-bumps and sat down on the dugout bench, I grabbed a rag to wipe the adrenaline from my forehead before it dripped into my eyes. I was trembling ever-so-slightly but beamed with excitement inside. No matter how I felt about an outing, I was always this stoic, robotic version of myself—that was the mask I wore on stage. It was my goal to bare no emotion and simply do my job. No matter how *I* felt, this was still just a pedestrian spring training game to everyone else and as such there was no room for any theatrics. Inside though, I was jumping up and down…I *knew* I had punched my ticket.

In Fargo, I had fled from every fight I was faced with on the baseball field and I resolved to never to be that person again. Fargo taught me that flight didn't work—I had to growl and show my canines when backed into a corner. I was trying to make a team full of former Big Leaguers and had to find a way to pull myself up to their level. Though I was merely a low-level independent player who hadn't thrown a pitch in two years, I still believed I belonged on that team. I was a somebody…I just needed an opportunity to prove it.

As I leaned on the dugout rail for the rest of the game, playing spectator for the final three innings, I thought about the inning and my glove. I didn't have an agent who would buy me a new glove each winter. Though I usually bought myself a new one each year and wrote it off as a business expense, I had asked my parents to buy me that one. I told them it would be my last glove, with the embroidered inscription carrying me until the end of my career, whenever that would be. A pitcher's glove can last five years if well cared for and only used in games. Maybe it wouldn't be my last glove. Maybe the new me could outlast it and pitch pain-free for the next five, six, seven years. I could dream.

A day or two later, I sat in the bleachers with a few other pitchers, retrieving foul balls as we played our last intrasquad game to no audience in TD Bank Ballpark. Final cuts would be made after the game, they told us, and a few players still had to go. A few hours later, I was in the coaches' office sitting across from Brett Jodie and Corey Domel, the Patriots' pitching coach. Brett started. "Dan, we hate to have to do this…"

Among the final three pitchers vying for the last spot in the bullpen, they were letting go of me and another, keeping a sidearmer who they wanted to use in matchup situations. Everything that had happened in the past two years suddenly flooded back, the memories piled high in front of me like a stack of pancakes. I relived them all at once. The scout in the stands in Southern Illinois as I walked off with Brooks; the phone call in Rockford; the intake exam in Dr. Kremchek's office; the deep purple color of my elbow as I tried in vain, the day after the operation, to squeeze a balled up sock. I tried to listen, as both had been fair and encouraging, but I couldn't. I now had a task that I was completely unprepared for: escaping from that clubhouse.

Years prior in Normal, during my first spring training, I barely spoke a word to anyone. If I hadn't made the team I could have just vaporized, returning to the fog. Players might have questioned if I was ever even there, if I had been real or just a specter. Somerset was different. My friend Matt Zielinski was on the team and I made a few others. I introduced myself to a number of players who were friends of other former teammates, and generally felt well-connected. Most players were veterans but made me feel at home nonetheless. I had to say goodbye to a *lot* of players—I couldn't just slink out into the night, though it was exactly what I wanted to do. I knew myself. You could hold me down and take a power drill to my elbow and I could probably manage to not flinch. But if one of my buddies gave me *that* look you give to your friends when they show up at your locker with their bags packed…I would flinch.

I took a beeline to my locker then to the shower, hoping that the running water would give me a chance to breathe. I'd buy a few minutes to collect myself and get it together. I took deep breaths and washed my face over and over. One of the older veterans, soaping up next to me, laughed as he explained that he was still working on my nickname. He promised that it would be done a few weeks into the season at the latest; he wanted to get it just right. My last name barely required alteration to become a joke and I had been heckled plenty throughout my career. I tried to not look at him as I replied. "I won't be around to hear it."

It took him a second before he realized what I meant. His eyes got wide and he apologized, explaining that he didn't know. He and I had spoken in the outfield a decent amount, so I knew he meant well. "Don't worry about it." I said. My voice was steady.

I finished my shower and said goodbye to a select handful of guys, then engaged my camouflage reflex as I slipped out. Matt texted me soon after and asked if I wanted to grab dinner. I declined. I climbed into my Honda Civic and hit the road. I didn't have a destination, so I just drove south. Fifteen minutes later, I pulled into a restaurant near the highway. I needed to eat and figure out where I was going. I had used up my favor with Andy, but knew I had to let him know what the outcome was. I needed more help but didn't want to ask for it.

"Hey. Bad news. They cut me. Thanks again for your help, I'm not sure what I'll do next, but I'll make some calls."

Almost immediately, the phone began to vibrate on the bar in front of me. I picked it up. It was Andy, and he was not happy.

"I can't believe they didn't keep you—I told them what you're capable of. Sit tight, Blew. I've got friends on other teams. Don't drive anywhere yet and stay near the phone."

I ate, but the food was tasteless. Before I could even finish, the phone rang again. I picked up.

"Call the pitching coach from Southern Maryland—he's by his phone now and expecting your call. He said if you're 92-93 with the hammer that I told him you have, he'll have a spot for you."

I got in my car and kept driving south. When I stopped for the night at my parents' house, I sat down and sent out the latest volume of *You're My Boy, Blew*. Re-reading that email, I laughed at the title—*plot twist* was a good way to put it. The 28-year-old me was right—there was one big positive from it all: I hadn't felt that alive in a long time. I missed the fear, the competition and the adrenaline even when it didn't work out the way I wanted.

Plot Twist.

Well, Somerset released me. If you don't know the term, it means to break one's contract. Turn in your uniform.

* * *

I hadn't had the displeasure of being the guy cleaning out his locker before. I had been released once, but it was via telephone. Everyone goes through it and it's like this:

The clubhouse is silent because guys see what's happened—you get called in, they give you the news, then you go out and start cleaning out your locker. You take your time so guys leave before you, so you don't have to awkwardly say goodbye to 20 people. You put on your most manly face and say adieu like it's not a big deal. It's *never* not a big deal.

I tell you what, though—I hadn't felt this alive in a long time. The nerves before each outing, the second-guessing myself, the anxiety knowing each performance is make or break. The implications—knowing that if you fail, you're gone—is what makes it exciting and the successes rewarding. The downside is that it's real life, and real life isn't a fairytale with happy endings all around.

The idea that my life wasn't a fairytale? It was both very true and utterly false. The longer I played, the more I was convinced that there was always some boobytrap waiting when it seemed my prize was within grasp. Yet, I was also somewhat convinced that I was a modern, real-life version of Forrest Gump. I kept stumbling into the right people and the right situations at the right times. There I was, trying to shed my elbow brace and sprint down that gravel road. I just needed a chance.

I was sitting in a Wegman's supermarket near Bel Air, Maryland, eating a six-dollar meal out of a white takeout container. The container wasn't normal Styrofoam, but some recyclable material that I assumed was made of something weird like free-range albino kelp. Wegman's are about as high-tech as grocery stores get, and they kept me fed as I lived on the road. I could buy a healthy meal and feel like a real person after sleeping on someone's couch for multiple nights in a row.

As I chewed my sweet potatoes, I replayed in my head the bullpen I had thrown for Southern Maryland the previous day. I had sprinted down to Waldorf, Maryland the morning after Andy arranged the tryout. When I arrived, I walked into the clubhouse with my baseball bag and immediately searched for the coaches' office. The clubhouse was filled with players killing time on the couches or in front of their lockers, waiting for their practice to begin.

The pitching coach greeted me and explained that I needed to find an open locker, get dressed and that he'd meet me out on the field in half an hour, once he rustled up a catcher. In the meantime, I had to sit and mingle with pitchers who knew I was there auditioning for their job. This was the second time in a month I had to be that guy. I had been on the other side of that in previous seasons—a guy would walk in around 3 p.m. and everyone would look him over as he quietly tried to get settled. He'd then dress, spike up and walk out to the field to hopefully replace someone on the team. There's little job security in pro baseball, and one's best protection was having great numbers. When a new player showed up to display his skills, you crossed your fingers and hoped that there were at least a few guys below you on the statistical totem pole.

I walked out of the clubhouse onto a concrete path that led to a door in the left-field wall. I hated walking on concrete with cleats. Though the signature clacking sound of cleats on concrete will always remind me of baseball, my personal hell would be running laps on smooth, polished concrete while wearing metal cleats. The cringe-worthy noise and sensation, the lack of traction, the careful, up-and-down walk to compensate—it was awful.

The sun was high in the sky as I shoved open the left field door. Reaching the comfort of the jade green grass, I reflected on what I was there to do. The home bullpen was right in front of me, an enormous mound with two pitching rubbers and a huge, yellow-painted wall adorned with a gargantuan Wawa hoagie. Though I hate cleats on concrete, I love Wawa convenience stores with all my heart. At 3 a.m. on a long bus ride, a Wawa soft pretzel and buffalo chicken cheesesteak with roasted red peppers, spinach and Old Bay? That meal brought me back to life time and time again. Wawa is to convenience stores what Wegman's is to grocery stores. They're both magical, transcendant places.

I got loose pretty fast and when I was just about ready, both the pitching coach and manager appeared. "Do your thing" they instructed. I calmly fired off five or six fastballs—wildly at first—then settled in and popped the mitt at the bottom of the strike zone. I threw clusters of curveballs, then my changeup, then a few more fastballs. After about 20 or so pitches with not a word said, I felt that I had accurately shown myself and turned to the coaches behind me. The manager spoke:

"That curveball of yours is good—it's enough in itself for you to be very successful in this league. With your hard fastball, you don't need the changeup that much; just command that fastball in and up and throw the curveball down. Guys in this league will swing at that."

I nodded.

"Do something for me," he said. "I want you to go curveball for a strike, fastball in, fastball up, curveball down. Let me see you do that."

I took a deep breath and prepared for target practice. I threw a hammer as hard as I could, dead for the catchers' mask. It tracked straight then, as it got close it finally bit down, breaking to his mitt for a strike. Then, the catcher set up inside to an invisible right-handed hitter; I drilled his mitt again. I then signaled up with my glove and uncorked a heater that he caught right at eye-level, making me three-for-three in my test. I drew in a big breath of air and locked my eyes on the catcher's mitt, the exact spot where I was going to start my final curveball before it broke, hopefully bouncing on the point of the plate. I started my delivery and the curveball "caught" just right as it left my hand. The catcher tracked it before dropping down to block it just before it bounced on the gravel a mere inch behind the plate. I was 4-for-4; I turned around.

"What else would you like to see?" I asked. The answer was *nothing*.

I had done exactly what was asked of me, exactly what they had told Andy would be enough to make the team. We met a few minutes later in the coaches' office, and soon after I hit the road. I sent out yet another email.

> Calls were made on my behalf and I drove four hours to audition for Southern Maryland today, another team in the same league. They have two guys who are iffy due to injury and they liked how I threw. On Tuesday, they said they might have an opening to sign me, but for today their roster is full. We will see. I'm going to hang around the Baltimore area and see what happens. I'm fortunate to have great friends who have been making calls to managers on my

behalf, which is how I got in front of Southern Maryland. Other teams know I'm out here and I pitched very well, twice, in front of another team, Camden.

After getting turned away yet again, I was out of options and there were no more phone calls to be made that would get me on an opening day roster. I had aged out of the Frontier League, so going back to Evansville or Normal wasn't possible. The Atlantic League was now two days from opening day, so rosters were being finalized as I spoke. The other two independent leagues—which I was really too old to be playing in—didn't begin their spring training for another three weeks. I had no other options and if two of the eight teams in the Atlantic League didn't want me...why would the others? I concluded the email with the following passage:

> Sometimes you're qualified but just don't get the job. Sometimes things don't work out despite good intentions. I'm not bitter at anyone and we will see how this shakes out. I will pitch somewhere this summer and I may be on a roster in a few days. You'll know when I know. This isn't the end.

The optimism in this email was the most inauthentic of any to date. Really, I was flat-out faking it. I always put on a brave face when writing my updates because lots of kids received them. If I hadn't written those optimistic, glass-half-full emails, I might have spiraled out into bitterness and blame. Though every word I wrote was true, they weren't *my* words, at least not yet. Nonetheless, I wrote what I thought I should feel, what I would say if I were counseling someone else in my exact position. *It'll work out. Just keep going. It's never as bad as you think. Annie is sending good juju. Something will happen.* As I pecked out keystrokes, I rearranged the words until they were in the proper order to keep me going.

Some nights I slept at my parents' house, others at Andrew's or Fred's in Baltimore, and others still in my sister's guest room in Northern Virginia. I was driving up and down I-95 each day not sure what to do. I needed somewhere to sleep, somewhere to train and someone to throw with. Everyone else was living their "big boy" lives, so finding a catch partner at two o'clock on a weekday was tough. I worried about getting out of shape and I didn't know how long I could hold on in limbo. I lived in coffee shops from sunup to sundown. At some point, I would have to cut bait and drive back to the Midwest where my life lived. I just wanted it to turn out like I had envisioned it in my head—I wanted a locker and jersey, to play baseball again. I didn't want it to be this hard and I didn't want to go home with my tail between my legs.

A week later, I had a potential offer to go to spring training with the Gary-Southshore Railcats, a very good team in the American Association. Andy had called them. Some bad memories came with a ticket to Gary, though: it was the place where I had experienced the worst moment of my career while with Fargo, albeit on the visitors' side. I considered it, because beggars couldn't be choosers. I wanted my chance, however, in the Atlantic League, which was the place for older players to prove they could hack it at the highest level. Countless guys in the Atlantic League had Major League experience and I knew I'd both learn a lot and boost my stock if I did well. I could handle it. If I succeeded in the Atlantic League, Major League scouts would know that I could get outs at almost any level. I was aging, so I felt starting back up in the Atlantic League was best for my career.

Twelve days after my release from Somerset, Andrew, a fellow strength coach, invited me to go to a baseball injuries conference with him in Washington, D.C. I agreed, as I had nothing else to do. After a long day in class, learning about baseball injuries from MLB team surgeons, I had no desire to drive home. It was a beautiful day out and I wanted to spend more time in the District of Columbia, a city I hadn't much explored. I ate dinner alone and spent the rest of the evening exploring the bar scene around Dupont Circle. Learning something and getting to know a new city was a small but meaningful boost to my morale. I left for Bel Air the next morning, needing a respite from my vagabond lifestyle. At my parents' house I'd have food, shelter and a chance to get off the road. As I took the exit for Bel Air, I stopped at Wegman's.

I polished off my meal of grilled chicken, rice and sweet potatoes while carelessly scrolling through social media. My phone had been glued to my hand as I hoped each day that it would ring with an out of state number. Players and coaches don't usually live where they coach, so I had been hoping my phone would light up with a call from someone I didn't yet know. I swear, in that last week I had gotten more phone calls from bankers and telemarketers than in the past year combined. It seemed like every five minutes my phone rang with an unknown number originating from Bismarck or Scottsdale. My heart would race only for me to pick up and find a robot congratulating me on qualifying for a loan I never wanted. To say that I had grown callous to all the unknown phone numbers would have been a massive understatement. What I didn't know, was that something had been brewing behind the scenes. This time, it wasn't Andy's doing. It came in the form of an email, a response to my letter about getting cut from Somerset. It started like this:

Dan, I know you don't know me at all…

The email was from a guy named Ryan Quigley. A few years earlier, I had opened up my private email list to my blog readers for a narrow window of time, allowing anyone who followed me on the web to sign up for my *You're My Boy, Blew* updates. Ryan was a pitcher himself, playing parallel to me in the Frontier League a few years earlier. He had a few different stints with MLB teams and had pitched to a sparkling 1.36 ERA for the Camden Riversharks in 2013. Now retired and informed of my plight, he asked if I wanted him to contact the Camden bench coach, Brett "Bono" Bonvechio, on my behalf. The answer was *yes*—I'd take all the help I could get. I took down Bono's number and left a voicemail myself. In my message I explained that I was still in the area and game-ready.

Tom, the thing about baseball is that it changes so miraculously fast. I've seen bases-loaded jams completely wiped out in just a handful of pitches. In the darkest situation for a pitcher—sacks full, no one out—he's still just two pitches from getting out of it. With the castle walls awash in enemy troops, a pop-up and a double play ends the entire threat in the blink of an eye. It never ceases to astonish me how the game turns an about-face on what appears to be nothing more than the pulling of random strings from up above.

An email from basically a stranger? It was my pop up and line-drive to short—almost comically easy in the face of what I'd been through. Perhaps that's why grown men like you chase it so long and refuse to let go. Baseball just has this insane power to make men instantly forget the bad times—the abuse—and come back home with open arms. The reason we hate it is the same reason we need it. The highs are worth the lows, even when it's unclear if it's only lows going forward. Every time you suit up, the game is the same and yet utterly different, fair and yet infuriatingly unfair. It's nothing like the ordinary lives men and women today live, yet it's exactly like the cutthroat, vicious, random world we've inhabited since the dawn of time.

As I placed my plastic knife and fork inside the now empty takeout container, the phone rang. I was slow to flip the downward-facing phone over, assuming it was yet another telemarketer. When I did, though, there was that name: Brett Bonvechio.

"Oh." I said to myself. "It's *that* call. It's finally *that* call."

A few minutes later, my email inbox showed an unread message containing my $1450 per month contract. I drove straight to my parents' house, printed and signed it. I had a locker waiting. I spent that night with my folks in the house I grew up in. In the morning, I'd drive home. I forgave the Baseball Gods. Why? Because they wanted me back.

Dear CJ, Set the standard.

I've known you and your father for a long time. I watched you grow up from a long-legged baby deer into a powerful, fast baserunner. Few high school players can whip a bat through the zone like you can, which is probably why you're shipping off in a year to play Division-I baseball. Your Dad was a friend and defender of mine, all the while being honest with me, even when it wasn't what I wanted to hear. Each year as I went off to play, leaving behind you and others at the academy, I came back with a more clear view of the world and how we all fit into it. Sometimes it was an experience, a challenge or a person who changed my perspective. In 2014, it was Wynn.

I was still beaming with excitement from the phone call with Bono and the new contract I had signed. I was going to be a Camden Rivershark. I woke up the next morning and again drove south, back down to Waldorf, to meet my new team for their road series against the Blue Crabs. I was greeted by three coaches: Manager Ron Karkovice, pitching coach Chris Widger and Bono, the bench and hitting coach. Bono basically did three jobs—player procurement, meaning he found new players like myself when the team needed them, hitting coach and administrator. He was in his early thirties and had just retired, switching to the coaching side of things. He had played for eight seasons in the minors and handled things in Camden in much the same way Pete had in Lake County. He was the glue, and all of us would come to respect the thankless work Bono put in. Widge, as he was known, was formerly a 10-year Major League catcher, winning a World Series with the White Sox in 2005. He was our pitching coach because, well, he knew how to handle pitchers. He was personable, laughed easily and everyone gravitated toward him. Karkovice was a former first-round draft pick, playing 12 years in the Majors himself, all of them with the White Sox. He was a bit gruff and we were acquaintances at best. I can't remember a single conversation I had with Ron and my memory of him is about as neutral as a glass of milk. Kark retired in 1997, two years after Widge began his Big League career with the Mariners. They were opponents for two years, though never teammates.

I was told that I would be in the starting rotation and that my first start would come against Long Island in the next series. I didn't know any of the guys on the team but it didn't worry me too much. Being an outsider was par for the course and I'd make friends soon enough. I'd have the entire Southern Maryland series to get acclimated, get my work in and watch. I landed the job with Camden because the team was struggling. After a 1-11 start, they decided to let a few underperforming players go and I was in the first wave of replacements. They also lost a few key players to promotion, including longtime former Major Leaguer Mike MacDougal, who was signed by an MLB club and sent to Triple-A. The majority of the roster, though, was simply not getting it done on the field. Most teams give their opening day roster at least 10 days to get acclimated and get into a groove. Because the Atlantic League was comprised of all older players, who had played an average of eight years of pro baseball, it didn't make sense to cut a guy after just a few chances. Atlantic Leaguers had proven themselves over a long period of time and managers understood that good players sometimes got off to slow starts. Yet, a 1-11 start was a whole different type of thing, and heads started rolling.

A former teammate from Evansville, Wynn Pelzer, texted me out of the blue two days into my stay in Waldorf. I hadn't heard from him since we played together two years prior, nor were we overly close during our time on the Otters. He saw in the transaction list that I signed with Camden, and informed me that he too had inked a contract with the Riversharks. Wynn had been in spring training with Sugar Land after taking a year off in 2013, but didn't make it through final cuts. His year as a reliever with the Evansville Otters in 2012 was his first year in Independent Baseball after being let go by the Orioles. He and I fell somewhere between acquaintances and friends. I knew that Wynn made me laugh, but beyond that, I didn't know much. He was also (if I'm being honest) a lot cooler than I was.

He texted me about the living situation in Camden, which, I

explained, was fraught with uncertainty. I was told I'd be be given three days in the team hotel when we returned from our road trip; after that I was on my own. Finding short-term, affordable housing that you can get out of if you get released, traded or signed is pretty much impossible. One of the reasons Camden had become a perennial loser was precisely this: They couldn't offer good players any kind of stability. I didn't have statistics on it, but my guess was that the majority of Atlantic League players had wives and children. The league offered the typical, meager minor league salaries ranging from $800 to $3000 per month. For a single guy it wasn't the end of the world—you'd break even if you budgeted well. But for a guy with a wife, child and mortgage, spending a third or more of one's paltry paycheck on temporary housing was out of the question. Other teams did a better job of having options readily available, so that when they found good free agent players they could set them up quickly. If the wife was going to come along for the ride with a young child, she needed somewhere comfortable and safe to live that didn't bankrupt the family.

Wynn flew in a few days after our text conversation, which meant that he didn't have a car. I didn't mind driving us both around once he got settled, as it was nice having someone I knew on an otherwise unfamiliar team. Wynn was African-American and stood about six-feet tall with a wide, sharply angled jaw. I never wore chinos, but Wynn wore them often in different colors with rolled-sleeve button ups and henley t-shirts. He wore a dog-tag necklace in a way that I just wasn't trendy enough to pull off. It was tough keeping up with him, because if I wasn't on my game I'd look like a slob by comparison.

We each had three free hotel stays courtesy of the team. When those ran dry we split hotel rooms on the team rate (about $70 per night), but started to balk at the expense. A lot of the Latino players had simply been sleeping in the clubhouse, most having purchased air mattresses from Wal-Mart. This wasn't legal but the ownership looked the other way. Some players stayed there, in the locker room, for the entire five-and-a-half month season. The idea of sleeping in the bowels of the ballpark seemed unthinkable—laughable, even. *I'd never do that*, I told myself.

A few weeks later, as our bank accounts thinned to the point of discomfort, Wynn wanted to take a sabbatical from the hotels to let his bank account recover. Then, he explained, he'd move into the Rutgers-Camden dorms when they opened in June, which was a new team-sponsored option. The dorms became available to players about a month into the season and the countdown was now at 10 days. For $450 a month, we'd each have our own room in an empty dormitory just three blocks from Campbell's field. The dorms seemed like the best option, but there was an expensive gap of home games until they became available. Wynn insisted he was done with the hotel, so into the bowels we went.

The clubhouse was dank, musty and often too loud to sleep. Players stayed up until two or three in the morning watching TV and YouTube, talking and listening to music. In regular intervals the ice machine would let out a jarring crash as freshly formed ice fell into the hopper. The fluorescent lights had a constant, audible buzz and the emergency lights couldn't be turned off, leaving it relatively bright 24 hours a day. Latino players had staked out coaches' offices as their bedrooms, laying claim to the darkest, quietest spots. It was first-come, first-served, and they lived there full-time, so we didn't challenge their domain. The only unclaimed land was the training room, which was the equivalent of sleeping in a janitor's closet, albeit a large one. I dragged my mattress onto the grimy tiled floor that never completely dried. The plasticky, blue tiles had a perpetual white scum on them from the useless in-floor drainage system. When our trainer, Dan, would drain the hot and cold tub, the water would run out the bottom, through a hose toward the drain, which often overflowed. Ice coolers would get dumped right on top of it to slowly melt away. Yet, it offered a closed door and darkness, both of which I desperately needed.

I learned a lot in my first night sleeping in the training room. Most notably, I learned to turn off the ice machine. If I didn't, the crash of fresh ice falling into the hopper would wake me up every two hours. I'd often forget it was on and fall asleep, just to be jolted out of a dream by a terrifying batch of cubes. If I turned it off for too long or forgot to turn it back on in the morning, Dan would give me an earful about not having enough ice for the game that night. I tried putting headphones in, but they hurt my ears too much as I laid my head on my pillow. I finally settled on sleeping with ear plugs in. The 10-day stretch in the clubhouse wasn't really that hard, though. Lake County had prepared me for it and I woke up each morning to shower and head into Philadelphia to explore the beautiful city that loomed across the Delaware river. Did I love the game enough to sleep in Campbell's field every night for a whole summer, like the Latino players did? Fortunately, I didn't have to find out.

* * *

Move-in day at the dorm was glorious and came with an awkward familiarity. I had graduated from college five years prior and here I was once again sleeping on those awkward twin-XL mattresses that were covered in a black polyester. Anytime I moved in bed, the mattress made that same noise those old nylon wind pants made as your legs brushed together while walking. I hated those nylon wind pants. The dorm, though, provided a much better quality of life and it was a major victory to start getting full nights of sleep again.

Camden, New Jersey is a dangerous place. When I'd meet a girl, I'd often invite her to game.

"No, thank you," was the typical reply. I'd press.

"I just don't feel safe in Camden, sorry." I'd explain that it was a huge ballpark with lots of people around, in an area canvassed by Rutgers-Camden University police. The ballpark was safe—I walked home each night in the dark and rarely even saw a person on the streets. They didn't relent as the image of Camden as a war zone was burned into their mind.

The Camden that everyone feared was on the north side of the Ben Franklin Bridge. Once, as our first baseman's wife flew in to visit, she took a wrong turn in her rental car just as she got close to the ballpark. A cop pulled her over a number of blocks deep into the slums beyond the bridge. "Mam, do you know why I pulled you over?" She didn't.

"You're being followed. I'm going to escort you out. Follow me and please don't ever come back into this area. You're lucky I was here today."

We were astonished to hear this story in pregame. Apparently, outside vehicles were quickly identified, followed, then boxed in by a second car. What happened next could be an armed robbery, carjacking, or potentially a murder. It was terrifying to think that our affable first baseman's wife had nearly fallen prey to that within her first 45 minutes of touching down. We respected the boundary of the mighty "Ben."

One day, Wynn and I jumped in the car and drove into Center City, the local lingo for the downtown portion of Philadelphia. We were looking for a good place to park so that we could walk around Rittenhouse Square, which we had heard was a good spot. Rittenhouse Square was one of the more posh areas with a beautiful, small park in the middle surrounded by highrises and majestic four-story concrete and brownstone townhouses. There were high-end shops, tons of bars, restaurants and unique coffee shops. We took in the sites and sounds and bantered to pass the time. Tattoos came up, of which Wynn had a few. I explained the origin of my single tattoo, a logo on my chest.

"You know, I got mine because it was a gift by some of the kids I trained; they paid for me to get my logo tattooed and I decided—for no good reason, really—to get it on my chest. It's sentimental and unique. Even though I don't think I'd get another, I like that no one else has it." I continued.

"But what I really don't get is how people get these generic tattoos. They're permanent, so why a person would want to get some cliché tattooed on their body is beyond me. Things like "Carpe Diem"—I feel like millions of people have that tattooed on their body and I just think it's sad. Come up with something original, you know?"

He looked over at me from the passenger seat. Then, he casually, calmly rolled up the sleeve on his t-shirt, revealing none other than Carpe Diem tattooed in a flowing, antique script font. My jaw dropped.

"Oh...man, I...I'm so sorry." I couldn't take what I said back, so I was just remiss to disparaging myself. "I'm such an idiot. I had no idea you had that. You know I respect you; I just get too opinionated sometimes." I made a mental note to never again have opinions.

He laughed it off. "How would you have? You don't know my tattoos. It's fine man, I have a lot of different things that I got for a lot of different reasons. I'm not worried about what other people think about them."

It was a glimpse into my high school side, the side that often judged without context. I apologized a handful more times then gave up, admonishing myself in my head. He wasn't mad, but I hated when I spouted off. I tried hard to leave that side of me in the past.

Wynn had been through a lot and chose at each juncture to rise above it. Growing up in Holly Hill, South Carolina, he earned a scholarship to play for the University of South Carolina. He wore the legendary Gamecocks jersey for three seasons before being selected by the Padres in the ninth round of the 2007 MLB draft. His time at USC was bigger than baseball, though. When he arrived on campus as a freshman he spoke with a sped up, difficult to understand dialect—a version of Gullah that was prevalent on the islands of South Carolina.

"Man, when I arrived on campus, people couldn't understand me. I had to change. I didn't want to be written off; I wanted to make good impressions on people because of the way I spoke. So, I took speech classes."

He gave me a sample one day in the car; it was a garbled mess of slurred, rolled-together words. Concerned about creating a negative first impression in college, he dedicated himself to improving it. Speech classes at USC helped correct the way he spoke so that he could be viewed as...*more*. I would never have suspected any of that, which I suppose means the classes worked. He was one of the most articulate teammates I ever had.

He also didn't speak like a stereotypical athlete in even the most general sense. Baseball players tend to represent the bell curve in the same way as any other group, though many assume the "dumb jock" label applies to 100% of us. Despite being characterized as shallow thinkers, there are always a handful of incredibly intelligent men in any given dugout. Yet, mannerisms tend to rub off on one another and bring us all toward the mean. There's a tremendous book of lingo in baseball and no matter how intelligent a player might be, he drives home from the season with a few more curse words, slang terms and "bro" phrases in his vocabulary. We all enable each other and perpetuate a common, vulgar lexicon. I swore more in a single month during baseball season than I would in an entire offseason.

In the clubhouse, all different types of music spews forth from the shared loudspeakers. In the early-going, the stereo is usually under veteran control, but as the season wears on, players just come and go connecting their phones to it. Rap usually wins out amongst genres and the N-word is prevalent in even mainstream, popular rap and hip-hop. I'd feel awkward sitting next to him as the word was used over and over in rap songs. Did he hear it? How did he feel about it? I never really understood why it was okay, even in its casual form. One day, I gathered the nerve to ask him. I wanted to know how he felt about it and I figured we were close enough where I could ask. This was an issue, I learned, in which Wynn drew a deep line in the sand.

"Wynn, how do you feel when they say the N-word in songs?" He paused.

"There's still racism where I grew up—*real* racism. I can't count how many times I was called that growing up and if I get in a situation with the wrong white guy today, it's still the first word they'll pull out. They know it's a dagger, so they use it. If you're not black, you'll never understand what it's like to be called that. It's just not okay. If I use it, if I sing along, then I allow it to be okay. It's never going to be okay."

For years, I sat in clubhouses and listened to vulgar rap music stream out of the stereo. I like some rap, but it's not one of my favorite genres. My view of the N-word was shaped as a kid while learning about slavery. I'm not overly sensitive to violence, but I am sensitive to cruelty. Forever associated with that word is a scene in a movie that I watched when I was in middle school. A runaway slave was caught and returned to his plantation. To make sure he never ran away again, they tied him to a chair and propped his feet up on another, his legs extended. He begged and pleaded, promising to never run away again. "We know you won't," was the reply. The slave master picked up his heavy sledgehammer, then gleefully swung it down onto his knees, breaking his legs backward into the space between the two chairs. I covered my eyes before the hammer struck and kept them closed as he screamed. Two decades later, that portrayal of cruelty is still chained to the word.

But maybe it isn't a big deal in mainstream music. I genuinely didn't understand and probably still don't. In asking that simple question, however, I learned that Wynn didn't compromise or look past the racism he endured growing up in the south. He wanted to be better than it. It would have been easy for him to bend and give popular music a pass. He didn't sit there judging others for listening, nor did he lecture anyone. Yet when asked, he was firm. He established his core values long ago and stuck by them, something I respected. As a privileged white kid, I have no perspective on what discrimination feels like. Even strong-willed people, however, acquiesce over time as they get worn down from years of resistance. Not Wynn. He remained strong in his beliefs and I felt privileged getting to know more of him and his story.

No one spent free time in Camden, as there were almost no businesses worth patronizing, save a pizza place and a Latin American restaurant named *Latin American Restaurant.* Nearly every day I took the PATCO train across the Ben Franklin Bridge to the 15th/16th and Locust stop, a 10-minute ride. I'd return on the 2:08 train, which gave me just enough time to drop my laptop bag, grab a to-go lunch of chicken, rice and plantains from Latin American and head to the ballpark. I felt at home. Kark, Widge and Bono gave us freedom as players, I had freedom in my dorm and freedom during the day to explore a new major city. I sat in coffee shops and wrote, working on articles to make extra money, new blog posts and emails. I started on two books, both of which remain half-finished and were essentially practice runs. I was holding my own on the mound, pitching to an ERA in the high-3.00s most of the season before it tipped into the 4.00s in the final month. I had some ups and downs but finished the year mostly healthy with an ERA of 4.04. It was a solid, average season. One thing I later came to understand was just how hard it was to be average, to be consistently decent in the higher levels of baseball. I wasn't proud of a 4.04, but I contributed to my team, didn't get released and did well enough to perhaps earn an invite back. Really, average is good, good is great and great is unbelievable.

One of the hard things about pro baseball is the look on your friends' faces when they struggle. In the dorms, it was Wynn and myself down the hall from another hilarious bullpen mate, Sean. Sean had his Australian girlfriend in tow and they carved out a nice little life in the dorms. We'd talk about cutters and nonsense in the bullpen each night and hung out in the dorms here and there. It was our little dorm room family, holed up in the high rise for the summer. That was, until the game started picking us off, one by one.

When you struggle on the field, everything that's bright and shiny loses its luster. A month in, Wynn began to change. He wore a more solemn mask, consternation etched on his face as his ERA rose. He laughed a little less and smiled a little less in the same way we all did when times were tough. Years later, he'd admit that he was worn down from bouncing between teams. Palling around Philly was fun, but he had things going on behind the scenes and with results on the field incongruous with his previous self, it felt like time to move on.

One day, I felt a tap on my shoulder as I buttoned up my fly, having just gotten out of the shower and thrown clothes on. There was Wynn, fully dressed and fully packed, a navy blue Padres travel bag thrown over his shoulder, bursting at the seams. He extended his hand for *that hug*, the hug that follows *that meeting* in the coaches' office. Tomorrow, his locker would be someone else's locker.

Life in Camden wasn't quite the same after his release. Our regular nightcaps at the bar across the street from the ballpark came to an end, as did our day trips to Philly. A few weeks later, I got the same bro hug from Sean. He decided it was time to move on with the next phase of his life, leaving me alone in the huge highrise dorm building. It was July when Sean left and I lived there for six more weeks until college came back in session. I kept my routine of daytime adventures in Center City and stayed busy, but being busy didn't replace my comrades in my empty skyscraper.

Seeing your friends get released was always confusing and conflicting, a flood of both sadness and relief. It's a lot like the "Citywide Special," a Philadelphia tradition at local bars. The Citywide has now morphed into all types of beer and whiskey combinations, but it began as a can of Pabst Blue Ribbon and a shot of Jim Beam. Each time a close friend gets released, you drink down the full can of sadness and disappointment. The clubhouse gets a little darker. But as you do, a reminder of our fickle mortality turns your attention to the shot sitting next to it. You pick up the glass and toss back an ounce and a half of relief that it was *him* and not you. It burns the whole way down. A period of reflection always follows, playing back the good times that are now lost.

With Wynn gone, I reflected on my own values, on what I stood for. My path in baseball hadn't been easy, but my road to success was always smoothly paved. I never wanted for resources, nor did anyone try to discourage or oppress me. I never had to change anything about myself to prevent others from judging me, from thinking I was stupid. I shared the story of Wynn's dialect with the other pitchers and they barely believed it. "No way!" They said. "He's so well-spoken." I hardly believed it myself, except when I thought harder about who he was. Wynn wasn't afraid to better himself or make a stand. He chose to leave Gullah in the past. Rap lyrics? Certainly not a hot-button issue. Yet, he refuses to give that word endurance, and sustain its hate-filled legacy. It's a peaceful, unseen but important protest. Quietly but firmly, he lives as an example of what he believes is right.

CJ, we tune our own moral compass, decide who we are and what our legacy will be. Those we keep close have the power to affect our heading, the direction of the rest of our lives. The philosophers Kant and Sartre believed that whenever a person makes a choice, he does so in a universal sense. Our ethical decisions are a statement on how we believe all of mankind should act if placed in the same situation. Your choice today is what the rest of us should choose tomorrow. Thus, we must be mindful of our actions as if they speak at a volume heard by the world. Though it would have been easier to give in, stay the same and become complacent, Wynn showed me a higher standard that summer in Camden, a standard set for all of us.

Dear Coach J, There were claw marks.

When you offered me that spot on your UMBC roster, you had no idea whether or not I'd hit my stride and bloom. I did. You also had no idea how two of your esteemed players would grow up in the game, spreading out across the country in separate directions just to find each other later on. As far as I could tell, Zach Clark had at least one legacy at our small school: Coach Jancuska's favorite player. When he came up in conversation you always lit up about how smart a pitcher he was, and what a great example he was for others. For a Division-I coach to talk about a player in such a way...I had to find out what it would take for others to talk about me in that same manner.

I latched on. Little did we know, we would end up becoming teammates again a decade later. Since he was—at least as far as I could tell—your favorite player, I figured you should know how it all ended, how your lessons of character and professionalism helped pave the way for both of us to make it farther than we should have, to leave deep claw marks on that mountain we tried to climb.

Growing up, I wondered if one day I'd ever become one of those confident people I admired. As a freshman I looked up to the upperclassmen—they were these big, tough, tall guys who walked with their chests puffed out. As a quiet freshman, I kept my mouth mostly shut and didn't put much effort into connecting with them; I wasn't worthy. Yet in my desperation to get better as a ballplayer, I was constantly asking around for an off-day throwing partner. Even when we didn't have team practice, I needed to get my throwing in because if I wasn't throwing, I wasn't getting better. Most of my teammates had no interest in cannibalizing an off-day and detached from the game when practice wasn't mandatory. Zach, a redshirt-junior, was rehabbing his second labrum tear. The labrum is a piece of connective tissue in the shoulder that deepens and stabilizes the shallow socket. Tearing the labrum results in a loose, painful shoulder and is a serious, career-threatening injury. Even the world's best surgeons admit that restoring a labrum surgery patient to his previous pitching ability is very, very difficult. About 50% of pitchers return to their previous level of performance after just one labrum surgery…and yet Zach had *two*.

He had undergone surgery first in high school, then again in college as a redshirt-sophomore. When he began searching for a partner to throw with over break, I jumped at the chance. I knew how you described him and I needed someone who could help me get there. Who better than the source?

Zach and I became catch partners on off-days and when school was out of session. He wanted to return to his previous, healthy self and finish his rehab protocol. I was merely trying to make *something* out of myself. If we talked during our throwing session, I don't remember what we talked about. Mostly, I just watched what he did and how he did it, taking mental notes at every step along the way. I often had teachers who didn't explicitly teach me anything. Rather, just through their presence I was forced to reflect upon myself and attempt to sharpen my focus. Seeing others perform at a high level challenged me to pull myself up to it, even when I didn't know how. Most of the managers I'd have down the road in pro baseball were this same way —they didn't go out of their way to teach, but I got better anyway. I suppose it was assumed that if one had made it that far, he knew 99% of what he would ever know. The 19-year-old version of myself didn't know much about pitching, so doing what Zach did seemed like a good starting point.

When Zach pitched, I leaned over the dugout rail and analyzed. I listened to the stories told about him and the traits others ascribed to him. His reputation was that of a smart, savvy pitcher who understood more about the game than anyone else. Clark played summer ball for a team called the T-Bolts, managed by a guy named Bobby St. Pierre who he spoke highly of. Naturally, I sought out the T-Bolts, spending a year coached by Bobby and the rest by Duff. Those summers with the T-Bolts were formative.

When Zach signed with the Baltimore Orioles, it was his prize for staying the course over a long, frustrating battle with his shoulder. As he moved on with his professional career—and I carried on at UMBC —we lost touch. But as I moved on to professional baseball myself a few years later, we reconnected. When I got signed in 2010, we were the only two pro players from our alma mater still playing. I called Tim O'Brien once in a while, looking for advice on ways to improve in the offseason. After talking through some of my woes from the previous season, he suggested I give a different mentor a call.

"When's the last time you talked with Zach?"

"I dunno," I replied. It's been a few years.

"He's done a lot of things with the Orioles. He's been to every level and has pretty much succeeded at all of them. He'd be a good sounding board for some of your struggles. I bet anything you're going through he's already tackled at some point." I nodded. He was right.

"You really should consider calling him—who knows what you could learn!" Tim was the biggest proponent of continued education I knew, and so I agreed. What could it hurt to dial him up? Okay. It was decided. It'd been some time and I didn't really know him all that well, but I'd call Zach.

It was the summer of 2011 as I held the phone to my ear, sitting beneath the stadium bleachers, hoping to stay out of earshot of my teammates. I had my black Dri-fit shirt on and my white pinstripe pants. We had a long gap between batting practice and the start of the game, so I wanted to see if I could catch him. Things had not gone well for me while wearing the pinstriped Fargo uniform.

"Dan?" He said in a somewhat silly tone, obviously knowing it was me. We had spoken a few times that offseason and had been developing a more normal rapport. Zach, though serious about all things baseball, had a goofy side.

"Hey Zach."

"Whatcha got?" It was his signature opener, asking what the latest news or talking point for the day was.

"Wellllllll…."

I was drowning in Fargo. I needed a lot of help and needed it *now*. Zach was in Double-A with the Orioles and I usually picked his brain on how to read hitters and situations. He would ask for training advice, as I had a lot more expertise in the strength and conditioning world. That day, we discussed preparation and mental strategies that might help me.

"I've been getting killed," I said. "I lost my spot in the rotation and my ERA is in double-digits. I need to right the ship pretty fast or I'll be out of here."

"What's happening? Why are you pitching so bad?" he asked.

"At first I wasn't pitching *that* bad, but then it became a pattern." I explained what had happened in the clubhouse in Gary, what Simi had said.

"Yikes," he responded. "But dude, I know how you feel. It's hard to come back from that. Staying within yourself and never getting too high or too low—it's what all the best players do. But it's easier said than done. Can you find a way to block it out, take a step back and relax on the mound?" I didn't have an answer.

"I'll think about it and see what I can find," I said. "Maybe there's a book—got any you'd recommend?

"*The Mental ABCs of Pitching* by this guy H.A. Dorfman is a pretty good one to start with," Zach said. I thanked him and asked what was going on with him.

"Well, currently I'm not even pitching. I'm on the Phantom DL."

"What's the Phantom DL?" I asked.

"It's when you're not really hurt, but they need roster space for another guy, so they make up an injury for you and put you on the Disabled List. I don't want to be on the DL, but I guess it's better than being released. They moved one of their big prospects to Double-A and I'm the odd man out right now."

"What are you going to do about it?"

'There's nothing to do. I'll just wait, keep going through my routine on the side and see what happens. I'm still on the team, I'm just not allowed to play. It sucks, but at least I have a job."

So he did—he stuck it out and waited his turn. For lots of players in his situation, those who were a "Senior sign" with only $1000 invested in them, Big League chances were slim. But because of how he handled himself both on the field and in the clubhouse, even despite Phantom DL stints and political demotions, Zach stuck around. The Orioles kept him and he earned his innings as a starter in Double-A and Triple-A. It was perhaps his reward for pitching well and waiting patiently in line. The Baseball Gods liked guys like Zach—he earned all of it. He was pious toward the Church of Baseball. Diligent and gritty, he was a good teammate and a fierce competitor on the mound.

When a player gets to the Minor Leagues, he enters a huge field of players with similar qualities. Everyone is comparable in size, athleticism and ability as the variance between them gets smaller. When people talk about how important the mental side of baseball is, they're not lying. Putting up good numbers is what matters most, and to do that it's not just about throwing harder than everyone else or having the nastiest slider. Baseball is a complex game, and one's baseball IQ determines if he maximizes—or minimizes—his physical talents. In competition for promotions and limited roster spots, players differentiate themselves in numerous ways. Zach differentiated himself through his *makeup*.

Makeup is comprised of a handful of traits—coachability, baseball IQ, savvy, likability, discipline, professionalism, sportsmanship, trustworthiness and the ability to perform under pressure, to name a few. Zach was disciplined, well-liked and trustworthy on the mound. The Orioles knew that no matter the competition level, he'd go out there and turn in a reliable performance that included throwing strikes, calling intelligent pitches, fielding his position, getting ground balls and generally giving any team a chance to win without burning the bullpen. Every team needs guys like that, even if they don't have superstar potential. He pitched mostly at 89-92 miles per hour— average velocity at the time—with an underwhelming scouting report that we discussed on the phone.

"How does your stuff rank on the Major League scouting scale?"

"Well, I asked once and they took me through it. It wasn't impressive, but being above-average on that scale means you're an above-average Big Leaguer, so it's pretty hard to be that good. Most guys are average or below at that high of a level."

It made sense—we were talking about the best 750 players on the entire planet. To be among the best at that hand-picked crop was a heck of a task.

"Basically, they said my command is the best thing about me—55-60 depending on who you ask. My changeup, curve and slider were all pretty similar—45-50 on the 20-80 scale. 50 means it's average for the Major League level, so 50 is actually pretty good in the grand scheme of things. My fastball is my best pitch—45 to 50 or so, that plays up because of late movement and my command. At its best it's probably a 55."

Being average at the highest level of baseball in the world? Guys got paid millions of dollars to produce average Big League numbers. It was all a matter of perspective, really, and he kept climbing the ladder because the sum of Zach was always greater than his parts.

A few years later, I was at home in Illinois, rehabbing my elbow when I got the news: Zach got called up and would be on the Baltimore

Orioles' Major League roster for their series against the Seattle Mariners. Not having a television in my apartment, I camped at Buffalo Wild Wings the next few nights, excited to see him get his chance. I knew that they usually got new guys their first innings in low-pressure situations, so I hoped for an early exit by one of the teams' starters. On May 1, 2013, nursing a Bud Light at the bar, I watched as the camera panned to Zach in the bullpen. He was *up*—throwing and getting ready for the bright lights. I wondered how he must have felt in that moment—he was living every kid's dream. His name would forever be in the *Baseball Almanac*. He was a Major Leaguer.

It was surreal watching him pitch against the Mariners on the big screen. He got through his first frame unscathed, a groundout ending a relatively pedestrian inning. In the second, he gave up two quick singles then hung a 1-2 changeup belt-high to Kendrys Morales. That changeup was driven to the wall, plating both runs. Two fly outs and a walk later, his debut—and Major League career—came to an end. It wasn't the outing he wanted, but he *did it*. It was a victory he'd always have, an accomplishment few in the world could ever claim. Somewhere, there was an undersized little boy sitting Indian style in front of a TV. He saw a 5'11" right-hander make it to the summit. Maybe he, too, could complete that climb.

A few days after being called up, he was removed from both the 25-man and 40-man rosters, exposing him to waivers, where any team could take on his contract. When we went unclaimed, he returned to the Orioles' Double-A team, the Bowie BaySox. His re-signing with the Orioles, however, came with a condition—and *that* is where his story really took a turn.

Phil Niekro, the hall-of-fame knuckleball pitcher, visited Orioles spring training regularly. He would tour the camp, talk shop with guys, and council the handful of young knuckleballers in their system. One such spring training, a coach remarked to Niekro: "The best knuckleballer we have is a guy you haven't seen before." Phil was introduced to Zach and watched him play catch with a knuckleball that I remembered well from college. His knuckleball was terrifying, taking jagged left and right turns without warning—everything about it defied the laws of physics and all that was holy. "Screw that!" was what most players said after catching his knuckleball for a few minutes. Standing in front of that thing—even with a glove—was downright unsafe.

Upon being designated for assignment, a fancy term for saying, "You've lost your place in our organization," the Orioles gave Zach a choice: part ways or become a knuckleballer. When I heard his ultimatum, I hoped he would choose the former and look for a contract elsewhere as a conventional pitcher. Despite not being a high draft-pick, he had proven himself at the highest levels of the Minor Leagues and cracked the Majors—guys like him often found work again in short order. If he chose to be released, I figured, he could remain a conventional pitcher and probably get signed by a new organization within a month. As a *makeup* guy, however, he saw it as a challenge. He accepted it, and set his mind on returning to the Majors as a knuckleball pitcher.

Most Major League knuckleballers start their journey back in a similar way, washing out as a conventional pitcher. These guys then beg for a chance to try their luck at re-climbing the ladder as a knuckleballer. Tim Wakefield and R.A. Dickey were two such notable, resounding successes. Zach quickly learned was that there was no instruction manual, and no coach with experience who could help him make the conversion. He knew how to throw a knuckleball on the sidelines that danced and scared everyone who tried to catch it. But throwing it for strikes, on a mound, over and over in games, getting professional hitters out? That was a completely different animal. After getting his feet wet, he was suddenly swimming in the dark with no direction, no life vest, and the shore nowhere in sight.

In our continued phone conversations, it became clear how hard the transition was. Teammates and opponents who knew him as a solid, successful pitcher didn't understand why he was suddenly lobbing the ball toward the plate. He'd go out there in a Double-A game, walk five batters and give up five runs, and his teammates just shook their heads. To go from a strike-thrower to a man shot-putting pitch after pitch toward the plate at 60 miles per hour…it didn't make sense. Everyone knew about Tim Wakefield, a shining example of the success a knuckleballer could have. But folks weren't privy to the developmental curve of a knuckler, to witness what failure looked like when trying it. The awkwardness of lobbing balls toward the plate—when everyone else fired them like BBs—was tolerable when it worked. When it didn't, everyone just cringed at how ugly it was.

"Niekro talks to me and tries to help me, but he really

only talks about pitching with it—when and where to throw it, when to mix in a fastball, all that stuff. None of that helps. I throw a great one, then I throw a terrible one. One day I throw a lot of strikes, the next day I walk five batters in two innings. I don't know how to throw the same knuckleball every single time —to locate it, how hard to throw it, all that stuff. Throwing it for fun when I was just screwing around, I didn't have to think about any of those things."

"I'm aware of how stupid I look; some guys I know have even come up to me and told me— they ask what the hell I'm doing. I'm working on it every day, but still get shelled by rookie ball hitters. I tried to keep some of my conventional stuff, mixing in a fastball or curveball at almost normal speeds, but then that messed with my knuckleball too much. I have a harder version, but it's tough to control and my slower one is better. Yet when I mix in higher-speed conventional stuff, then go back to the slow knuckleball, that doesn't work, either."

Maybe Zach's predicament was self-inflicted. Refusing the assignment would have been easier, and maybe his can-do attitude trapped him. I got updates every few months and checked in to see how it was going. It was July, a little over a year later, when my phone rang. I was in Camden and had just come in from BP. Seeing his name on the caller ID and having nothing but time to kill, I took the call and walked through the Campbell's Field hallways to post up outside. I never got tired of the views of the Ben Franklin Bridge and of Philly. I put a brick in the door to keep it from locking me out and leaned against the tan outer walls of the ballpark.

"What's up man?" I asked.

"Yo. So I got released by the Orioles. They let me go yesterday. I figured you'd be a good person to talk to; I'm thinking of playing Independent ball to get back."

"Sorry to hear that, dude. Are you sticking with the knuckleball?"

"Nah, I think I'm ready to go back—see if I can convert into my old self. I haven't thrown a ball hard in over a year now, so I'm sure it will take time, but I know I can do it."

"Well, would you want to play for Camden? I can walk back inside and ask Widge right now. We'd probably take you—we need more starting pitching, even if we had to wait for you to get stretched out."

"Actually, yeah. I was looking at either Camden or Somerset, since both are close to my house. I could commute and be home each night."

I walked back into the clubhouse, found Widge, and asked if he would want to sign Zach. After a quick internet search to pull up his stats and a brief explanation from me about his conversion back into a conventional pitcher, Widge emphatically said yes.

I was proud to have made it to the top of the Indy leagues, but it was a place with no further upward mobility—a dead end. If our careers were graphed out, mine was a slow, methodical climb with two big valleys for my elbow surgeries. His was also a slow climb with a sharper, much higher peak at the top. It was on his tumble down from the top where he intersected with me. Zach arrived the next afternoon and just like that—nearly ten years later—we were teammates again. For the first time we were both in the same precarious position, with the exact same goal: get out of Independent baseball.

The vast majority of Atlantic League players were like Zach— veterans who sported a long résumé in the upper Minors or Majors. Atlantic League teams were picky and only wanted those released from the highest levels. Few lifetime Indy players got chances at all, and even fewer moved on to MLB organizations. There was a stigma with lifetime Indy players like myself. It was as if your name wasn't called on draft day, you'd never have value no matter how much you improved. They wanted to see a history, a record that someone else thought you were good, social proof that other teams saw *something* in you. It was true that most players plateaued in their early-20s, but there were always outliers. I was one of them. I tried not to dwell, though, on the reality that it would be a long-shot for a team to take a chance on me. An average-sized right-hander with two Tommy John surgeries and no MLB-affiliated history? I tried not to think about it. I just kept doing my best each day and left it at that.

We played catch like we used to in college. It was the same now as it was then—quiet and purposeful. We worked on getting him back to his old self, only this time, feedback was flowing in both directions. The last time a throw from him had hit my mitt, I was merely a 20-year-old kid. Nearly 30 with some battle scars, my outlook was different. I knew a lot—not everything, but I had experienced enough success and failure to learn who I was as a player. In college, I was physically building myself from scratch, and I shed my skin so often that it was impossible to keep track of who I was. Yet by 25, I was fully formed and my days were spent learning who I was, who I *wasn't*, and how to refine the things that I did well. Zach and I were different pitchers, but by the time we became teammates again, we both had a good idea of what made each of us successful.

We played catch in pre-game for merely a few days before he was right back in the fire, starting a game for us on a limited pitch count. The velocity wasn't where it used to be—maybe 85-88mph—but he pounded the strike zone in his those first starts with sinking fastballs at the bottom of the strike zone. Even though he had spent nearly 18 months lobbing grenades, he hadn't forgotten how to do what he did best. Maybe it would be like leaving for college—you come home and your room is still exactly as you left it. Sure enough, after four or five starts, he had an ERA in the 1.00s and scouts were starting to call about him. It appeared that our time as teammates would be short. The old Zach—the Zach that had made it to the Bigs—was back.

With just a month under his belt as a conventional pitcher and with a mere three weeks left in the season, Zach's elbow started barking. Soreness and perhaps some pain was to be expected as his pitching arm converted back from mortar tube to sniper rifle. The pain, though, didn't subside. As the end of the 2014 season loomed and elbow pain began holding him back, the decision was made to shut him down until next season. Widge wanted to give him a full off-season to get back into "real" shape, let his arm calm down and look forward to a great 2015 season as a rotation centerpiece. He would be ready for a full workload and a leadership position on a pitching staff that needed guidance. It was a sensible call, the *right* call.

Lacking a pitching coach and taking over as manager for 2015, Widge wanted Zach to play a bigger role. When building his pitching staff that off-season, he was part of the process, helping to source new players and give feedback on returners. My numbers were average—a 4.04 ERA with pedestrian walk and strikeout tallies. I was a starter when I signed with Camden, then had a minor forearm injury that cost me my spot in the rotation. I pitched the second half of the year as both a reliever and spot-starter. It was hard flip-flopping between roles, something I had been warned of but hadn't yet experienced. Your arm never gets a chance to acclimate and adapt when throwing two innings today, a single inning tomorrow, then five innings a handful of days after that. Yet, I did whatever the team needed and gave my best no matter the hat I wore. As 2014 concluded, I just wanted another chance, another year. The first year returning from surgery was always hard—you were back, but still weren't yourself. Post-surgical pitchers are like cast iron pans—they can do the job and cook you dinner but get vastly better with time and seasoning. Would Widge offer me a spot back with the team? I hoped so, but knew I was on the bubble. I later found out that Widge was about 50-50 in keeping me or letting me go. Who finally convinced him to give me another chance? It was Zach. He vouched for my makeup, among other things.

"You know what you're gonna get with Dan. He'll show up on time, he's disciplined and he competes. He's low risk, he's hungry and you know what you'll get with him every day he goes out there." In February of 2015, Widge called. I was going back to Camden.

The off-season went as planned. I arrived in camp in great shape with major improvements, honing the command of my changeup and curveball. Despite having a good fastball, I needed to be more than just a one-pitch pitcher. I also showed up healthy, which was a pleasant rarity. When Zach arrived, though, they tore away the tape and packing peanuts to find a few broken pieces. His elbow pain became shoulder pain, and it hadn't subsided.

He started the year on the Disabled List, with a shoulder that he described as "not right." It was vague and enigmatic. He had seen a world-class doctor in the winter and gotten world-class rehab, but as he heated up in February to prepare for the season, his shoulder just refused to cooperate. No one wanted to arrive hurt—spring training was always supposed to be a fresh start, a time when wear and tear hadn't yet set in. But his shoulder just wouldn't get right. I watched him scramble to find his footing. Entering the second month of the season, he still hadn't found it.

After another month passed, I was sitting in Widge's office. I wasn't being released—far from it. I had done what I intended on doing and was a leader in the bullpen that year, earning the setup man role in a dominant first-half. But our team had been playing sloppy, lifeless baseball and post-game speeches about effort had become a regular thing. If Widge was getting on us, it had to be bad. Finally at wits end, he addressed the team, giving the speech that required me to visit him in his office. Following yet another lazy, ugly loss, he shut the clubhouse door and told us all to listen up:

* * *

211

Before you take the field tomorrow, every single one of you needs to come into my office and tell me that you want to be here. Based on the level of effort I see out there, I genuinely think that many of you don't want to be part of this team. So, everyone is going to come talk to me tomorrow. If you want your release I'll give it to you and we'll get someone here who wants to play hard. And if not, I expect things to improve. But, every single one of you needs to come to my office and tell me personally if you want to continue being a member of this team.

It was this speech that forced all of us into his office for a private meeting. As I sat in a black pleather office chair, I mulled over what I would say to him. When my parents would shame me after screwing up—telling me how disappointed they were—the guilt always straightened me out. I never needed to be screamed at or threatened—letting down personal heroes was always enough. When Widge gave us those same, "disappointed manager" speeches, they were met mostly with deaf ears. The guys who were showing up late, taking batting practice out of uniform, giving a lazy effort in pre-game and showing zero hustle in the game...they didn't respond to it. In Indy ball, a player who saw the end of his career looming might check out mentally; nothing would check him back in.

Widge lived locally in New Jersey and would regularly bring his son to the ballpark. He wasn't built like a typical catcher—listed as 6'2, 220 during his playing days—but it was clear his baseball IQ and personality was a major part of what took him so far in the game. He didn't want to take a bigger coaching job somewhere that would pull him back onto the road, away from his family. He had spent enough time away from his kids during his decade in the Bigs. It was easy to see where his heart was, because it was clearly focused on other people—his son, his daughter, his wife and all of us. He also had a presence that made all of us feel at ease.

Most managers were distant. What made Widge different was that he was *close*—accessible to us players in a way most managers were not. He would regularly come down to the bullpen—where he spent most of his life—and shoot the breeze with the pitchers. He'd play cards with guys after batting practice. When he spoke, everyone perked up—he had decades of stories that no one wanted to miss.

Many of us felt that he walked a little too far on the players' side of the line. Would he be able to turn off the affable, likable persona when guys had to be set straight? Could he release the infielder that he played cards with on a daily basis if he both failed to make plays in the field, and refused to take extra reps in pregame? Could he put the fear of God into an outfielder who strolled in three minutes late? He had spent so much of his life as a player that I think he was still figuring out how to draw a deep enough line in the sand. I'm sure it wasn't easy.

I was selected to the All-Star team that year and would later finish with a 1.80 ERA, 59 strikeouts against 12 walks in 50 innings pitched. I had finally developed into the pitcher I knew I could be. I didn't care if we were bottom-feeders, Camden was *my* team as much as anyone's and I wanted to stay. However, I did *not* want to be a part of what was happening. The Baseball Gods would have pillaged our ballpark—at times, the whole thing felt like slow-pitch softball. I knew the standard we were supposed to uphold. As I sat there with Widge, I was conflicted by whether I still wanted to be a Rivershark. I didn't want to be part of a team that had no standard.

> You know that I want to be here—I don't even have to tell you that. But, I hate how things have been going and they haven't gotten better. Every day I watch guys take BP out of uniform; guys who are making errors in the game don't take a single ground ball in pre-game; there are no consequences for showing up late; there are a bunch of players on our team who should have been released weeks ago. I hate that I'm put in the position to say that, but it's true. I want to win and I also want to be pushed. I want to play knowing that if I don't do my job, I'll be sent home. That's how I made it this far and I need that to keep moving forward.

I took a breath and continued.

> You know, I don't know if I'll ever get signed out of here; I may never get a chance at a higher level. For some of these guys who have made it, this is just a fun, last hurrah for them. But it's not for me. If I'm

going to go out with this as my peak, I don't want it to feel like some beer league where no one cares. *I care.* I want to win and I want to feel like I'm part of something legit. This may be *my* Major Leagues and I may never get a chance to go higher. With the way things have gone, it makes me not want to come to the ballpark. So, I'm not sure I want to stay here. Maybe I should be traded somewhere else. But this is my team and it's not fair that I should have to go. Camden has been good to me and I want to win here.

He leaned back in his chair. As I waited for his response, I glanced up at the big whiteboard behind him, covered with a hand-drawn baseball field and names written in stacks at each position. All of baseball was just a big depth chart. He let out a long exhale.

"You're right. On all of it. I think a lot of guys have gotten too comfortable and stayed too long."

We talked for a little while and Widge conceded that he was probably too close to us. It was tough for him to release players—he wanted to give them chances to turn things around, nor did he have replacements waiting. He was spread thin, basically a one-man show. Widge had been doing the jobs of numerous people, acting as both pitching coach and Manager, player procurement direction and, at times, GM. He was wearing too many hats. He assured me that things would change, but also that I should speak up more for what I believed in. I explained that I was an Indy-ball nobody—I couldn't command attention in a room full of Big League service time. It wasn't my place.

"You're wrong," he said. "You set a good example. You carry yourself in the same way that Clark, Garrison, Murph and D-Ray do. If something isn't right, it's your job to speak up. It's as much on the players to turn this around as anyone." I nodded.

I thought about my role, my status in the pecking order. In a clubhouse like ours, guys with Big League service time were the oak trees and I wasn't sure what I was. As our meeting wrapped up, we discussed the complexion of the team going forward.

In 2010 and 2012, Brooks had often confided in me about player roster moves. I felt honored that he trusted me enough to share confidential information, but I hated hearing it. It made daily life as a player even heavier. I'd walk around knowing that one of my teammates was a bad start away from being released. Or, I'd know that his replacement was getting on a plane tomorrow and the deal was already done. It's not easy laughing at their jokes and pretending that you don't know they're the walking dead. I could practically smell their skin rotting as they just sat there, oblivious. This is the reason managers typically keep their distance—if they didn't, the stench would consume them. In the final few minutes of my meeting with Widge, Zach came up. His frustration with Zach had been mounting.

Struggling and trying to find his old self, Zach had been wearing Widge out, asking for lots of input and shaking his head when he didn't like the answers. At the same time, he was getting unsolicited input from pitchers whose opinions he didn't want. His goal was to return to the old version of himself—the guy who was a good, respected pitcher, the guy he was for 30+ years before converting into a knuckleballer. He could feel his old self in there and was picking up all his old bread crumbs. Yet while retracing his steps, the crumbs had simply run out. No one else knew what the old Zach felt like except Zach, but today's Zach couldn't find him. He was lost.

When I'd sit in the bullpen or stand with a group of pitchers during batting practice, Clark would come up and they'd talk about how "if he only listened," or did this or that. The other pitchers didn't like having their advice thrown back in their faces; there was discontent sown all the way up to Widge. Initially, I laid back completely, though it was hard for me to sit idly by. I wanted to help. After a few weeks, however, I offered a small piece of advice as he went through his throwing routine. He snapped at me. Point taken.

A year later, I'd come to understand with greater depth what he was going through. I'd face similar issues and receive similar discontent from my pitching coach in Long Island. If Zach didn't want input, then it was his right to receive no input. I was only trying to help, but help wasn't what he wanted or needed. He knew what his old self looked like and only he could resurrect it. I decided being his friend—rather than his pitching coach—was the best route for both of us.

We remained road roommates and I never stopped looking to him as a mentor. It was exciting that he got to watch me pitch—he had only images of me as a 20-year-old and the cliff notes of what I told him on the phone. Yet, it was hard to watch him fall apart in front of me, especially as I was doing so well. A cortisone shot and a month of rest got him onto the mound. Once up there, though, he just didn't have it. He'd walk off the field after another bad outing asking himself, *what am I doing?* It was a dreadful question that all of us asked ourselves when we felt powerless to do what we used to do so well. A few days after that conversation with Widge, I had just showered and was sitting in front of my locker.

"Dan-O."

I turned around and there he was, Baltimore Orioles gear bag packed tight and thrown over his shoulder. I knew what that meant. After a quick hug, he was out the door. There was nothing meaningful said—just goodbye. At that moment, being the last guy from our alma mater still in the game, I felt alone. I didn't like that I had outlasted him. It was a burden witnessing what might have been the end of his career. The next day, Widge found me in the outfield during pregame. I asked him how Zach took the news.

"Relief, honestly. It seemed like relief, to me. I think his shoulder, his wife and his baby daughter back home, all of those things were really weighing on him. He took a deep breath and took it okay. He knew."

Widge walked off, back to the turtle where he could keep his distance. I drank down a second Citywide Special, then finished my running. I had to be ready to pitch that night.

Coach, you always said that what we'd learn in the dugout would prove to be much bigger than baseball. The game was merely preparing us for real life—to be good husbands, fathers and employees. Yet, we don't want it to merely be preparation for some other thing—we devote our lives to it because we want it to be *the* thing. Few of us go out like champions and it was hard watching Zach go out with a whimper. We scratch and claw to hang on when, in reality, at some point it's less painful to just let go. A year after him it would be my turn, in an eerily similar fashion no less. There are deep marks in the side of that mountain, and neither of us went out with much fanfare. Yet, Zach accomplished great things—not only on the mound, but in spreading his knowledge and good will around to other players like myself.

Going out on a low note is something I've thought a lot about. If you don't fight that voice until it's so loud your eardrums burst, if your fingernails aren't ground and bleeding as you slide to reality, the journey wouldn't be as fulfilling. You gave me a chance back on that dark night at Harford Community College, even though the radar gun didn't light up with the proper numbers. Neither myself nor Zach ever wasted a chance. He could have given up after his debut, said no to reinventing himself. But he didn't. He kept going and accomplished so much despite long odds. In the end, it didn't go the way either of us wanted. Yet, now with some distance and perspective on the matter, I believe that the claw marks and that final whimper—they were a sign of a race well-run.

Dear Dan, You ran free.

As you stood in your white button-down shirt and black slacks, you were sure diplomacy wasn't going to work. Moments before, everyone was on the front lawn having a good time. A rare night off from baseball allowed you to shoot down to the University of Maryland to visit Fred. You hadn't seen him in a while and it was a chance to reconnect. Baseball brought you together as kids, but the craziness of your D-I baseball schedule forced you apart. With just a year to go until he graduated from engineering school, he threw a black and white party at his College Park townhome. All was going well until five thugs walked straight through the front door. You all looked at each other—stunned—and rushed inside.

Back out on the lawn a few minutes later, it became a standoff. Fred took the point and began to reason with them, calmly, gently. You and his other close friends stood at his flank, watching as the intruders scowled back. Fred met their hostility with a soothing voice: "Guys, listen, we're sorry but we just can't have you here. This is a closed party. I'm sorry."

They shouted expletives back but Fred refused to break character. He stayed calm as they became more and more agitated. It was clear they wanted to fight, but needed someone to fight with. You scanned their hands for weapons. You didn't see any—they had to be concealed. No way they walked into all of that without *something*. You formed a plan. Any second, they'd pull out a knife or a gun and rush Fred. They wouldn't get there. Your hands trembled as you shifted your weight onto the balls of your feet. You'd reach them first.

The voice first showed up years prior at Harford Community College; there was no record of it before that day. Crouching down, it looked you in the eyes as you packed up, pleased with yourself that you now had a home in college baseball. It scolded you for not seeing who you really were—a mediocre ballplayer at best. There was a whole world of players better than you, it said.

You have four years. Do you want a desk job?

No sir.

Four years. Don't you waste a single day.

Seven years after the standoff in college park, you were searching for a parking spot, your green Honda packed with all of your belongings. It was 1:40 in the morning and you'd have to circle the block at least two more times. Finally, you gave up and parked on the curb. You knocked and were greeted by Lindsey, your new roommate. Her dog, with his black coat and greying snout, squeezed by to inspect. He accepted you and you walked in. You were home.

Maybe Maryland didn't feel like home because it just represented the sameness, the old you that was best left behind. Returning there meant climbing back into your childhood closet. UMBC, located in Catonsville, a Baltimore suburb just 10 minutes from downtown, was close to the city but too far to be immersed in it. When college came to an end, staying meant failing. Returning to Maryland meant you hadn't made good on your promise to the voice. As your elbow healed you got a job as a strength coach, passing time before you had a ticket out.

Over the next four years you didn't live in the same place longer than six months. You'd pack up all your things, break the lease and head back out. No posters on the wall, everything temporary. Your life was never here and always there, though it was never clear where *there* was. For a while, it was exciting. Thirty-plus states, a free tour of the country? You were happy, did well for yourself and kept moving.

American Pharaoh won the triple crown that same year you moved back for a second season in Camden. The Preakness Stakes, held every year in Baltimore, always fell during baseball season. Though you were never able to attend, the highlights were endlessly looped as pride swelled for the historical local race. You said you always played for yourself, that no one else pushed you to stay on the field or put in more work off of it. It was always for *you*, you said. But would American Pharaoh sprint down and around the bends of that track without a jockey's relentless whipping? Does a wild horse run faster without fences, beset on all sides only by meadows and countryside?

Can any of us become champions without a jockey?

It's unclear what version of our story is real, what account of our attitude and interpretation is accurate. This is because of the voice. Who are we, anyway, to audit ourselves? What if we're all just uniquely color-blind to the world in front of us, seeing it only through the shades, the filters with which we screen and smooth the truth? I've looked back on your emails to friends and family and could not discern who wrote those words. Was it you? Was it how you really felt? Or was it a syrupy confection meant to encourage those who would read your thoughts? Did that concocted version later become the truth? Can the veracity of something shift over time?

A United States quarter is a sandwich of two layers of cupronickel—an alloy of copper and nickel—pressed into a sandwich with a core of pure copper in the center. Our story is much the same. The first layer is what you actually experienced, actually felt. The second is what you told others—your interpretation of what happened and how it affected you. Sandwiched in between is the version I found as I searched through the wreckage looking for our black box. All three versions are pressed into one, three versions of the same events all inseparable from one another. There was no black box.

I still cannot tell if you were truly a wild horse as I've claimed. Was the voice the jockey on your back, whipping you around that track? Who is the voice in our head? If it's such a crucial guiding force, where was it on the night that you readied yourself for an unarmed knife-fight on the lawn of Fred's College Park home? Where was it in Camden? Where was it in our youth, before Coach J pointed his radar gun at us? Were you weak and the voice a projected attempt to be strong? Or were you always strong and the voice was merely your own?

Fishtown is a northeastern neighborhood in Philadelphia, a stone's throw from Center City. Rapidly gentrifying, it's barely recognizable just a few years later as the posh Northern Liberties neighborhood has leaked further and further into it. You vowed not to bounce around again upon returning to play for the Riversharks, and so you searched, finding Lindsey. A former lacrosse player at Temple, she understood your situation and agreed to a month-to-month lease. Each morning you walked to a different coffee shop, sipped a different cappuccino or cortado, then packed your laptop and walked to find lunch. You ate cheesesteaks from Steve's and occasionally lounged in the hammocks of Spruce Street Harbor Park. You wrote and explored, absorbing like a fern the vibe of the first major city you'd lived in. Some days you took the train, its rails located on both sides of the Ben Franklin Bridge as it crossed the river to the ballpark. Other days you drove, paying the five-dollar toll for the privilege of stressing it's light-blue support cables. The ballpark was tucked beneath the bridge, waiting to be rocked to sleep by it each night. To others, it was a struggling team with dwindling attendance. But to you it was a special place, a place where you found yourself as a ballplayer. The voice did not follow you over that majestic bridge.

That season, you mindlessly did what I always knew you could do. You pitched. You executed. You attacked and did not back down. You needed no bullying or coaxing to do any of it. With experience and confidence comes the ability to gaze out onto one's land and see all of it at once—every hill and valley. Situations that used to bring out the voice no longer did. You surveyed game situations with an easy clarity. Even when you hit the inevitable slump, you remained calm. You explained in an email that you knew it would pass—it was because you finally knew who you were. Even in the face of a very rough string of outings, you didn't panic:

> I've failed to do my job recently. I've given up the winning run in three recent games in which I pitched the ninth inning of tie ball games.
>
> *Game One.* I gave up a single, then a bunt to second, followed by a single for an RBI. We lost 2-1.
>
> *Game Two.* I got two quick outs, then gave up a solo home run to a guy who hits maybe four in a season. We again lost 2-1.
>
> *Game Three.* I surrendered a lead-off triple, struck the next two guys out, then gave up a jam-job pop up down the line to lose 3-2.
>
> I didn't do my job and when I don't come through, we lose. Thing is, earlier this week I entered in the eighth and put up a zero both times. We won each of those games by one run. In both of those outings I

threw the ball terribly—didn't locate well, fell behind in the count, and couldn't throw offspeed for strikes. They were shaky performances. Yet, I got three outs and held the lead.

Ironically enough, I threw more quality pitches in all three of the blown games than I did in those two successful ones—I just got burned the one or two times I left balls in the middle of the plate. It's still my fault, but baseball is just like that—somedays, you throw a ball down the middle when the game is on the line, and the guy grounds into a double play. Other days, he hits that ball 425 feet.

Baseball is somewhat like poker. Even if you make the right play, you still might lose out on sheer luck. Sometimes, your stuff and your performance stinks and you come out on top. Pitchers can control the pitches they make, but not where the ball goes after it's hit.

I'm inclined to think that the mature, experienced tone was real. You sounded different in a subtle way—you'd been there before, and you could see how you fit into both the present and future. Because of that, you didn't have to constantly escape into the distance, consumed with ways to get better. Maybe it was because, for the first time since you were a kid, you played the game truly for yourself. Not for anyone else, for the future, or for the bullying voice in your head.

In the past, if a teammate wanted you to go out on the town, the voice would guilt you into staying in and laying low. *Nothing good can come of it*, it would say. *Rest up and do something productive.* Yet that year, you had good teammates and went out with them more, just like you had with Wynn. You went out with Sean Gleason, watching him say and do things you'd chuckle about for months. You both still pitched well the next day.

There was more to life than just baseball. You dipped extra animal crackers in your sixth inning coffee, and laughed a little harder at everyone's bullpen antics. It was the first time you forgave yourself for not doing more. You let yourself have fun and in doing so, experienced the present for perhaps the first time. In all the years prior, you had been so focused on *getting there* that you never let yourself fully be anywhere at all. Yet in Campbell's Field and on the streets of Philadelphia, you were—for the first time—at your destination. It wasn't yet the end of the line, but there was no jockeying voice choosing your path. You alone decided where you went next.

It wasn't surprising that Fred negotiated his way to a peaceful resolution. After what felt like an eternity, the group of thugs wandered off, back into the night. With the exception of Fred, all of our heart rates slowly returned to normal. His had seemingly never elevated. He knew his strength was in diplomacy and never reached for anything else. If Fred had tried to be anyone but himself that night —tried to rise up, puff out his chest and be the person he thought maybe he needed to be, who knows what would have happened. But, he never wavered. As for you, though flooded with adrenaline and fear, you knew exactly what you'd do had the brawl begun. No inner monologue directed Fred, nor did one direct you.

The voice in your head helped build you into who you are today. Though it often stood you up and dusted you off, it wasn't always a healthy influence. You were at your best in Camden, acting without conscious thought while enjoying the first stop on your journey that felt like home. You weren't your best with the jockey on your back, nor did you need it when the situation was dire. Your instincts, your experience, your inner strength was enough. You finally knew yourself and knew that you were best out in the open—no fences, no track, no jockey. The best version of you ran free.

Dear Lucas, You were the only one who saw it.

It's April 10, 2017 and we're a few hours from starting our normal daily routine together—opening our academy at 3:30 p.m. to give lessons and help kids get bigger, faster and stronger. This past weekend and nearly every previous year for the last seven years, I would have been driving somewhere to start yet another baseball season. That always meant you were left managing our two-man business completely by yourself. It was a six-month assignment that you never complained about. You just wore it while I pursued my dreams.

When I officially pulled the plug a few months ago, I tried my best to hide how I was really feeling. You and I certainly weren't going to make lavender tea and talk about how I was handling retirement. I had a hard time focusing, had a hard time understanding where the rest of my life was going. To say I was distracted at work was an understatement and I wasn't sure how well I hid it. You asked me later if I was okay. I said *kind of* and left it at that. I've lived too privileged a life to complain and whine to you about my personal identity crisis. At least, that's been my excuse for keeping it inside. The one good byproduct of leaving baseball was that your share of the load got a lot lighter.

I didn't realize how heavy my burden was in trying to keep fighting that fight all these years. The weight was heavy. You were the innocent bystander, having to put our entire business on your back while I was away. I always promised to help manage the business remotely, but I think we both knew those words were hollow. When I was away, there was never a time when I was completely free, at ease and able to relax. I had to do well both for myself and for the time I was stealing from you and from the kids in our academy. If I left the nest, I had better do what I said I would do. Otherwise, I was wasting everyone's time.

Somehow, you were there for one of my most profound performances on the mound, a moment in time when I was at my mental and physical best. In over 500 professional games, only a handful of my friends and family got to see me on the mound. Geographically, I was rarely close to anyone and when I was, who knew if I'd get the call that night. Though you had sat through eight full innings that day in Long Island, even you almost missed it.

We were down to our last strike that Sunday on the road in New York. With the bases empty on a windy day, our cleanup hitter, Mike, was in the box with a 1-2 count. We were down 2-1 in the top of the ninth. Our last hope was hitting about .220, so it didn't look good. Widge had called down to the bullpen at the end of the eighth: *if we tie it, Blewett is in the game*. After two quick outs, the opposing closer cruising, the game looked surely in the hands of the Long Island Ducks. You, realizing the same after the bottom of the eighth, walked out of the stadium to charge your phone. It was a near-certainty that I wasn't going to pitch that day.

Mike didn't bow down. Fouling off two-strike pitches until the count eventually ran full, he didn't let the Ducks' closer shut the door. The foul balls kept coming, reaching double-digits for the at-bat before finally it happened. From 330 feet away in the left-field bullpen, I heard the familiar *THOCK* of a baseball caught flush on the barrel of a maplewood bat. Seconds later I heard the loud, hollow *BANG* of a baseball colliding with the second-tier of outfield advertisements.

That loud bang was Mike taking their closer deep to dead-center on what had to be the dozenth pitch of the at-bat, tying the game at two. His deep drive smashed into the plywood-backed Pepsi sign towering beyond the centerfield wall, some 400+ feet away and 20 feet off the ground. I heard it as I was lazily playing catch with our bullpen catcher, preparing for the one percent chance that we'd tie the game. *YEAHHHH!* Everyone cheered from the bullpen box. *Oh Crap.* I had to shove my way past the excitement to get my arm loose as fast as I could. I only had one out (typically 2-3 minutes) before I had to be jogging across the outfield into the game. I fired off pitches as fast as I could and pulled my game face down over my normal one.

The 4,500 fans were so stunned when that ball left the yard that they let out a massive collective groan. You had just walked out of the gates when you heard it, and quickly ran back in to see what happened.

What you heard as you re-entered the ballpark was the very reason you were there: *Now Pitching for the Camden Riversharks: Number 13, Dan Blewett.* The fans weren't done reacting, though—I had a lot more in store for them. On that sunny afternoon I was the pitcher I had always wanted to be.

I always enjoyed the competition of higher-energy, packed ballparks like that of the Ducks. In the Atlantic League, the best places to play were Sugar Land, Somerset, and Long Island, and it didn't matter whether you played for or against them. All three teams had fantastic ballparks and droves of passionate fans. Adrenaline was higher, stakes were raised, and it was plainly more fun when people cared about what happened on the field. I didn't mind that the Long Island Ducks fans cheered against me, I just liked that they cheered at all. Back home in Camden, we were lucky to draw 1,000 fans on a good night.

There was a lot of energy that Sunday afternoon in Central Islip, New York. I had just enough time to warm up, the fear of not being ready hastening the process. I planned to use my eight pitches on the game mound for finishing touches, but I was ready. I could go from sitting cold on the bench to ready to pitch in about four minutes, which usually meant two hitters. If I had more time than that I could get a drink, take some breaths, stretch between pitches and spend more time mentally psyching myself up. I took pride in being able to pitch any time I was summoned. This time, if I hadn't been ready, I would have had no one to blame but myself. Mike's home run was so unlikely that I never seriously considered that I'd be pitching that day.

After finishing my warm ups, I dug my cleats into the clay and stared down one of the "farther" home plates in the league. Some plates seemed close and others farther away, despite all being exactly 60' 6" from the rubber. It was an odd perceptual phenomenon, but any pitcher will tell you the same thing—sometimes the plate looks close and other times it looks distant.

The first hitter was a friend of mine named José Morales. He was our catcher in Camden the previous year, a Puerto Rican player who had enjoyed some big-league success with the Twins. He was always encouraging to me, treated me like I had something special. Coming from guys who played at the highest level, that always meant a lot. As my opponent, I knew the scouting report—he struggled with breaking balls and would chase them out of the zone. So my plan was to go after him early with fastballs; if I could get to at least one strike, I'd finish him with curveballs. Sure enough, I fired the first fastball in for a called strike, paving my road to the punchout I wanted.

A few pitches later, as he waved at a sharp curveball in the dirt, the ball bounced away and he took off for first, reaching safely on the archaic and stupid "dropped third strike" rule. The winning run was now on first with no outs. The next hitter bounced one to first for out number one, advancing the pinch runner who had entered the game for José. Their substitute speedster now stood just a single away from victory. I clenched my teeth, lowered my brow and bore down against the next two hitters. I induced an unremarkable fly out to get the first one, and then a harmless groundout to end the threat.

As the setup man pitching in a tied away game, it was my job to keep pitching with the score tied, at which point we would hopefully score and my work would be complete. The closer would trot onto the field and finish it off. That was the plan, but we didn't score in the tenth. So back out I ran, defending our right to play an 11th inning.

In the tenth I got the first out right away—a routine fly ball to right field. Getting the first out meant a drastic reduction in the likelihood of a run scoring, so it was a good start. The next batter was the best player in the league, a salty Major League veteran named Lew Ford. Lew was nearly 40, but still hit .350 every season. He was a stalwart in the Mexican League and Dominican Winter league, earning MVP honors there. The Long Island natives loved him, as he was their veteran, their rock, their ace in the hole. He even had his own special introduction beyond just the normal 10-second music clip. The announcer came over the P.A. System:

Now batting: Lewwwwwwwwwwwwwwwwww Forrrrrddddddd!

The crowd would drag out his monosyllabic name with the announcer; it was pretty cool. Lewwwww Ford continued to hustle out stolen bases despite his advanced age. He did not appear to get old like the rest of us. In that moment I both hated Lew Ford because he was my competition, and loved him for the added stakes he brought to the table. I played the game precisely to be in situations like that one, to be the guy squaring off against *the guy*. The crowd came to watch Lew be Lew, and I got to compete against him *and* the crowd of thousands of people who expected me to lose. Lew and his posse versus Blew, the unknown pitcher with a paper mache' elbow. It was a classic underdog story.

He was an exceedingly tough out. Aside from the experience that comes from seeing thousands of pitches each season over a 20-year pro career, he had a level of focus unlike any I'd encountered. On that day, he dug in like he always did. He fouled off each of the first two pitches I threw, falling behind 0-2. I had a chance, but I could see it in his eyes that he was locked in, his every fiber focused on me and the gleaming white baseball that was about to leave my hand.

Good curveball down? *Foul ball.*

Good fastball up? *Foul ball.*

Tough fastball barely off the outside corner? *No swing. Ball.*

Finally, I caught a fastball really, really well off my fingertips and let it fly at chest-level; it was HARD. He swung late and foul-tipped it, the ball barely glancing off my catcher's mitt. Lew jumped up in the batters' box, realizing I had nearly gotten him. As I looked back at the box score, ensuring that I recounted this story with accuracy, I chuckled reading the pitch-by-pitch: *Foul, Foul, Foul, Foul, Ball, Foul, Foul, Foul, Ball, Ball, [put in play].* I was sharp that Sunday. I'd throw 34 pitches total, of which 26 were strikes. To Lew, I got ahead 0-2 and had him fighting for his life as soon as the at-bat began. But, being the pro that he was, he fought back, beating me on the 11th pitch, a 3-2 fastball low-and-away that he lined into right field. As he rounded first, I mentally tipped my cap to him. *Well-done. You got me.* It will forever be one of my favorite at-bats, even though I didn't prevail. I was locked into a battle with a seasoned veteran, and at no point was it clear who would win. Both of our best was on display, an even match for all to witness. I saw him in my home ballpark in Camden a few weeks later, and I told him how much I enjoyed competing against him—how win or lose, he brought out the best in me. He didn't say much, agreeing that competing was what it was all about; he gave me a gracious handshake as I continued on to the clubhouse. I appreciated feeling challenged while simultaneously challenging my opponent.

I still had two outs to get, now with a base-stealing threat on first. Pitching to the next hitter, I quickly induced a mile-high pop-up to third base. But as I watched it swirl in the high sky, what happened next changed the course of the game. Our third baseman who just an inning earlier had hit the game-tying home run to dead center, dropped the pop-up. He didn't even get a glove on the darned thing. The strange thing was, despite pop-ups being sure outs at this level of play, I knew as soon as I looked at him that it was going to fall. Right off the bat, I looked up at the ball then down to see what fielder was converging and where I had to go. As I glanced over at Mike, I could see this look in his eyes that said, *I want no part of this pop-up.* It bobbed and weaved in the coastal wind before emitting a loud *THOP!* as it collided with the hard dirt a few feet behind him. He barely had to move to catch it; my jaw dropped. This was a guy who—from all reports—was a phenomenal third baseman in his prime. Fifteen minutes ago, he had shown everyone just how good he could be. Now, I had to get a fourth out against a first-place team in the 10th inning on the road. Lew Ford posted up at second base, representing the winning run. Once again, I went into shutdown mode, and this is where it really got fun.

The next batter was the Ducks' first baseman, their five-hole hitter and big power guy. As all six-feet, six-inches of him strolled slowly toward the plate, the crowd of four-thousand plus rose to their feet. They howled, clapped and cheered, sending the ballpark into a roar. They were sure their big bopper would send one deep and end the game. The Long Island faithful had the man they wanted up at the plate. I knew this guy well—a few of my teammates had played with him and they shared his scouting report at the beginning of the series. The consensus was that he would consistently chase fastballs up in the zone, but would rarely connect. He had a lot of power, but a relatively slow swing and would only hurt you down in the zone. I was mad about the pop-up, and had nothing but contempt for the guy stepping up to my plate. I oxygenated, flaring my nostrils as I pulled hateful breaths of air in and out through my nose. He, along with the fans on their feet, were going to sit back down very soon.

Wearing a scowl as I came set, I threw that first fastball as hard as I could, right at the belt. With the whoosh of a heavy barn door, he swung and missed. My catcher put down fastball a second time, and I again reared back and fired it right past another equally late swing. It was now 0-2. My catcher then put down curveball; I shook him off. I was living or dying with my best pitch—my hard, high-spin fastball. I pulled in one last aggressive breath and threw the absolute piss out of the ball. It punched the pocket of the catcher's mitt with an echoing pop that could be heard the next county over. The crowd reacted:

OHHHHHHHHHH.

On that third consecutive swing and miss, the crowd let out a huge, loud, shoulder-drooping sigh of disappointment. It was the most unbelievable thing I'd ever experienced—I took the wind out of the sails of an entire ballpark all at once. I *loved* it.

I swatted my glove at the ball as it was tossed back to me, watching their mighty power-hitter walk back to the dugout in shame. I struck out their big hitter in 30 seconds on three overpowering fastballs—

probably the three hardest of my life. Sometimes, players make statements with their performance. It was undoubtedly the strongest, loudest statement I had made during my life in baseball. That mound was *my* mound, and *I* was controlling the game. The crowd tried to wrestle control away from me when that pop-up hit the ground, but I took it back with those three fastballs.

The game did *not* have a fairytale ending. The next hitter blooped a ball into left field on a fastball that was probably the wrong pitch. I was feeling so confident, so aggressive that I chose fastball when even the most mediocre curveball would have resulted in an inning-ending strikeout. Instead, I gave him just enough of a chance to put the bat on the ball and a dying quail ended the game, falling just in front of our left-fielder. The loss, though, didn't overshadow the moment. I showered, ate and you and I hit the road down to Washington, D.C., to spend an off-day touring the capitol. A few days later, you flew back to Illinois to take care of our academy.

The version of myself who showed up to pitch that day could have pitched in the Major Leagues. The reality, though, was that I needed to be that guy 100% of the time and I simply wasn't. The man who pitched that day was born too late and spent too much time on the bench waiting for another chance. I'll always have the memory of that game, a trophy for finally assembling myself into the pitcher I knew I *could* be. I'm thankful that you got to be there. It was fitting because it wouldn't have happened without you.

I had help from numerous coaches and mentors along the way, each swooping to my rescue in the nick of time. They left me with a hammer and nails or a lantern and map. Neither of those, though, had any value unless I had the ability to go, unless I had time to follow the map. On April 7, when those 17 days transforming our new facility were up, you shoved me out the door and took care of the rest. If I had been forced to choose between my career and our academy, it would have torn me apart giving up either. You took that decision off the table, giving me the time I needed to become the best version of myself. I couldn't have found him without you.

Dear Annie, It swallows you whole.

You and I never talked about baseball that much, at least as far as I can remember. In high school, our relationship was tenuous at best. I'm not sure why I pushed you away and didn't treat you the way a big brother should, but I hope I've made up for it since then. I think I just needed space and an escape from the house we grew up in. Maybe the introvert in me felt boxed in or maybe I was just a typical moody teenager. Regardless, we turned it around after high school. Yet, even as we got closer, we never talked about the ins and outs of baseball all that much. I don't talk about it with many people, really, and I'm not sure why. Maybe because I felt it was all just minutia, stuff that without the years of context wouldn't be relevant to anyone else. In this book, you've probably learned more about my life as a ballplayer than you did in the two decades watching me play.

Perhaps part of that is the compartmentalization that people in high-stress jobs are forced to develop. I'm sure there are lots of things Ryan never shared—and perhaps never will—about his time in the military. Even though he's your husband, there's still just a depth of information that most will never be privy to in jobs like his and mine. I don't want it to be that way and never did, however it just always felt like...where would I start? Would she even understand? Is it worth mentioning if I already have a solution? What good is venting, anyway? Finding the context for so much of it often felt impossible.

So here we are—I bottled up so much of it over the years, both good and bad, that it had to go somewhere when it was all said and done. Despite upping your game in my last season with daily deliveries of good juju, the end was still a mess. I watched my career unravel before my eyes. I trusted you enough to tell you all of it...but I didn't. I think *this* will help explain where I was, mentally, that final summer.

* * *

It was chilly night as Kevin and I sat in the bullpen box, perched atop the right field wall, watching our teammates under the lights. It was 8:30 p.m. on a typical weeknight in late May, and we were approaching showtime. The starter had an inning or two left, which meant all of us relievers were beginning to stir. It was a close game, which, at the time, meant that Kevin and I were likely *not* getting the call. Earlier in the season, I was one of the guys they trusted with a narrow lead. I had pitched as the setup man the previous year with Camden and entered this one—2016 with the Long Island Ducks—in a similar role. Not so much anymore, neither for me nor for Kevin Vance, a former farmhand of both the White Sox and Arizona Diamondbacks. Kevin was a new buddy of mine, the kind of teammate I gravitated toward. I meshed well with guys who appreciated dry humor and deeper conversations. Vance, sporting long, black hair that he slicked back, was finishing his Master's degree online during the season. In the Atlantic League, having even a bachelor's degree was rare because so many players had been drafted young, selected in the early rounds. Vance is dark complected with a deep, rumbling voice and a build similar to mine, both of us shorter and more muscular than the average lanky pitcher.

Ordinarily a guy who laughed easily, he nor I had been feeling overly chipper. We commiserated in slumping. We'd given up too many hits and were greeted with a quick hook on far too many of our recent outings. It never felt good entering a game and making a bigger mess of a situation you were supposed to clean up. Our manager played match-ups. If a reliever went in and gave up a few hits, he was quickly pulled for another. Yet, it had nothing to do with our manager —match-ups or no match-ups, neither of us were doing our job.

The common baseball player doesn't talk much about his struggles. Slumps are *not* Tyrannosaurs. Yet, we ballplayers do what *Jurassic Park* taught us—we stay still, don't make a peep and hope it loses interest. Maybe if we do that, it will walk away without eating us alive. Maybe it's superstition, machismo, or just plain fear where if you talk about a slump you're perceived as enabling it, giving it power, and psyching yourself out. It's true that we don't want to give power to the fear and doubt. It's true that no one wants to hear our excuses or whining. It's also true that you get labeled a *head-case* if people see you stressing or changing things in an attempt to get out of a slump. Yet, the cycle of silent rumination doesn't convince the T-Rex that he should leave. No, no—rather, it convinces him to hang around and wait it out until his prey sneezes and panics, running into the open where he's gobbled up whole.

I didn't want to complain or make excuses, I just wanted to purge and vent. Everything was riding on that 2016 season, and I'd been absolutely blowing my chance to get out of independent ball. Kevin was a decent bullpen philosopher, plus his ERA was similarly ugly, so I knew he could empathize. No one else was around and it felt safe to break the seal on the topic.

"It sucks going out there and not doing your job," I said. "I haven't had a clean inning in like two weeks now." I shook my head as I looked at my cleats. "It wears on you."

"Yeah," he replied. "It's the absolute worst. People have no idea how hard it is to pitch *bad*."

There is something especially rancid about underperforming as a pitcher. Much like the kicker in football, all eyes are on you and everything is your fault. All action starts and stops with the pitcher. Though a huge amount of what happens is beyond our control, it doesn't feel that way. We all know that bloopers fall in, swinging bunts happen and good pitches become hits, but it doesn't change the fact that *we* blew the game. Kevin, staring at the damp wood floor of our bullpen box, looked over at me and continued:

"You know, when I'm done playing and have a 9-5 job, life's gonna be easy. Baseball prepares you for everything because there's nothing worse than when you're pitching like crap. You let everyone down—your teammates, your coaches, the fans, your friends, your family, yourself—*everyone*. All you want to do is just contribute to a win and there are times when no matter how hard you try, you just can't. The worse you pitch, the more things seem to go wrong. In the work world...deadlines? Meetings? Come on."

It was true. Willpower, intentions, preparation—none of it made one bit of difference. Baseball is a uniquely terrible combination of luck and skill. Good pitches sometimes went for game-winning hits and bad pitches sometimes went for easy outs. The same ground ball that costs me a run gets snared by the third baseman for another pitcher. Why couldn't my ground ball have found the shortstop and become a double-play? Why couldn't my 3-1 fastball have been popped up? Why did it have to be a grand slam instead? It's easy to focus on the bad times and think, *why can't I get a break?* In reality, the same good and bad luck is evenly distributed amongst us all. When things are bad, however, we focus on the bad. When things are good, everything is just so darned easy.

Knowing what sensible, logical players like Vance and I knew about luck and slumps, we should have just kept our mouths shut and rode them out. The bad luck would subside and we'd get our fair share of line-drive double plays soon enough, right? The problem is that sometimes we just need to vent and feel like someone else is in our corner. Yet when everyone on the same team is in competition with each other, it's difficult to know who a player can trust and who he can't. Open up to the wrong teammate and he'll spread rumors about you being soft. Open up to the coaching staff and they might think you're a head-case and need to be replaced. Open up to your spouse and you might just toss the weight from your shoulders onto theirs and make the whole thing worse for everyone. It's complex, and often leads to the same outcome: players suffering in silence.

That year in Long Island was *so* important for me. It was the culmination of everything I had worked for. The pressure I put on myself to finally break through and not blow my chance…it was heavy. It just so happened that it was the first year I had a girlfriend during a season. Our relationship depended, in large part, on my performance on the field. Meg was from Long Island. I met her the previous season when I was playing there on the visiting team. We lived apart the rest of the year, flying to see each other on a monthly basis like so many long-distance couples do. Part of my decision to sign with Long Island was because of her. When spring training rolled around, I moved into her one-bedroom apartment.

After the best season of my career with Camden in 2015, I wanted an upgrade. Camden folded after that year for financial reasons. My contract rights were transferred to New Britain, an expansion team. New Britain was far from everything—my family and friends in Maryland, my business back home in Illinois, and Meg in Long Island. I was an All-Star there, and felt that I had some leverage. So, I asked both teams if a trade to Long Island was possible. The Ducks drew big crowds, signed great players and were a well-run franchise. I wanted to be a part of that, to be pushed by a team that took care of their players and expected to win.

Meg was pretty and smart as a whip. An architect, she had a very thoughtful, logical mind, something I could relate to. She had icy blue eyes from which I could not look away. Though it would have been in our best interest to *not* live together—since most of our relationship had been in short bursts and via FaceTime—we figured that we needed to give it a shot and see how compatible we really were. As my arrival date got closer that offseason, the anticipation grew. I was looking forward to having her around in real life, rather than as a computer screen. I eagerly awaited my chance with a championship team in a new city. Things were looking up. Then, my shoulder began hurting.

Banged up is perhaps the most apt baseball term for how players hobble off the field at the end of a long season. Though 2015 was my best year in the toughest league I'd played in, I limped to the finish line. Just as the elbow pain I pitched through in the All-Star game subsided, shoulder pain cropped up. My shoulder was never a problem, so I thought little of it and kept pitching with a max dose of anti-inflammatories in my system. Games 110-140 of that year were tough, but I managed okay. I drove home banged up, but intact.

The Arizona Diamondbacks saw me pitch in the Atlantic League All-Star game that year—I pitched one clean inning with two strikeouts. After the season, their head Independent League scout, Chris Carminucci, called me. It was the first conversation I had with a MLB scout since I was 21. *I'm on to something,* I thought. *I'm close. I might finally get my shot.*

"Hey Dan, I saw you in the All-Star game; you were good."

"Thank you," I replied,

"No, thank you. Thank you for being good," he said with a laugh. "Some of the guys we go out to see aren't what they're advertised to be."

He was fast-talking and direct; exactly what I'd expect from a busy scout. I was invited to throw in Arizona at a workout for free agent players, just before spring training. They wanted to see me again up close, and he explained that I had the ability to pitch for them if the situation ended up right. They might need a reliever at Double-A or Triple-A in 2016, and it was possible I could be that guy. Maybe I was finally good enough for someone to overlook my age, injury history and status as an undrafted player. Despite two Tommy John surgeries, maybe I'd finally caught up.

Upon arriving in Arizona a few months later, I was disappointed to find a *lot* of players at that same workout. It was definitely not a short-list, hardly even a medium-list. *You're here for a reason. They don't waste their time. All of these younger guys have nothing to do with you.* I reminded myself that I was only in competition with myself. There was a sea of 22-25-year-olds, none of whom would fill the role I was auditioning for. They wouldn't send a 22-year-old to Triple-A, nor would they send my 30-year-old self to Single-A. *I'm here for a reason. I'm on their list for a specific role.* The day went like this:

I arrived at the complex at noon.

The workout began at 1:30 p.m.

Position players hit and fielded first, finishing at 3:45.

Pitchers started at 4 p.m.

I was number 32 out of 55 pitchers. Each pitcher got 15-20 pitches.

My turn came at 9 p.m.

I waited nine hours to throw my 15 pitches. It was a long day by any standard, but the ten or so scouts were just as intently focused on the last pitchers as they were on the first. I appreciated that about them— they were thorough, re-affirming the idea that every player was there for a purpose. A lot of pitchers grew agitated and anxious waiting so long, but not me. Experienced pitchers learn to only worry about what's within their control, to be the best version of themselves no matter the circumstance. I rationalized that I typically entered a game around 9 p.m, so I was basically just pitching the seventh or eighth inning as usual. After I got my chance to throw in the starlight, Mr. Carminucci was brief but positive.

"Hey Dan."

"Hey." I shook his hand. "Thanks for having me."

"Yeah no problem. You were as advertised: 90-92 with a "plus" curve. We really liked your cutter. We'll be following you during the season. Thanks for coming out."

I grabbed my stuff and changed into shorts for the drive back to my hotel. My curveball had been my special pitch my whole life and I threw some good ones that night. The cutter was really my fourth-best pitch and I was surprised that the scouts liked it. An older coach in the bullpen had shown me a new grip that night as I got warm. My cutters had sucked as I got loose, but after he politely showed me a new grip to tinker with, they started biting hard. Not one to experiment in important situations, I made an exception and threw the new grip in front of the scouts. I had nothing to lose, so why not? Thanks, old-timer, wherever you are. I don't remember your name, but you were my spirit guide that night.

2016 with the Ducks was supposed to be my year. All I had to do was repeat my performance from 2015 and be myself when the

Diamondbacks again poked their heads around my ballpark. What I had done in Camden, at the All-Star game and at that brief workout in Arizona…it was enough. They knew I was 30, that I was only six feet tall, that I topped at 94mph, not 98. They knew who I was and still had me in the mix. If I continued to just be myself, I might get my chance.

"You can't try harder. No matter what you do, you just cannot try harder."

Those were the words of coach Jancuska, said to me as an impressionable 19-year-old. Baseball is a game that punishes those who let their mind get in the way of their body. Trying harder—forcing action and outcomes—only make a player worse. In classes with Dr. Templeton, we read the philosophy of the Samurai warriors that preached the same things. *Non-action. Wu Wei. Mind like water. Create an unfettered mind.* If we try to interfere with what we've taught our bodies to do in practice, we'll strangle ourselves. If we let fear and doubt seep into our mind, we'll be distracted and overtaken by it. The only way to stay alive as a Samurai was to have a clear, free mind that could simply react to his sword-wielding opponent. Ballplayers are the same. When we *see ball, hit ball, throw ball,* we play at our best. We need to forget consequences and just throw the stinkin' ball where we want it to go. Don't *try* to do things, just do them. Coach J watched countless young players like myself fail trying to throw a perfect game all in one inning. I vowed to stay the course and take the most important summer of my life one pitch at a time. *Don't try harder.* I resolved to just be myself. Being myself got me there and would be the only way I'd get any further.

My shoulder was painful the next day when I woke up in the Aloft hotel in Phoenix. I was almost thankful they hadn't signed me on the spot because I would have reported for my first day of work banged up. Thankfully, it was only February so I got a bit of rest and felt okay when I reported to spring training with the Ducks. A week later, however, I was having trouble just getting through a game of catch. Whatever had crept up on me at the end of the 2015 campaign was starting to look and feel more serious than I had thought. Little aches and pains went away like little aches and pains do. But for that pain to have stuck with me all winter…it was *not* good.

"Blewett—please shut off your alarm." Jack Snodgrass, my

roommate, grumpily but politely asked me to silence my obnoxious phone that wrenched us both from sleep. Jack is a free-spirited, quirky dude. A 6'6" left-handed starter, with long hair and an intense love for WWE wrestling, Jack was a typically weird lefty. He was also a deep thinker, so we had our share of late night philosophical debates. We were in New Britain, Connecticut and it was opening day, 2016. I reached for my phone, trying to be a good roommate. I nearly dropped it as a bolt of pain shot from the inside of my shoulder to the touchscreen. Not a good way to wake up. I rolled over for a few more minutes, hoping maybe I just slept on it wrong.

I stumbled over to the bathroom and brushed my teeth. There was a dull pain in my shoulder as my morning breath gave way to minty freshness. I ran the shower while I brushed, then, with toothbrush held between my back molars, stepped into the steamy downpour. I finished brushing, spitting sudsy white toothpaste carelessly onto my feet. I then put my toothbrush on the ledge of the shower as I grabbed the shampoo. From it's tiny bottle, I poured a third of it into my left palm, then screwed the cap back on and set it down. I wiped the shampoo across the top of my scalp and as I raised my right arm to meet it, another bolt of pain shot down. I was going to pitch with that arm later that night, and yet reaching for my phone and shampooing my hair caused 7 out of 10 pain. Everyone's pain scale is different and a 10 out of 10 is what—getting eaten slowly by a hyena? Who knows. But it *hurt*. And, it hurt doing stupid everyday things that had no business hurting.

I learned some tricks of the trade, one of them bagging my arm and rubbing Cramer Hot Stuff all over it. "Hot stuff" is basically petroleum jelly mixed with a high concentration of capsaicin, the substance that makes peppers hot. I'd slather on a ton of the reddish goo—the hottest of three intensity levels—then cut the bottom out of an ice bag. I'd then take the bag and pull it all the way up to my armpit, taping it at the top of my bicep. Then, I'd tape the bottom of it where it stopped in the middle of my forearm. This was essentially a mini sauna suit, forcing my arm to sweat and pull more of the capsaicin into my pores; it burned like crazy. After the game, I was careful not to get into a hot tub, a mistake I only made once. The one time the hot water hit my capsaicin-soaked skin, I snatched it right back out and looked down to see how much of my skin had melted off. God, did that burn. It did a great job, though, of both warming up my arm and masking pain.

It was a cold night in New Britain. When my name was called over the walkie talkie, I yanked off my jacket and hoodie before tearing off the bag. I got warm and ignored my arm; I had a job to do. I threw a scoreless seventh inning in an opening day victory. I couldn't shampoo my hair but I *could* throw a baseball 92 miles per hour.

I pitched four of our first six games, each with significant pain. Even though my initial results were good, inside I began to panic. I could *not* make it 134 more games like that. When you pitch with a style like mine—using velocity and brute force over location and finesse—you become very vulnerable to changes in your physical ability. The strategy and locations I used at 91-94 simply didn't produce outs while pitching at 89-92. My 94 always seemed to "play up," going by a hitter like 96 or 97. Now it was playing *down*; something was awry. Before I realized what was happening, I was getting hit and hit *a lot*. Pitches that used to get swings and misses were now getting put in play, and the poorly-located pitches I used to get away with were now getting hit hard. Although I was still able to pitch through my shoulder pain, the ball wasn't coming out the same way it used to. I was like a race car with one bad spark plug—I could still drive, just not as fast. Usually though, it would be an uncomplicated situation—I'd pitch and do therapy in the background to stay on the field. I'd eventually get through it; business as usual, right? Not this time. Things were different.

As my results on the mound got worse and worse, coming home to Meg each night got proportionally harder. I was good at compartmentalizing my life and not taking baseball home with me...or so I thought. In reality, I never had anything to compartmentalize. I didn't have a wife or kids to tend to. Meg was my first serious girlfriend during the season. She'd wake up early and head off to work as I stayed in bed to sleep off overnight bus rides and late games. When I arrived home at night, she'd already be in bed, waking up to say hello, give me a smooch and ask how the game went. Did I need to vent at 11 p.m. in our brief conversation? Did I need to vent all day on the weekends when we played at home, when I'd actually have time to spend with her before or after the game? I didn't feel like it was a good use of either of our time. I'd solve it in my head myself, just like I always had.

I was captain of a sinking ship and Meg was a passenger in first class. I'd have dinner and a dance with her when I could. I put on my best suit and an almost genuine smile when I was with her. The whole time, a huge portion of me was preoccupied with the vast amount of water pouring in below deck. 24/7, my brain was trying to find ways to patch the hulls and purge the ocean water before we sank. She was smart, though, and could tell when my mind was elsewhere. She'd politely ask if I wanted to talk about it, if she could help bring me back to the present. I'd give her a superficial version and change the subject. She didn't need to hear me complain, nor could she relate to what was happening. Everything I worked for in two decades in baseball would soon be at the bottom of the ocean. I couldn't compartmentalize; too many hulls had been breached.

I knew that if I didn't start trending in the right direction, I was going to get released. The Ducks were a winning team and didn't accept mediocrity, so sooner than later it was going to happen. When I talked to the GM on the phone in the off-season, brokering my own contract, I told him specifically: "I want to play in a place where I'm expected to pitch well and if I don't, I expect to be released." I didn't regret it one bit—it was truly how I felt, as the pressure in pro baseball helped me thrive. Camden lacked that culture. I entered a new level of focus and determination when I felt my life on the line. The fear made me better.

Meg was kind and supportive but had never dated an athlete before, certainly not one playing for her well-known hometown team. Everyone on Long Island loved the Ducks, including me. I wanted to stay there so badly. The team was winning and the clubhouse environment was terrific. The front office was filled with great people, there were few egos amongst the players and everyone got along well. The Ducks had good facilities and took care of us players, the fans were passionate, and I felt like a part of something special. I wanted to keep my relationship with Meg afloat. Most of all, I wanted my chance. I knew that if I didn't pitch well, my window would close. The Diamondbacks would need a pitcher, look me and my numbers over, then move on to the next player. I was too old for them or any other team to wait around for. It was my turn on stage. I had to be good *now*. To do that, I had to ignore my arm pain, the embarrassment I felt about my rising ERA, the thought of getting released, the uncertainty with Meg, and the fact that I was blowing my chance. I had to pitch with a clear mind. *Mind like water. Dominant and Confident. Attack. This pitch. You're here for a reason. Ride it out. It will get better. Be yourself. Don't force it. It's still just a game. It's still fun. Don't try harder. You're good at this.*

I stepped back off the rubber and tried to not look toward the dugout.

Out of the corner of my eye, I saw him. *No, no no no no. Please don't walk out here. Please let me just clean this up myself. Just one full inning—I need a full inning. Ugh.*

Our manager, Kevin Baez, called for time and began his medium-paced walk out to the mound. He signaled with his left hand to our bullpen; my night was over. I had faced three batters and allowed all three of them to reach base.

"That's it, Blew." KB extended his hand, into which I gently deposited the red and blue seamed baseball. The Atlantic League had unique baseballs with alternating threads of red and blue; they were beautiful. I walked off toward our dugout on the first base side as Jarrett Casey, one of our lefty relievers, began jogging in from right field. It was the second time in as many outings that Jarrett would come in to try and bail me out of a bases loaded situation I had created. Just a day or two earlier, he had struck out the side on my behalf, stranding all three runners; it was an incredible gift. If it wasn't 10% of my paycheck, I'd have bought him a nice steak dinner.

I'll never forget that moment, sitting in the dugout watching Jarrett fall behind 1-0, then 2-0 to one of their big hitters. Reliever code was such that we all tried our hardest to bail each other out, and Jarrett had been my knight in shining armor. I certainly didn't expect him to get out of this jam, too—the stats said that teams scored an average of 2.3 runs in a bases loaded, no one out situation. I had no illusions, nor did I deserve any more heroics. As if on cue, his 2-0 fastball cruised in and was met with a thunderous *CRACK*. I watched the baseball transform into a golf ball, then an aspirin as it rocketed into the black sky at a steep upward angle. As it crashed into the very top of the scoreboard, the loud *THUD* silenced the crowd of 5,000. The ballpark was quiet enough that a fan or two probably heard the deflating sigh I let out as my ship slipped beneath the ocean surface. I smirked, though—the grand slam was an almost comical way to mark the end of my time in a Ducks uniform, one heck of an exclamation point. *Yep. That's about right. It's officially over.* Jarrett profusely apologized, but I stopped him. He was my hero that season. "Dude. You've bailed me out over and over. Please don't apologize—you've saved me way too many times already. No one can get out of every jam."

A few hours later, I slowly opened the bedroom door and sat down on the edge of the bed next to Meg. I let out another deep breath of disappointment as she wriggled awake to greet me. I didn't want to say it, I didn't want to give my fears any power. I refused to create a self-fulfilling prophecy. But nothing I had been trying had worked. I was no healthier nor was I pitching any better. I had been working at home and in pregame on mechanical fixes to help alleviate the pain in my arm. I had paid for a pitching mechanics analysis from a biomechanics expert in California, taking video of myself in the bullpen and sending it to her. The mechanical adjustments I needed to make didn't hold up in the game. It was all but impossible trying to change the way I threw during a game while getting pro hitters out. My pitching coach wasn't supportive of it, either. "Blewett's all messed up in the head," was his sentiment as I tried, in desperation, to get healthy. Dottie, the athletic trainer, was wonderful to me, but the daily therapy and medication I received hadn't helped. I had kept it to myself until finally telling her. Daily ice baths and contrast baths calmed me down, but not my shoulder. It was too inflamed, too far gone.

A few weeks prior, I had told KB in his office that I was still capable of pitching well despite having some shoulder pain. I was intentionally vague about my condition, but wanted to make it clear I wasn't making excuses for myself. At the time, I genuinely believed my words. I wasn't walking guys nor was I falling behind in the count. I just couldn't get anyone out. I felt that perhaps my mindset was off and explained to him that I would find my old, aggressive self. Yet with that grand slam, my ERA was somewhere around 7.50 or 8.00. I'd been utterly unreliable and believed it was over. As I sat next to her, watching her sleepy blue eyes pry open, I just needed her to know. I needed to say it.

"How'd the game go?" She asked. I paused and stared at the white sheets, stained a deep blue in the darkness.

"Not well. Look, I just need to tell you." I took a deep breath.

"I'm going to get released."

We sat there in silence for a while. She looked me over as I wondered what she was thinking. I had little else to say. I didn't want to utter those words and give them power. After a long deliberation, she spoke.

"Well, what does that mean? Did they tell you that?"

"No," I said. "But tonight...it was awful. It just had to be the last straw. I'm sure it's coming soon. It has to, as badly as I've pitched."

A day later, I still had a job and we departed on a weeklong road trip. I pitched a few times and had yet another meltdown inning. I assumed the axe would come when we returned. On the last day—a Sunday day game—I pitched the final inning in a blowout win against the Southern Maryland Blue Crabs. Mom and Dad had driven down to watch, and after I finished going through the hand-slap line, I went over to the railing to talk with them. A group of little boys ran over, asking me if I'd sign their tickets, programs and baseballs.

"You know I'm on the other team, right?"

"We don't care!" They replied.

I signed all their stuff as Mom smiled. She always smiled when I signed autographs; she saw me in those little kids. I answered Dad's questions about the pitches I had thrown that got swings and misses. I answered Mom's questions about how I was feeling. I told them what I told Meg. When I had nothing left to offer, Mom just smiled. When I wasn't pitching well and didn't want to talk, she had a habit of holding a smile as she made long, lingering eye contact. It was a beam of positive energy she shined on us Blewett kids, hoping to erase our looks of disappointment like a laser did an unwanted tattoo. None of us knew it at the time, but it was my last inning, last pitch and last autograph. After I hugged them, I walked across the field to the detached clubhouse to shower and get on the bus back to Long Island. The sun was still shining, though I wasn't sure why.

The mental side of sports is complex. We hit snags and roadblocks, are tested and challenged. Sometimes, I did things that were obviously counterproductive. I wish I had shared more of my struggles when I was going through them, rather than clamming shut. But there's a tiny percentage of people who can both empathize with and truly understand the struggle. Those I was closest with—our family, Lucas, Andrew, Fred, Meg—none of you got the real story. Complaining about how hard it was to be a fawned after, privileged, successful pro athlete? There was nothing to complain about. Maybe I just didn't know how, or assumed it'd be met with blanket advice. I'd call Duff, Goose, Zach, Andy and Tim. I could vent and explain to someone who'd lived it. Those conversations were life-giving. Baseball is hard in myriad ways that often don't explain well over a cup of coffee. Players have to maintain an image, a front, a shell, a series of hulls to stay afloat. You don't talk aloud about the slump or the injuries. You don't give it power. The irony, though, is that keeping it within eventually cracks the shell from the inside out. The mental side of the game can consume a man whole, in silence, before he even realizes it.

I didn't like the way I went out. I didn't like having to leave such an amazing group of players. I didn't like that it forced Meg and I apart. I didn't like not knowing that my final pitch was my final pitch. I wanted to look around and soak it in, but I wasn't privy to what would come next. If the Baseball Gods had any logic behind their moves, it's been fuzzy, at best.

Difficult or not, I always just wanted one more game, one more inning, one more hour in my cleats. Maybe that's why the sun was shining that day in Maryland and why Mom smiled so wide. That day, like all the days before it, was the one more I wanted.

If there's a bright side, it's that you won't have to sit in 98 degree heat for three hours, waiting for me to pitch a mere half-inning in four minutes flat. To this day, I still can't understand how anyone endures daytime baseball games. We players curse the early wake up, the sun and the heat, thriving in the coolness of night. Yet, you did it without complaint. I should have repaid the favor by letting you and everyone else in. It would have been easier. The next phase, however, will be a breeze. You can send the good juju to others who need it. Though it always did the trick, I won't be requiring nearly as much.

Dear Andrew, It's the costume.

Our history as friends sure has been weird. It was a long, winding road between preschool and D-I baseball. I think the reason we ended up in the same place was because beneath our street clothes, our identity was the same. Baseball was the reason we both got out of bed. Throwing a ball was my favorite thing in the world and you grew up into a strong, capable collegiate catcher.

All of us, though, are one day forced to leave our jersey hanging with a lonely drape, in what is now someone else's locker. I remember when I turned my back on #13. As I walked out with my black gear bag flung over my shoulder, I didn't know it would be the last time. I might have lingered if I had. You took the plunge into the real world sooner than I did and I counted myself lucky to get that extra time; I didn't take it for granted. The voice in my head bullied me when I felt like giving up, sometimes guilting me into putting one foot in front of the other. After I got home from Long Island, though, my arm just wouldn't stop hurting no matter what I did. As I fought to get back on the field, the script read by the voice changed to something I'd never heard before: *It's time to retire.*

What? No. I don't want to retire. I'll get healthy again. I've got a bunch more years left and my chance is coming. This could be my tipping point—I'll get my chance if I get healthy.

No. It's different this time. It's time to retire.

The voice always gave me what I needed—*always*. Years prior, when I called you sitting beneath that tree, the voice was the last to speak with me. He made me stand back up.

Is that who you are? You're gonna just quit now? You're just like everyone else? You can't do the surgery again? Yes you can. You know you can.

It's two more years…

So what? You've got the rest of your life to be normal. Two years is nothing.

You're—you're right.

Good. Then stop pouting and be a man.

For the first time, though, I felt like what he wanted from me was wrong—it was what the weak side of me would have wanted, the side I always ignored. Quitting was the path of least resistance...wasn't it?

Why are you doing this to yourself? You're miserable. Just retire.

No. I can't do that. I'm not a quitter.

Every throw kills you.

I can keep going. My arm will be fine.

No it won't. Your arm is ruined and you know it.

No it's not. Something will work, it will heal up.

Nothing's working and you know it. Just retire. It's time.

I can't. That's not who I am. That's not who we are.

I went back and forth like this every day in the fall and winter. I *was* miserable. At the end of the summer, I got back into a men's league game and sat 88-90. I had called Goose and told him I might be ready. He told me to think about it, that I sounded hesitant. The next day, my arm blew up again and I could barely lift it above my head. After that, it never stopped hurting.

When I picked back up six weeks later, giving it rest that it desperately needed, the time in my relative youth when I could throw 90mph indoors—with no adrenaline and no one watching—was long gone. It had been normal for me to throw my preseason bullpens at 86-89, even though I threw harder in real games. This time, though, the voice was right—things were different and this rehab stint was not like the others. I exhausted myself just trying to break 80 and felt optimistic if an 82 or 83 showed up on the gun. I was working at 120% just to throw 90% as hard as I used to.

Just retire. It's killing you. You don't want to do this anymore.

I don't remember the exact day, but it was sometime in late January. Jon, my catching phenom, came in to catch me on a weeknight between lessons. Ordinarily, I'd only do my throwing before we opened. I chose to throw during our busy time because I felt if onlookers were watching, it might help me get some adrenaline and break through. I didn't want those who paid me to train their kids thinking I was no better than them. I would always rise up when eyeballs were on me.

After I threw the last pitch of my forty or so and thanked Jon for his help, I sat down on the turf mound and slumped over to collect myself. Sweat dripped off my nose; I was gassed. Jon had been catching me since he was 13, starting as a fill-in when I felt too guilty to interrupt Lucas' busy days to have him catch me. Jon had caught me throwing 89-91 in years past, something almost zero 13-year-olds could do. His dad was so proud he asked me to sign the ball, a memento of the first time Jonny caught a pitch above 90. As I sat, I wondered what he must have been thinking, watching me wilt and die in front of him. In the two years when I threw my hardest, my changeup was 85, sometimes 86 miles per hour. Here I'd just finished a bullpen where the hardest fastball I could muster was a measly 81 miles per hour.

After a few minutes, I had to get moving. I grabbed my black Rawlings mitt and my water, picking myself up to go prepare for the pitching lesson I had to give. In the batting tunnel next to me, Charlie, a 16-year-old stud pitcher, was warming up for our lesson. I watched as he effortlessly threw fastballs at 70, then 75, 78, 80, 82, 83 miles per hour. I watched the ball cruise out of his hand, the same way it used to cruise out of mine. There was no strain, just electricity and life—life that my arm didn't have anymore. I started my baseball marathon 22 years prior and had been in motion for a long time. Yet on that night, there he was—passing me with a pace I couldn't possibly match. I felt myself slow to a trot and then to a walk. He was the future. I was the past. Suddenly, the voice was back and this time I knew he was right.

You and I ran the same sprints, did the same stretches, ate the same foods, and practiced the same movements over and over until we were bored to tears. Then, we did it all over again because we wanted to perform well on game day. Green grass and future greatness got us out of bed. I remember that first morning when I no longer had baseball to look forward to. I didn't know why I woke up and what I should go do. No one prepares you for that door to suddenly be slammed shut. One day you're an athlete, the next you're not. After pounding our fists to be let back in, we finally wandered away. You just don't walk away from something you've done your whole life…you wander, lost. It took me a while to figure out where I was going, to start walking again.

In 2012, I was lacing up my cleats in the clubhouse when Brooks walked through; he was clearly in a good mood. "Put on your baseball costumes, boys! We've got a game to win!" I enjoyed his brand of humor and especially liked the costume reference—it was a funny way to refer to the jersey and pants I'd wear that night on the field. Later on, I began pondering the significance of the term. Was my uniform a costume? Was I merely an ordinary man masquerading as a ballplayer? Or, was it the other way around?

Superman wore a Clark Kent outfit—it was his way of disguising his true identity among humans. He was his real self when he wore his Superman tights and cape, not the other way around. Kent's clothes gave the appearance that he was like everyone else in the city of Metropolis. He wasn't like everyone else, though—far from it. It didn't matter if he was eating breakfast in his boxer shorts or flying faster than a speeding bullet to save someone—he was Superman 24 hours a day, 365 days a year. Anything else he wore was simply to hide who he really was.

For lifelong athletes, everything revolves around our sport. It's like the movie *Groundhog Day*—we live that same day over and over for decades (only we do so willingly). Would it really be accurate to say that our street clothes are our *real* clothes? I think for many of us, our uniform is a sweat-wicking billboard, an advertisement for our calling in life. A pair of jeans and v-neck t-shirt could never define us in the same way. For two decades I sat down at my locker, took off my costume, buttoned up my real clothes and laced up my spikes. I then grabbed my hat and mitt and walked down the tunnel to the field. My metal cleats clacked loudly on the concrete, announcing my presence to the world. When we had a bat and ball in our hands, you and I knew our place on this earth. We were most ourselves out in the sun, not inside a classroom or cubicle.

Months later as I began to turn a corner, I manufactured this idea that baseball had merely prepared me for my true calling. The life-lessons it taught were setting me up for the *real* thing, I thought. About a year later, I decided that speaking and writing were what I was meant to do. Baseball had just been a vehicle to set me out into the world with a story in hand that I could shout from the rooftops. I took solace in this mindset and believed it...for a few months. Then, I came to my senses and stopped feeling sorry for myself. Being honest is important for truly getting over something.

It's awfully convenient for us to fail at something and then declare our next exciting endeavor to be our true calling. We fall in love, break up, then meet someone new and declare him or her to be the one we had been waiting for all along. We then fail or grow tired of that one and the cycle continues. I settled on that belief because it was easy, because it was comforting. It's hard to come to terms with failing to reach the ultimate destination of a two-decade-plus journey. In the end, though, that was what happened—*that* was the truth. If baseball would have let me, I'd be happily in the Major Leagues collecting gargantuan paychecks, my mind at ease that I was born and destined to be there. No one who knows me would have given it a second thought, either— baseball has always been my thing and yours. Players don't turn down million-dollar free agent contracts to search for something bigger.

Letting go of the game is hard because we don't know what costume we'll wear next. As athletes, we're both blessed and cursed that our uniform—our true clothes—puts our soul on display. We wash that uniform after every game but it never comes off. I thought I watched that side of me die that day in the bullpen, but I was wrong—it never will, not until I'm in the ground with it. It will live on, covered up only by the uniform of whatever I choose to do next. You're a successful coach. I'm not yet sure what costume I want to wear. I think, though, that both our parents knew this all along. It was why they drove us from one field to the next and drained their bank accounts on the latest high-tech bat and glove. They knew the pinstripes were our real clothes, the rest little more than a silly costume.

Dear Andy, I let go.

A hitter pops the ball high into foul territory, watching helplessly as the third baseman coasts over and camps beneath it. Then, as the hitter starts walking back to the dugout—he's surely out—the third baseman loses it in the "high" sky. It falls to the ground, and everyone in the dugout erupts at the batter's good fortune: "Got new life! Put a charge into one!"

Life for a ballplayer comes in various forms and I felt like I was always in search of it—I struggled to sleep at night unless I knew I had another day ahead of me. If a pitcher had an ERA below 4.00, his value to the team was proven—he still had life. If a pitcher was healthy, could still throw hard and pitch whenever he was asked, he still had life. If a pitcher had a resume' long enough to ensure that some team would call him next year…he still had life. I didn't always have those things—sometimes I wasn't healthy and other times I couldn't get the job done.

In 2012, after I blew out my elbow in an Evansville Otters uniform, you took me under your wing and welcomed me unofficially to the coaching staff. I felt like I had some kind of purpose, even though I was neither a player nor an actual coach at that time. It reduced the sting, gave me a tiny shot of life. A gust of wind or high sky couldn't give me what I needed to stay on the field.

A little over a year later, you made the call that you promised you'd make and got me a tryout with Somerset. I made good and got my invite. When they cut me, I figured we were square; I wasn't about to ask for yet another favor, another call. So I sheepishly texted you just to let you know the news. There was an unspoken understanding regarding these favors—I'd ask for and accept one, maybe two. If I couldn't make it happen, that was *that*—eventually, the training wheels

250

have to come off and a player has to make it on his own. Not you. I got the feeling after that text that you'd have made ten additional calls if that was what it took. Because of that, at the end, quitting felt like the most ungrateful thing I could do. So many others gave me life and I'd just throw it away?

My final year was the hardest, probably because I was so very aware of how close I was to my lifelong goal. "I'm good, coach" still felt like the right move. Just taking the field had always worked—I always found ways to be good enough in years prior, where if I could physically pitch, I pitched well. It just didn't happen that year. I *sucked*. It was a helpless feeling as I watched my entire career crash and burn. Injuries were beyond my control, sure, but I had learned long ago how to handle them. Yet when I had the power to pitch but not pitch well...it was something I didn't know how to fix. My plane was spiraling, the engines failing, and I had no parachute. So I just watched the altimeter and waited for impact, mostly because I didn't know how to let go. It was part of who I was that I'd keep gritting it out, fixing myself, dusting off my uniform and standing back up. There was no ejector seat. As I tried to come to terms with it, I couldn't find anyone with the proper perspective. It took someone who really knew what it was like, who had been through it himself. Then one day in January, the phone rang. Goose always had impeccable timing.

In Florida, there is a seafood restaurant in St. Pete Beach called Crabby Bill's, which became the unofficial banquet hall for Goose's Gildea Raiders. With just a day or two left in the Raiders' annual Florida trip, he would bring us together at Crabby Bill's for a team dinner, with strict instructions to order anything we wanted, in whatever quantity we wanted. Guys who had been there before let the newbies know that Goose meant it—that we should eat absolutely as much as we could. I crushed about $100 worth of seafood alongside my buddies. Goose would roam around the 25-man table, tell us stories about legendary Raiders who got signed, did extraordinary things, had run-ins with police, or woke up the entire hotel with late-night craziness. He was one of the best storytellers I'd ever met, with a big belly-laugh that couldn't be ignored. Goose would throw down his Gold American Express card and laugh off the $3,000 bill. It was a spectacle, a microcosm of who he is and his larger-than-life persona.

Ten months or so after my second trip, I texted Goose in January asking what the details were for what would be my third trip with Los

Raiders. He texted me back asking me to call him a bit later. So, I did.

"Danny! What's up, my brotha?"

"Hey Goose. So what's going on? Just wanted to check in with you about Florida and Los Raiders."

"Well, unfortunately there's not going to be a trip this year. My health—I've been to the doctor a lot recently and they're just now figuring out what's wrong with me. As much as I want to be there, it's just not going to happen this year. It'll be the first time in over 20 years that the Raiders won't play in Florida."

We talked through the specifics—or lack thereof—of what was going on with him. He didn't have a lot of answers except that his beloved trip was going to be an impossibility for a while. I'd later learn that he did the same thing I was good at doing—he didn't let on how he really felt about it. Goose and I spoke a handful of times per year and I'd send him an update of how I was doing every now and again. I always assumed he had bigger fish to fry and probably already knew how I was doing anyway. He tracked all of us, keeping tabs and making calls to higher ups in the background. Goose was omnipresent at worst, omniscient at best.

As my career progressed, though, he was always there. When Lake County collapsed, Goose was my first call. When my elbow blew up a second time, he listened. In fact, he was almost dismissive of my injury and the gravity of it, a lot like the way my mom and dad would shrug off a runny nose. "Okay. Just let me know when you're ready to get back out there," he said in his booming voice. It was a huge deal but he knew I'd handle it. When the time came for me to get back into baseball, Goose put me in his passenger seat and drove me to my tryouts. When those teams cut me, he jockeyed for new ones to give me a shot. He was a part of my fight to keep going but just like his health, something in me declined over time.

Rehab and the grind of staying healthy had taken its toll in a few different ways. Back as an overly eager 19-year-old, I was excited about extracting every last drop of ability from my body. I was borderline psychotic about training, as I'm sure you knew. I gladly committed myself to *arm care*, the blanket term for the tedious but important shoulder, rotator cuff and elbow exercises that all pitchers need to both throw hard and stay healthy. Five days per week for the rest of my baseball career, I did a litany of arm care exercises, stretches and drills to help me become a better player. I never would have made it as far as I did without them. At the field, I did exercises. When the game was over, I did exercises. When I was back in my dorm or apartment, I did more exercises. I wanted to be the best and part of the agreement with the Devil was *exercises*.

In my last two years, I became aware that I was physically where I needed to be. I just needed to stay healthy and maintain the routine I had built for myself. I no longer had to keep pushing myself harder and farther in the gym. Instead, I devoted more time and energy into becoming mentally tougher, smarter and savvier. My focus shifted to pitching strategy, focus, mental conditioning, and the *details* of it all. As my work ethic was applied less to being a physical monster, and more to becoming a mentally smart and tough pitcher, I had to make sacrifices with my time. As I eclipsed the decade mark of arm care, the daily dosage of them became harder to swallow.

When the Ducks released me, I drove home and my car broke down four hours into the trip. It was a Friday afternoon, so naturally the new radiator wouldn't arrive until Monday. I could show you the repair bill, but you still might not believe me that I broke down in Somerset Pennsylvania. It wasn't *the* Somerset, but the coincidence was just… annoying. I had a lot of time to think as I spent three mind-numbing days in that middle-of-nowhere town. I couldn't make this stuff up.

I kept telling myself I would get healthy again, but a few weeks later I could tell I wasn't putting in the same effort that my younger self would have. Signs were right in front of me, impossible to ignore. I hung on and kept grinding out tedious rehab and strength training workouts, along with my painful throwing workouts. Running? UGH.

I still wanted to play—I had things to accomplish and was closer than ever, if I could reclaim my place in line. The goal was to get re-signed either before that season ended or the following year. What if I got healthy and had the best year of my career? It was certainly possible—I'd done that after my surgeries twice before. Yet, as the shoulder pain refused to subside and I gave up on a 2016 comeback, the cold of winter strangled me. In January of 2017, I ground to a halt. I hated what I was doing—every single facet of it. I was in constant pain. I hated lifting, I hated stretching and I hated those goddamned shoulder exercises that I'd done for hours each week for more than a decade. Throwing—the thing I loved the most since I played ball in my backyard—was *miserable*. I hated all of it. Yet I also wouldn't, couldn't say that out loud.

My story had a fairytale ending…didn't it? I still believed it did, but I was so burned out, so tired of being in pain. The voice in my head that urged me to retire wasn't wrong. I was breaking down. My shoulder hurt with every throw, and the pain was not only shooting down my arm, but also affecting how the ball came out of my hand. It was...*different*. I didn't want to do the rehab. I didn't want to lift those stupid weights anymore. I didn't want run and stretch or do any of it. I was out of gas. The burden of preparation—this big weight all high-performers carry on their shoulders—had caught up with me.

Then, my iPhone buzzed. Goose had sent out a group text, asking what a few of us guys were up to. I thought for a minute about what my response would be, but decided there was no way I could send some cryptic, vague text without him immediately calling me to sort it out. Not wanting to lie or explain myself over text message, I called him.

"Hey Goose."

"Danny! What's up, my brotha?" It was his signature greeting.

"Not much. I got your text."

"Yeah, yeah. Pete [a scout friend of his] is looking for guys who need a spring training job, so we've been seeing where everyone is at. How you doin'? You healthy?"

I didn't want to lie to Goose. But, I thought if I lied and ended up getting healthy before anyone knew the difference, then telling him I was healthy would ultimately prove to be the truth, right? That was how I operated sometimes—I'd do the right things to heal up while I kept quiet about it, then when I got healthy no one would ever know I *hadn't* been healthy. It was kind of like when someone asks if you're lost—as long as you find your way back, no one cares how you got there. I was tired of that, and lying to go into a game was different than lying now.

"I'm not great," I said. "My arm hasn't been responding well."

As I thought carefully about what would be next out of my mouth, I felt the words get sticky in my throat. I paused, trying to figure out what I was going to stay next. He picked up on my distress right away.

"Take your time," he said.

"I believe I can get healthy. My voice cracked a little. "But..." My lower lip started to tremble as I paused again.

"But, I just don't want to. I don't want to put in the work."

I was so ashamed. My eyes welled up. I stared down at the dark oak table in the office of my baseball academy. I had to pull it together, as I was meeting Lucas in a few minutes to interview a potential new employee. I walked out and ascended the stairs to our loft area where we stored old equipment, team uniforms, dust bunnies and miscellaneous junk.

"It's just...I just can't quit," I said. "But I want to. I just don't know what to do, because I'm not the guy who quits. It wasn't supposed to end this way. I was going to be *that guy* who stuck it out and made it." I started sobbing.

"And that can't happen if I quit. But I just can't do it—I don't want to do this anymore." Goose stepped in and did what Goose did best: *he talked*.

"Danny, if you were a quitter, you would have done it years ago, back when people counted you out. You got hurt and didn't complain; you just silently did the work. You kept going. They counted you out years ago. *Years ago*...and look how far you made it! I've known quitters, and you're the farthest thing from it. This day just comes for everyone. And the reality is, if you were going to make it, you'd have made it by now. You're what now, 29?"

I was 31, which was about 60 in baseball years. Literally *everyone* assumed I was two years younger than I was. I choked out a laugh as I corrected him—it was only fitting that I'd sneak one last correction in. He continued.

"Even more so. At 31, if it was going to happen, it already would have happened. They're going to take the younger guys, the guys who aren't as banged up." I nodded.

"But I could have been *that* one guy, that guy who hangs on and gets his chance."

"You're right," Goose said. "Maybe you could have if you were lucky enough, if someone who really liked you just needed a guy to fill in. But there's more to it than just performance—you know that. I hung around 'til I was almost a decade older than you, so I know how it is."

"But," he continued, "I don't think your tears right now are tears of sadness or regret. They sound to me like tears of joy. I think you're ready—you sound ready. It's going to feel—for a long time—like someone ripped your heart out. That's how I felt for a longgggggg time when I retired. You have to let it hurt, you have to *feel it*. You have to embrace the heartbreak because it's a reminder of how great the game is. You won't get over it for a while, but you can't ignore it. No, I can definitely tell you those are tears of joy. You got what you needed out of the game, you did everything you could and this day comes for everyone. It came for me just like it's now coming for you."

That was it. I gulped, knowing he was right.

"Danny, you know why I took your call all those years ago? Why I invited you to Florida? Hundreds of guys called me hoping to play with the Raiders. But when you called, I asked around. People told me about you, about your desire to keep playing. It was no coincidence that I chose you. I played the game the same way you did and I felt the same way when I finally let go. You and I are kindred spirits."

I thanked him, took a deep breath, wiped my eyes and hung up. A few minutes later Goose sent me a text. It contained a short message to keep my chin up along with the following poem:

The Men That Don't Fit In
  By Robert W. Service

There's a race of men that don't fit in,
    A race that can't stay still;
  So they break the hearts of kith and kin,
    And they roam the world at will.
  They range the field and they rove the flood,
    And they climb the mountain's crest;
  Theirs is the curse of the gypsy blood,
    And they don't know how to rest.

If they just went straight they might go far;
    They are strong and brave and true;
  But they're always tired of the things that are,
    And they want the strange and new.
  They say: "Could I find my proper groove,
    What a deep mark I would make!"
  So they chop and change, and each fresh move
    Is only a fresh mistake.

And each forgets, as he strips and runs
    With a brilliant, fitful pace,
  It's the steady, quiet, plodding ones
    Who win in the lifelong race.
  And each forgets that his youth has fled,
    Forgets that his prime is past,
  Till he stands one day, with a hope that's dead,
    In the glare of the truth at last.
                    * * *

He has failed, he has failed; he has missed his chance;
  He has just done things by half.
Life's been a jolly good joke on him,
  And now is the time to laugh.
Ha, ha! He is one of the Legion Lost;
  He was never meant to win;
He's a rolling stone, and it's bred in the bone;
  He's a man who won't fit in.

I walked back downstairs to find Lucas and Lindsey—our potential new hire—chatting in the office. There was no way I'd be able to hide my crying eyes, so I said *screw it* and owned it. I sat down and half-explained that I'd just had an emotional phone call. Lucas caught me up on what had been discussed:

"I was just telling Lindsey what our open hours might potentially be this summer, and how things might work." He turned to Lindsey: "If Dan's away again playing, I'll be doing lessons and coaching, which means we need to balance the schedule so we don't have to close when I'm out coaching my team." He then stopped and looked at me: "Anything to add?"

"Well," I took a deep breath.

"I'm retiring."

Baseball was *heavy*. The longer I played, the harder it got and the heavier it became. I left that office lighter, though not precisely feeling free. Though I'd certainly miss it, I knew that I didn't need to play more baseball. All of what I'd bottled up and piled on my shoulders I now had to release; I wasn't going to carry it any longer. It seeped out for the next year in various forms—I teared up at random times, in random places. It was a slow process of purging a lot of hard times and grieving a major part of me that had passed away. We all make life transitions, and we all make them in our own unique way. I felt embarrassed that I was taking it so hard, sniffling about my deceased baseball career; it was *not* what tough guys did. Other players I knew walked away with a clean break and it didn't mean they loved the game any less than I did. Others still didn't talk about how they truly felt and I admittedly gave the same abbreviated, surface version to anyone who asked how it was going. The way I experienced the game and the way I internalized the struggle was unique to me. I listened to Goose's advice: *Let it hurt. You have to feel it.*

He helped me understand that the word "quitter" is not easily defined—it requires context, requires backstory. Though we might want to, it eventually gets too dark outside for even the best of us to keep playing in the backyard. For me, it was time—I just needed to come to terms with it. It was almost a blessing that my shoulder continued to hurt for the next year, sending a jolt of pain every time I threw on my backpack, opened a car door or pulled a hoodie over my head. It reminded me that I didn't go willingly. Feeling healthy would have been hard.

Andy, keep going—keep managing, keep enjoying the game. There will be other guys like me who need your help and there are enough men who fit the 9-5 world. I was thankful for the honorary role as coach, for the calls you made to get me those final three seasons and for the times you let me vent. "If anyone can do it, it's you," you always said. It kept me moving and gave me new life.

Dear Mom and Dad, I grew up.

As I was thinking about how I would start this letter and in it what I would write, I came to a realization: what started in Maryland, ended in Maryland. Thank you for being there on that tired day in June, watching me throw what none of us expected was my final inning, my final strikeout, my final pitch.

Because of you, I only ever played for *me*. Looking back from age 31, I've come to realize how much of a gift that was. Other parents push their kids down that road as they begrudgingly drag their feet. Those parents find fault and make it more than it is—a game. You told me that I did well even when I knew I didn't, and that you loved and were proud of me. You both were always in the bleachers, cheering and urging me on. Those were the things that allowed me to ignore the real pain that I dealt with on an almost daily basis.

At age fifteen and beyond, throwing with pain became my norm. With no antidote and no one to blame, I endured it without complaint. Throwing a ball pain-free was a luxury, one that I appreciated because of its scarcity. Long-tossing with Dad over at John Carroll High School was where I developed my love for throwing. I'd air it out, the ball gaining altitude out of my hand, cruising up toward the forest in the background. My throws would reach their apex five or ten feet above the canopy of trees 400 feet away. One day, I hoped to see the ball disappear into them. At 14 years old, I knew it was impossible yet threw as if it wasn't. After 250 feet or so, Dad had to get it back to me with a fungo bat. As I gained arm strength, even his batted balls took two, three or four hops before I collected them in my mitt and reloaded my cannon. Though it slowed down our game of long-toss, we were both content to take our time. There was nothing either of us would rather do.

A gentle yet powerful stretch flowed through my biceps and down my arm, culminating in a distinct sensation when all the speed and power at once reached the two finger pads last in contact with that little white ball. That feeling—when a ball left my fingertips just right —is my time machine. When I close my eyes, it places me right back on that muddy field with Dad, in the backyard with Kevin, in the outfield about to gun down a tagging runner at the plate, and in Camden about to end a threat with a hard, letter-high fastball. Whether I was throwing 64 or 94, that feeling was the same.

It's not up to me to declare who I am as a person—my actions and words speak for me. Yet who I was as a pitcher is not readily apparent to most. As I explained to Keller, reaching my potential wasn't possible until I truly understood myself. It took 28 years to figure that out but when I did, it was as if I pulled the emergency brake on the game; everything slowed down. My action was non-action. I no longer forced triangle-shaped pegs into star-shaped holes. I'd like to tell you who I found that I was, who your son grew up to be:

I was not a finesse pitcher. If I tried to slow down, be precise and hit my spots, I got laughed off the mound. I had to pitch with my foot on the gas pedal at all times to even have a chance. My strength was pitching inside to righties and away from lefties. My fastball appeared to both rise and speed up on hitters, so I thrived pitching up in the zone and was not a ground ball pitcher. If I listened to traditional wisdom and stayed at the kneecaps or stayed away from righties, I'd find myself walking off the mound early, shaking my head. Everyone gives well-meaning advice, but what's food to some is poison to others.

I could finish hitters off with my curveball or changeup, but I used them mostly to get contact in the middle of an at-bat or a ground ball when I really needed one. When I needed a strikeout, I used the rising appearance of my fastball to my advantage—I could always win at the letters. I challenged hitters early, pitched inside and finished them off upstairs. If I was aggressive and unafraid, I could really pitch. If I thought too much, eased up or tried too hard, I struggled. It seems too simple to have taken me so long to figure it out, but the learning process, the growing process…they were both long. After all those years and all that digging, there I was. Two decades since I began, I'm now moving on, about to find out what costume I'll wear next.

As I look back on this slow forging process, most of my memories are of those who shaped me. Countless people pushed me forward, helping me get a lot more than I deserved. I remained a kid into my thirties and that was what made it such a complicated, difficult process moving on. It was as if I was plucked from a remote village and dropped in the middle of New York City. Where would my place be in this new world? How did it all work? Many ballplayers feel depressed, anxious, and scared when they retire, as their sport is all they know. I didn't want to voluntarily lay what was the largest part of me to rest. I didn't want to grow up. To do that, I needed someone with the right experience, the right perspective, to help me understand that it was okay to let go.

"They counted you out years ago. Years ago. And look how far you made it."

Goose could empathize with how I felt letting go—he'd been through it all himself. As I got choked up I told him that I, if anyone, was the person who just didn't give up. That was who I was, who I am. I started to cry, explaining that I just didn't want to do the work anymore, that for the last nine months, my shoulder hurt on almost every throw. Something I loved so much, I had come to hate. I felt so ashamed to say those words. They felt so wrong coming out of me.

He reminded me that I didn't give up underneath that tree in 2012, when everyone else would have, and that I built a business at the same time, giving 100% to myself, to Lucas and to each kid who came through our door. Under that tree, I got up, ran down the road and committed myself to a second Tommy John surgery. I endured another 18 horrible months away from the game, just to gain these past three years. It was worth it.

Yet at some point, we draw the line, and it was clear to me—no matter how much I tried to will myself to keep going—that my body could no longer do it. Each day in these last nine months, I felt more and more that the herd was thundering on too far for me to catch up.

We shared some good times.

You watched as the second pitch I threw in pro ball got turned around, careening off my leg. I got the out and you cheered. I wasn't a hockey goalie nor was I blocking a punt, but you clapped anyway, as if corralling that line drive with my leg was my intention all along.

You watched as I established myself later that summer with a string of great starts.

You watched as I dominated St. Paul in front of a packed house, providing myself with the first deep breath I'd taken in over a month.

You watched as I had my big moment, mowing down two hitters in front of two dozen scouts up in Connecticut. Our family name was on that All-Star jersey.

You watched me run around the bases as a little kid and finish games as grown man.

Goose told me that I was ready, that my sobs through the phone were joy, not sadness. I sure don't feel that way right now. Right now, it feels like my heart is being ripped out. I know that he's right, that it's not sadness. It's just all the years of bottled strife, sweat, and sorrow purging as I realize that it's now over. I walked off the field two nights in a row in 2015, having given up the winning run. Getting walked-off two nights in a row is almost a privilege, that someone trusts you to be out there in tie games in the ninth on the road. Yet, I was terrified that I might get a loss on a third day in a row. I jogged out there in a lot of hard situations and somehow got through them. Fans don't realize how often a player walks the plank on his way to the mound. The game face covers up the fear of the sharks circling below.

Too many times, I made peace with my career in the bullpen before entering the game. My first response was *please, just let me get through this.*. Then, knowing I was going out there no matter what, I followed it with, *if this is it, you throw every pitch as hard as you can and you go down swinging.* A few of those times, I walked off the mound not knowing when or if I'd return. Other times, I took an extra deep breath as I escaped unscathed, at least until tomorrow. No kid should have to do that even once. I did it seemingly every other year.

My elbow gave me everything he had. Two partial tears, years of tendinitis, and two full tears that put me under the knife. I never cursed him, yet he never complained. He and I were in this together. I remember looking down on him in 2012, and even though he couldn't nod back, I knew; we'd do this again, together. More than any other body part, I put him through the wringer. The scars are in many ways my trophy. I always assumed I would have finally walked off the mound with an elbow injury. Rather, I think it makes sense that after all I put my elbow through, he held his ground at the end. I finally have one successful surgery.

I don't know what the next chapter of my life holds. I hope I can somehow inspire a few kids who have already been counted out—maybe they'll reach their potential. I think I reached mine, even if it wasn't the fairytale ending I wanted. At my best, I believe I was good enough to have gotten Major League hitters out. Yet, it takes more than that to get on that golden escalator, and climbing up the side didn't quite work.

I love you both so much. Thank you doesn't say enough. These twenty-two years playing baseball, they were made possible and made great because of you.

Dear Alexis, It wasn't fair

I watched you grow up from this gangly, smiley, not-so-little girl, into a big-time D-I collegiate volleyball player. It wasn't surprising where you ended up, because I knew where you began. I was your strength coach and you were a nearly 6-foot eighth grader with more potential than anyone I'd ever met. From day one in my small, lackluster facility, you put in the work.

The confluence of talent and work ethic is a beautiful thing. The trendy saying goes: *Hard work beats talent when talent doesn't work hard.* You had the talent and despite an intense volleyball schedule that took you all over the country, you never missed a workout. No one would have denied that a little rest would have done you good, that you could have slowed down and taken a little more time to be a kid. But you didn't. Your goals were too big. And when you inked a full-ride scholarship a few years later, it all made sense. When talent works hard, no one beats *her*.

Our goals for you changed when you signed that letter of intent. We tried to manage your body and your health, while still pushing to prep you for the next level. You no longer had to chase college recruiters or championship trophies. You simply had to arrive on campus in one piece. Considering all you had accomplished before even getting your driver's license, that didn't seem like much of a task.

I still have a flashbulb memory of that grainy smartphone video. You went up and routinely smashed another thunderbolt into your opponent's court. On the way up, it was business as usual. But on the way down, your foot—which had made that landing a thousand times —rolled inward. Your knee followed and in a flash, the rest of you was in a heap on the ground. I didn't have to ask what the prognosis was— when knees cave in like that, the surgeon goes in to pick up the pieces.

It was a mess, and though ACL reconstruction is a common knee surgery nowadays, nothing is ever certain.

But you showed up in my facility a short time later, like you always did, ready to get back to work. You'd soar to at least your previous heights and rebuild a better you. What Lex always did, Lex was again going to do. It wasn't as easy, though, as we assumed it would be. We got you back to jumping 10 feet, but over time, pain cropped up and then insidiously grew. When the doctor went in for a second operation —this time to repair your meniscus—the outlook was a breeze by comparison. "In six-weeks, I'll be good as new!" I believed you. And for a short time, you were right.

Half a year later, back to smashing volleyballs at terrifying speeds toward your opponents, your shoulder decided it was her turn. "The doctors said it's just rotator cuff inflammation. Rehab, some anti-inflammatories, and I'll be back on the court in no time!" Your boat had sprung a new leak just as we finished patching the old one; a pattern was emerging. Meanwhile, girls who didn't put in half the work were running around, happily digging, diving and spiking. It wasn't fair but I never heard a peep about unfairness out of you.

The fastest sprinter is often the first to pull a hamstring. The hardest thrower is the first to blow out his arm. You jumped higher and hit harder than everyone else. "She's just so strong that she's able to put more force through her joints, and keep going longer than others. Her strengths are almost—in a sense—keeping her down." As your doctor explained this to me, I realized that your problem perhaps had no solution. Race cars don't last 100,000 miles; rather, their engines blow up. But you went off to college just the same, determined to make your parents even more proud. The work ethic, the passion for the game— none of that wavered. A few years later, however, when you were just a college sophomore, the news got to me through the grapevine. I shot you a message: "Hey. I've heard rumors...can I call you?" You responded that you needed a few minutes, I think you were in study hall at the time.

It was a cold December day as I sat on the couch in my apartment, skimming through Twitter as I waited for the go-ahead to call you. I had been ruminating on my own career struggles, fighting on a daily basis with an aggressive voice in my head that was telling me it was time to retire. I had just turned 31 that offseason and the battle with that voice was crushing me. I was so engrossed in that mental fight— so focused on myself—that I lost sight of the bigger picture. If a baseball player started playing at age 8, his maximum shelf-life (with only a handful of exceptions in the history of baseball) was about 32 years. Almost no one could stick in pro baseball past age 40. I had gotten 22 years, about 67% of the maximum. Kids who loved the game as much—or more—than I did were cut from their freshman teams, varsity teams, or weren't recruited to play college baseball. Even fewer were good enough to sign professionally. And if they did make it through fifteen years of amateur baseball and turned pro, most guys were forced into retirement by 25 or 26. I made it into my 30s.

When I got you on the phone, you explained how your knee had continued to give you problems. The nagging injuries weren't huge ones, but there were lots of little ones. Your knee was just never *right*—always hurting as your meniscus continuing to degrade. "The doctors said they don't want to operate on my knee again. They also said that continuing to play would jeopardize my ability to walk for the rest of my life. I'd end up needing a knee replacement in a few years. They want me to give up volleyball and I think I have to."

Here you were being forced into retirement at 20 years old. At age 31, my inability to let go seemed, well, *selfish*. If anyone had the right to grieve a career cut short, it was you. Who was I—with an additional decade under my belt—to talk about how hard it was? Others got a lot less than I did. I had picked nearly every apple off that tree…and I was going to sulk because I couldn't get the last one, still hanging from the highest branch? How entitled was I? There you were, handling it like a champ while I was silently torn apart.

Perspective and context. Perspective and context. *Everything* that we hope to understand requires both perspective and context. I knew my context—what I'd been through wasn't typical—but my perspective needed adjustment. That conversation with you reminded me how much I had gotten and that I needed to be a lot more thankful for it. We can lose sight of the world around us when we're too inwardly focused. It was hard letting go because of all the work I put in and the relentless setbacks. But that was no different for you, and I didn't have half the resolve you possessed at age 14. I spent my childhood being a kid. And when I think about it that way, you turned pro a long time before I did. And that's probably why you later revealed that you were somewhat ready to walk away.

I began feeling burned out for the first time in 2015 as my elbow began hurting again. The grind through my second elbow surgery took a lot out of me. It was extremely involved and detailed, giving me the best chance at coming back again. The odds were not in my favor, so I had to give it my all and I did. But I think I started running out of gas after that, in part because I burned most of it up that second go-round on the operating table. I had built the physique of a grown man that no longer required as much attention in the weight room. I knew for a fact that I didn't have to push as hard, or train as intensely to be my best self on the field. Hard training also bothered my elbow and shoulder, so I had to adapt what I could and couldn't do. I also had so much going on with the academy that I felt mentally cluttered and distracted, especially when trying to choke down workouts that I knew weren't as important as they used to be. I knew what I had to do to be my best self, and I wanted not one extra drop beyond what I needed. In many ways, this is the right way to look at training—we want the optimal dose, exactly what we need and nothing more. But it can also be demotivating, as the slope gets slippery as we pare away layer after layer, to figure out what the bare essentials really look like. One only discovers the minimum effective dose when it's lowered so much that it stops working.

I was disappointed to hear that you felt so burned out at the end, that the love you had for volleyball had all but dried up. You were a victim of circumstance and your own can-do attitude, gladly signing up for every challenge because you wanted to be great. You piled on more and more until one day the weight crushed you. It was your choice, but you just didn't know that all of it would slowly steal your joy. Baseball was just a game to me for a lot longer than volleyball was for you. It wasn't fair that you had to walk away from the game so young. It was even less fair that it beat you down so much that walking away was for the best. The word *sport* comes from the Latin *des-porto*, which means "to carry away." Sports are literally meant to carry us away from our troubles, not cause them. If we make our sport our job, we destroy its true purpose.

Shame. I felt shame in not wanting to work as hard as I approached the end. But it was how I truly felt—I didn't love the endless tedium of the daily grind. I wanted to not be in constant pain anymore. And at the very end, the mountain of work I had to climb just to *maybe* get my shoulder healthy and *maybe* pitch as well as I used to...it was impossibly high. I had created and ascended my personal mountains so many times that when I saw that last one, every fiber in my body just said *no*. But who *was* this version of me who said no to that climb? I didn't know him. I'm sure you didn't know the version of you, either.

I struggled to make sense of it. In the end, we both had to choose happiness, pick ourselves up and carry ourselves away from what had devolved into too much suffering.

Even when I was healthy and doing what I loved—pitching in front of a few thousand people—there was still an inconvenient truth: baseball was the most fun in the backyard, with a stick for a bat and a rolled up, taped up sock as a ball—it was *pure*. Though I cherished my first uniform, first glove and every shiny, high-tech bat my parents bought for me, it wasn't the same game when organized and officiated by grown men in black masks. The love we athletes have for our sport is, to say the least, complex. It grows and matures with time and we leave the honeymoon phase just like a marriage. It becomes *work* and even when we put in that work, it often doesn't love us back. I've learned that with time, even the most tarnished parts of the story get their shine back. Lex, I've always been proud of you. You left it all out on the court, something few people can say. And even though it ended too soon and for the wrong reasons, I'll keep my fingers crossed that you look back with fondness at the hard times in your story. They built you into a tough, resilient person. You'll keep working on a new passion, I'm sure, with your brightest days still to come.

Dear Emily, I was here.

It wasn't that I didn't want or try to open up. It wasn't my intention to keep it to myself, to glaze things over and suffer in silence. I just didn't know where to start, why I felt the way I did and what would help it. Telling baseball stories? That wasn't what I needed but it was also all that I had. I didn't know what my story was but I did know that I had to sift through a lot of wreckage to find it.

You understood better than anyone—even when I was on the couch next to you, sometimes I was there and other times I was not. The need to create, to do more and be more—it mentally removes me from a room. The gears in my head turn at a deafening volume and it's not clear what grinds them to a halt. Yet, if I hadn't been utterly present, compartmentalizing and living moment to moment, I wouldn't have made it through any of this. Looking into the distance usually meant I'd have to count weeks, months or years spent on the bench. Because of my arm, I missed almost five combined seasons. Being present kept me sane and kept me focused on what I could control. Little, I learned. I could control little.

Did I refuse help? Did I make all of this harder than it needed to be? Did I wall myself off? I don't know. Things I can't say, I write. Things I can't write...I don't know where they go. As you sat, staring into the blank eyes of your boyfriend, wondering where I was, I can tell you now with certainty: I was *here*.

I was on the mound in Farmingdale, looking into the blackness of night, hoping what I assumed was coming next, wouldn't. I was on the bus in Gary, desperate to jump out and walk home. I was sitting, watching from the bench as my first All-Star game passed me by. I was thinking of my brother, wishing we were on speaking terms so I could tell him about a good game I had. I was in a lot of dark places, examining and arranging the pieces, trying to figure out how I could wash myself clean of them.

Yet, I was also punching out a hitter on a high fastball before gazing out at the blue Ben Franklin Bridge, waiting for my infielders to finish tossing the ball around. I was listening to *A Hard Rain's A-Gonna Fall* by Bob Dylan on the bus at four in the morning. I was listening to Annie say "Holy Buckets you were great!" as I hugged her after a game. I was posing for the team photographer in my uniform, feeling like somebody important. I was eating a sundae from the Franklin Fountain on the street corner one sunny off-day in Philadelphia. I was trying to muffle my laughter in the bullpen, so that it still looked like we were paying attention to the game. I was in Maui, sipping coffee in the dugout between innings as I stared with sleepy eyes out at the ocean. I was taking pitcher's BP after we threw a shutout. And I was walking through the hand slap line after I recorded the final out of a game.

I'm sorry I wasn't there; I tried to be. In the depths of where I was, I couldn't bring anyone along—not yet, not until now. I was trapped—I was here.

Dear Baseball Gods, I'm ready.

I've come to learn that whenever we experience a big life change, there's never a point when we're truly ready for it. We scratch, we claw, we delay and we bargain our way to obtain a little more time. Just one more day. Just five more minutes. Though I will admit that I'm not ready at this moment, I'd concede that I'm prepared. Being an athlete prepares you to improvise. Anything can happen in a game and so I think that *prepared* is the best we can hope for when the book of life decides it's time for the next page. As I look back on how I got here, I realize that I'm really just the product of my mentors. Each one held the lantern, explained the map and gave me provisions when I lost my way. Making it as far as I did would have been utterly impossible otherwise. It wasn't just coaches and father figures guiding me—it was my peers, too. As I struggled to move on from the game, I was picked up yet again by an unlikely hero of mine—a teammate who, at first, I couldn't stand.

As I scanned the room, my eyes stopped on Sean, his head bobbing to the beat that streamed through his headphones. We were surrounded by beautiful people in headphones, dancing in a completely silent room. LED lights traced the earpieces, marking each person with color that changed from neon green, to blue, to red. The walls were lined with old hardcover and leather-bound books, the furniture in front of us made of dark wood and leather. I smiled. It was Vegas, after all. Why *wouldn't* such an astonishing nightclub have a silent disco room, aptly named *The Library*? At that moment, I realized that being there with Sean…I was in the right place at the right time.

Sean Gleason was drafted by the Orioles in the 20th round in 2007, pitching seven seasons in their minor league system before being let

271

go. After his release, he played a few seasons in Mexico before becoming my teammate in Camden in 2015. At first, Sean and I were not on good terms. I kept to myself and preferred a relatively calm clubhouse. Though music flowing out of the sound system was a constant, there was typically a lull period after BP where the clubhouse had a relaxed vibe—the calm before the storm. But when Sean arrived…all of that changed—he was *loud*. Every day I'd walk in to find Sean cranking the music to 11, *(are we in a nightclub?)* dominating conversations *(does he ever shut up?)* and generally being the center of attention *(is every day the Sean show?)*.

I vented to Zach, who had played with him in the Orioles organization.

"Give Gleas a chance." He urged. "You have to try and go deeper with him. He's kind of crazy, but I promise you, it's a good crazy if you put in some effort to see him for who he really is."

I always trusted his opinion when it came to his personality assessments, so I begrudgingly tried to lighten up on my internal criticism of Sean. Zach watched, analyzed and took his time before deliberately drawing any final conclusions on a person. He wanted to be completely sure before making a final determination on whether or not he liked or trusted someone. Yet, as we stood in the outfield, chatting during BP, Zach struggled to convey to me who Sean really was beneath the loud, abrasive exterior.

"Dude. His personality is…it's without explanation sometimes. But in a good way."

"What do you mean by that?" I asked.

"You just can't sum Gleas up by any standard word or description. He's crazy, but crazy doesn't do it. He's loud, but lots of people are loud. He's unique but he's way beyond that. The best I can think of…is *madman*. He's a madman…but in the best possible way." I tilted my head sideways, raising an eyebrow.

"I still have no idea what you mean."

"I—I know, I know. That's my point. You just won't understand until you give him a chance and really get to know him. And you should—because Gleas is one of those guys who if he cares about you, he would literally take a bullet for you. He's one of the most loyal people I've ever met and he's a good teammate."

Loyal? Good teammate? I wasn't so sure. *Madman* was definitely about as close as one could come to a single, unifying adjective. Sean was completely and utterly unfiltered, saying bold, brazen and often out-of-line things. He'd rather talk to—and get rejected by—every woman in the room rather than sit idly in the corner. "Swing for the fences." Going out with him, you had to prepare to calm other patrons down if he offended a girl or pissed someone off. He didn't look for trouble, but just like my initial assessment of him, it was easy to be irritated with his behavior. At the end of a night out on the town with Sean, you'd drive home shaking your head and laughing aloud at what went down.

Physically, Sean was built like bulldozer at 5'11" and 215lbs; he would have fit right in as a linebacker or a Viking swinging a battle axe. In his prime as a relief pitcher, he threw as hard as 98mph and pitched with an aggressive attack-mindset. He was a savage in the weight room and loved to work out. In essence, Sean is a guy who lives life *hard*. He threw hard, trained hard, and partied hard on the rare occasions he went out. But as his layers peeled away, I found a great teammate beneath. Sean was the first guy in line to build you up when you were down.

In a world where you compete with your teammates for victories but against them for promotions, players tend not to pick each other up as fervently as they might under other circumstances. Every player wanted to win while also being acutely aware that if a teammate outperformed him, it would jeopardize his chance of being signed away and promoted. Not Sean. If he sensed you were down, he held nothing back picking you up. He didn't care if picking you up meant you'd be more capable of outperforming him.

One of our first conversations was in center field while shagging BP. It was spring training and I had thrown well in intrasquad. I wasn't a fan of Sean at this point, but he sought me out in the outfield just to let me know what he thought of my first outing:

"Dude, you were out there throwing FUEL! Our hitters couldn't touch you. And you've got that hammer curveball, man! You're stuff is *good*. How have you not played in affiliated ball before? You've definitely got the tools. You're gonna be out of here quick if you pitch like that once we get going."

I was floored. It was *not* normal to be talked to like that. In past years, once I had gotten close with teammates, they'd open up and sometimes say similar things, that I deserved a chance and was good enough to earn one. But no one was eager to give praise to strange new teammates, especially not an outpouring of it. Yet when I wasn't pitching well in the middle of that season, he was constantly in my ear, drowning out any doubt I had.

"Blewett. You gotta say screw it—ups and downs happen. Just keep doing your thing—no one can touch you! You throw those parmesan pellets in there! Guys have no chance!" I couldn't not laugh when he'd say stuff like that to me. He'd pepper in signature Seanisms like "parmesan pellets," a combination of slang terms—"throwing cheese" and "throwing BBs"—that basically just meant that I was throwing hard. He'd mix those in with genuine praise and affirmation. "You were making those guys look STUPID! That hammer—your curveball is nasty, Blewett. I wish I had your curveball." I heard a new rave review of my pitching ability on a weekly basis. The guy I had been rolling my eyes at was boosting me up without any ulterior motive whatsoever. He just wanted to tell me that he thought I was good. *Note to self: I need to stop hating Sean and start being nice to him.*

Zach was right about his big heart, too. I saw it when he struggled that season in Camden. He carried our team as a starting pitcher in the first half, but got tired and was hit hard for the better part of July. His ERA ballooned and he was hurting; you could read it on his face. When I'd talk to him about it, though, he never once lamented about his unsightly statistics. Rather, his disappointment and frustration was all about letting down everyone else.

"I just want to help the team. I've been going out there and we lose when I pitch; it sucks. I don't care about my stats—I know they're bad. I just want to help our bullpen get some rest and start winning games again." In a game that was all about stats, all about the statistical plaque that held the key to each of our futures, Sean was an old-school team player. He wanted to win, he wanted to help his teammates out, and he wanted loud, celebration music playing in the clubhouse after the game. It was sort of an unspoken rule that when a team lost, it would be silent and sullen in the clubhouse. To play loud music was to act like the loss didn't matter. In reality, we were all professionals and didn't have to sit in silence every time we lost. But nonetheless, the silent clubhouse was a *thing*, and no one wanted to rock out more than Sean.

I visited Las Vegas in 2017 as a getaway. I was not handling my decision to retire very well and needed new scenery to clear my head. I flew out to Vegas in March, just two months after the call with Goose, to write and make sense of things. I felt isolated in my Central Illinois home. I had no one there who could empathize with my struggle letting go of baseball. I felt I had to write it all down and needed space to do it. I'd be able to move on once I told my story, I thought. Until then, the physical and emotional toll, bottled up at different points of my journey, would continue to be trapped inside.

I chose Vegas for two reasons: First, I wanted to play poker to see if I liked it as a new competitive and intellectual hobby. Second, I loved the people-watching and energy Vegas could provide. I wasn't looking to do crazy things, but I didn't want to be locked in a dark place feeling sad, either. I wanted to be out, in the sun, around people in a hustling, bustling, energetic vibe. Writing always helped me make sense of things and being around people helped remind me that life would go on.

I knew Sean lived in Vegas, but I didn't plan on texting him once I arrived. It was a solo trip and I intended to keep it that way—I just wanted to write and think in peace. After a day in Vegas, however, I decided I'd dial him up; it might be good to reminisce, I thought. A Colorado native, he had lived in Vegas because of his ex-girlfriend. Upon making the call, I was greeted with a barrage of clarifications:

"Do you want to go to dinner? Get drinks? Go clubbing? A show? Gambling? Women? What do you want to do? We can do anything you want; just name it."

"Well I need to eat, so let's start with dinner. No shows; no clubs; I have a girlfriend at home so no women, and I don't want to gamble except when I play poker by myself."

"Alright. I know a good place where my friend is working tonight. I'll set it up. See you in a bit."

We ended up at a hybrid Japanese and Mexican restaurant and his waitress friend brought out nearly everything on the menu. We slowly chomped through countless mini-courses as we reminisced about the good ol' days. I wasn't there looking for reassurance, but I knew that I was going to have to live with the chip on my shoulder that I retired as merely an independent league player.

"Dude you can't worry about that. You had a good career—you know how good you were and you have nothing to be ashamed of. So what if you never played in affiliated ball? You had the ability but injuries just got in the way. All of us knew you were good enough. Sometimes guys get overlooked."

"I guess so. I just, I figured it would have ended differently."

"Give it another shot, then. You had the numbers; someone will sign you."

"I can't. My shoulder is legitimately ruined. Today, for example—I packed up my laptop to head back to my hotel. As I grabbed my backpack to put it on, pain shot down my arm. I can't open my car door, pick up anything more than a few pounds or do much at all without pain. I could barely break 80 when I called it quits."

He shook his head. "Well, then you did everything you could. You had a good career."

I was okay with not playing more baseball. I'd forever miss being on the mound, in the dugout, on the bus and in the clubhouse. I loved the life, the travel, the camaraderie and the adrenaline. There was nothing like walking off the bus into a secret door of a big, majestic ballpark. I felt special, even if there were no reporters or screaming fans and my autograph wasn't worth a penny. We sat at the bar a while longer, slowly picking at our small plates, our stomachs nearing capacity.

"Ultimately, I just wanted to feel respected by other good players. I wanted to be valuable to a team, to feel like guys were happy I was going to enter a game. I dunno, I think I had that. And I know if things were different I might have gotten a shot at a higher level."

"There are politics behind who gets signed, who gets money, who gets promoted. No one knows what scouts see or don't see sometimes. But you couldn't control any of that, and you controlled what you could."

I know I was bitten by injuries, time and circumstance. Was I unlucky? Perhaps. Was I a victim? No. Quite the opposite—I was privileged to make it as far as I did, being a late bloomer with a lot of injuries. I had a lot of help and good fortune when I needed it. People stuck their necks out for me. My path to the top was circuitous, but circuitous meant scenic, circuitous meant memorable, circuitous meant I was extra thankful for a clear line of sight.

I had no interest in going to a nightclub but as dinner wrapped up, Sean sent a few texts and got us into Marquee—a busy, enormous club —for free. "You just have to check it out—the place is insane." I reluctantly agreed. After cutting the line and taking a unique elevator up to the top, we wandered into the dark spectacle of the main level. The popular electronic group, Galantis, was playing on the stage, sending the packed house into a frenzy. It was cavernous and dark, strobe lights and loud music shocking the senses as bartenders served up $36 well drinks. Everyone in the place either moved with 100% purpose or none at all, and I felt that if I lost Sean I'd never find him again. My cell didn't have service and time didn't seem to pass while we there there. The black walls gave no clues to the time of day and the entire spectacle was a bit beyond description. In the shadows behind Galantis, a three-story checkerboard of tall, thin, athletic women danced and contorted to the beat, each occupying her own little unit of what looked like a cubby system for dancers. *Was this a real place? Was this real life?* I smiled as I gazed in awe at the grandiosity of the club.

After an unknown amount of time passed, we made our way up to the library, which was located on the top floor. The narrow stairwell led us to a man sitting at a small table handing out over-ear headphones. We grabbed ours and joined the silent party, everyone rocking out without a sound piercing the air. Sean did what Sean always did—he went all in, bobbing and weaving to the beat, dancing alone and with any girls who wandered near. He was unabashed at being himself, at having fun and not letting the grind of life bog him down. Though I couldn't muster a dancing state of mind, I bobbed my head and joined Sean in not wasting the moment. Sean *never* wasted a moment. He could compartmentalize and find ways to enjoy himself no matter where he went or what had happened on the baseball diamond.

I thought back to my rookie season, living with my host family in Normal. In spring training I barely left the house, keeping my head down so I'd stay out of trouble and on course. I did the same thing in college, rarely making appearances at parties, rarely allocating time to be a social creature. I had goals and at the time, the only way I knew how to meet them was to put 100% of myself into it, blocking out the rest. My tunnel-vision was enough to guide me in the only direction that mattered. But every time I met up with Sean, I was reminded that there was another way. He was a lot of things I was not and every time I went out with him, I vowed to let go and live life just a little bit harder, like he did. *Don't waste moments. Go out with the guys. This is the stuff you'll miss when it's over.*

As I gazed around the library, I reflected on some of the incredible experiences baseball had given me. I'd experienced every emotion on the mound. My favorite, though, was fear—the fear of failure, the fear of embarrassment, the fear of injury, the fear of disappointing myself and others, the fear of losing it all and the fear of what would come next. Fear drove me to work harder and find new ways to break through, molding a scared kid into a man. Though Kevin and I had some fun times in the backyard, playing baseball with a tennis ball, our game lacked that fear. It was what I looked forward to in spring training and what I now miss the most. The hard times, the fearful times, those were the only ones worth sharing. Being warm is only valuable when you're cold; being comfortable is only valuable when you've been aching. Waking up with purpose and climbing over obstacles has always been my version of happiness. The pain, the surgeries, that day in the clubhouse in Gary—those weren't happy times, but they were huge boxes of purpose dropped off at my doorstep. Once the packing peanuts were discarded, I'd find a better version of myself at the bottom of each.

After a while, Sean grabbed me. "I'm over this room. Ready to move on?" I nodded and we returned our headphones to the man at the tiny front desk. Sean was the only person who could have led me to such an absurd place. It was thirty minutes of zen as I reflected on just how amazing my time in baseball had been. I looked back on all of it with a shiny fondness. I got deeper into baseball than I should have. I visited countless states, played in dozens of new ballparks, met lifelong friends, dated beautiful women and figured out who I was as a ballplayer. Though the rest of my miles would be walked without metal cleats protruding from the soles, I felt at peace with who I was. I still had to figure out who I was going to be, but I'd unpack that box when I got home. As Sean and I descended the dark stairwell back to the main floor, I put my hand on his shoulder. "Thanks for bringing me here." It was all downhill from there.

Sean chose to stay a little while longer, so we hugged and I departed to walk back across the Vegas strip to my hotel. I was sure I'd see him again, though I didn't know when. He was the right friend at the right time on more than one occasion, never ceasing to put his own problems aside to pick me up and illuminate my path with his unique light. My plane departed for Chicago a day later, and I felt a little more clear. As the 737 flew high above the Rockies, I knew somewhere beneath me there was a new mountain to climb.

Baseball Gods, if you're really up there, I want you to know that I'm grateful for everyone and everything, good and bad. I believe I did my best to live up to the standard set by the legends, the ghosts of this game. The kids at the ballpark didn't know that my signature wasn't worth a dime, but they still just smiled, excited and sheepish, as they extended a baseball and a Sharpie. They didn't know enough to realize I was playing a silly game, delaying what others would call "real" life. Yet, their excitement wasn't about me—it was the lure of the jersey, the lights, the dreams we all grow up with. It took hold of me just as it now takes hold of them. A fortunate few of us get to cling to our dreams long past our youth. I was one of those lucky few, even if I went out with a whimper, even if the back of my jersey wasn't embroidered with a household name.

Yet, I don't think you were actually up there guiding line drives into my shortstop's mitt when I needed an out. Duff? He believes in hustle, in grit and respect for the game—not ghosts who give and take on a whim. I did things the right way because others showed me the standard I should live and play by. I made the best of things, both listened to and battled the voice in my head and tried to leave it all out on the field.

Baseball is special precisely because of the uncertainty, the fog we walk through in crossing those white lines. The magic is in the line drive double plays, the borderline strikes and the 2-0 fastballs that good hitters sometimes pop up. It's in the swinging bunts, the broken-bat singles and the bloopers that go for game-losing hits. The fairness and unfairness alike is what made that one extra day in the sun worth it.

I'll miss the green grass, the beautiful ballparks and the smell of a new baseball glove. I'll miss the high fives given to kids in the crowd and my teammates after a win. I'll even miss the hecklers on the road and the challenge of putting myself back together. The electricity that flowed through my arm as a high fastball left my finger tips—I can still feel it when I close my eyes. I won't have to miss that.

Maybe you had a hand in the strange coincidences, the good luck and the amazing people who showed up just when I needed them. I'll concede that ground balls did sometimes bounce in mysterious ways. Yet, I now know for certain that where I ended up was not merely by chance, nor was it chosen for me. It's with that knowledge that after all these years fighting to stay, it's now time for me to go—I couldn't stay stuck here forever. Now that I've gone back and seen how lucky I was, I'm ready.

Epilogue - Dear Reader, Someday never comes.

After that silent disco with Sean, it was clear to me that I was ready to start this process. I had already begun writing, but I hadn't really started leaving the game. Yet, that night gave me perspective and reminded me just how many weird corners of the earth I had set foot upon because of baseball. I still don't know who *the voice* is, but I do know that he's been silent as I've done my work, as I went back. I stayed here for two long years because I knew it was the only way I'd be able to one day leave for good.

I departed Vegas reveling in how many great people punctuated this run-on sentence that was my life in baseball. When my flight touched back down in Chicago and I meandered back to Bloomington, I forged ahead. I spoke with many of my teammates and realized that the process looks and feels different for everyone. What is universal, though, is that we all feel it. A massive weight is lifted, and is replaced with an equally massive hole…at least for a while. My first task was to find clarity on what the rest of my life might look like. The writer that had been incubating beneath my jersey all those years took over. I sat down behind my laptop and began molding together the pieces of this book.

I began to identify as a writer somewhere between 2010 and 2012, my first few years after college graduation. I began blogging in 2008 on the advice of my friend and mentor, Nick Tumminello. Nick is a personal trainer and world-renowned educator in the fitness field. I interned for him in 2008 and 2009, trying to learn things I could use on the diamond. One day, he offered some very matter-of-fact advice:

"Dan, you need to start blogging."

"Why?" I asked.

"Because it's where the internet is going and it will help you establish yourself as an expert in the fitness or baseball industry. Just do it and thank me later."

"Okay" I said.

A glaring question loomed: Who in their right mind would read my blog? Who would listen to the yammering of a formerly mediocre college baseball player with a blown elbow? I didn't know, but forged ahead anyway. Occasionally, an encouraging comment would slip into my inbox, letting me know that someone was not only reading, but nodding their head. I kept going.

Blogging was purely instructional. At some point, however, I began writing as a hobby, journaling in the back of the bus on my MacBook. Those journals, half-finished books and email updates were practice for me as a writer. Incidentally, those *You're My Boy, Blew* email updates also became an important time capsule of my exploits; reading through them was fascinating. I didn't realize until the fifth and final edit that my perspective in those emails wasn't objectively accurate. I wrote those emails while wearing a mask of optimism and courage, courage that I know for a fact I was often faking.

Though everything in this book is true, there was no black box and the entire story is, as I explained in the letter to my previous self, a composite of three different perspectives. Together, they formed my account of what happened, how I responded to it and how I internalized it. In writing this, I've come to understand how subjective even objectively true events can be. The version of myself I projected in my emails explained that the mental side of the game is the hardest part. In those emails I chose to be inspirational, to show the youngsters who might be reading how I kept my chin up. I put on brave mask for them and in doing so, my real face often became brave. Because of this, it wouldn't have been fair to let the 33-year-old Dan write this book alone. In the two years that elapsed, my perspective on who I am and what my story means, it evolved in ways I couldn't have predicted.

Growing up, I watched The Twilight Zone marathons with JD and my Dad on New Year's and the Fourth of July. Rod Serling's opening monologues never failed to amaze me. He could tidy everything up in a neat little bow before telling his philosophical stories on the nature and limits of human beings. One such episode, "The Masks," involved a dying man who was passing away in the middle of Mardi Gras. He was old and wealthy with just one night left to live. In his will he stipulated leaving everything to his daughter, her husband and their grown children, all of whom he described as wicked, selfish people. To claim their inheritance, each had to wear a special mask until the clock struck midnight. The masks were custom made for each of them, bearing a grotesque resemblance. As the clock ticked past midnight they removed their masks, excited for their newfound wealth. One by one they looked in the mirror to find that their faces had permanently taken the disfigured, hideous shape of the mask they wore.

What I wrote in my journal and email updates wasn't exactly the truth—it was the truth of how I knew I *should* feel, how a stronger man would reframe the situation. Maybe the voice was the same—the stronger, more aggressive man I wanted to be. Or maybe it was me all along. The emails, though, were the truth of how I'd advise a young player facing the same challenge. In some cases, I believe that the mask we wear for the world is the face we'll reveal when we take it off. I put on the mask of a more optimistic man and when I took it off at the end, the face that looked back had taken its form. I'll never sugar-coat the world for myself or others. Yet I began choosing a brighter lens, a more optimistic and brave mask for myself a long time ago. I carved that mask as a hybrid of the many traits I admired in my family, coaches, friends and teammates. It's up to each of us to choose our own mask and in doing so we must be careful, for our face will eventually conform to its shape.

As soon as the words *I'm retiring* left my lips, the massive weight of preparation was lifted and I immediately felt lighter. We players take for granted just how much we do to keep ourselves operating at 100% and not one single percentage point lower. Though I only once in a while miss playing, the issues of identity and the emotions I bottled up on those dark days were—and still are—not quickly resolved. They had to be dealt with someday, but at the time I just deferred them and kept moving. One of my favorite Creedence Clearwater Revival songs is *Someday Never Comes.* Unfortunately, the message in the song doesn't apply in this situation. Someday *did* come. It kicked in my front door.

For an athlete, the grieving process is difficult to talk about. I didn't know who could relate, nor is it the cultural norm for athletes to admit that they feel sad, that they feel weak and scared for the future. No one counsels us on what it will be like when we get kicked to the curb after our last game. For every athlete who speaks up and explains that, well, *it sucks*, there are perhaps a thousand others who never mention how alone, depressed and confused they felt. Part of it is that there's just so much backstory, which is why I was so glad I dialed up Sean, even though we didn't talk that much in my visit to Vegas. He knew what the game meant because he'd devoted his own life to it.

My family, my closest friends and the rest of those dear to me—most were kept on the outside, given a skimmed, watery version. It was just that without running miles 1-25, how could a person understand what it was like to quit at mile 26, with the finish line nearly in sight? I saw an insurmountable pile of work to relate why I felt the way I felt. This book serves as the mostly complete volume of mileage. If you're the parent, coach or spouse of an athlete, I hope you have a new perspective on just how much the silly ball and bat means to us...the pinstripes don't wash off. If you're an athlete yourself, I'm sure you either have, or will, live many of these same experiences. And if you have no personal connection to baseball or the world of sports, I hope you turn these final pages feeling included, an honorary guest on my journey.

Every athlete's career is both vastly different and utterly the same. Some are ready to walk away and others aren't. Some view it as their sole reason to wake up in the morning whereas others approach it part-time. There's no wrong way to do it—sports are what we want them to be, a diversion from the tedium of everyday life. I chose to dive in and for me, it's why it's been so hard to walk away. I believed that my story had some special ending and that belief kept me going. Though I bailed water and replaced planks as fast as I could, my boat still sunk.

Even knowing what it's done to me as I tried to leave peacefully, I'm glad I made the choice to be all-in. I hope you, Dear Reader, make that choice for something in your own life. We all have things that eat away at us—things we know we should, could, or wish we'd do. Whatever yours is, go do it—it's never too late to get started. Let the standard set by others guide you, but never allow yourself to be limited by it. Though I'm not sure if the Baseball Gods will lend you a hand, I do know that the voice is right when it demands we stand back up. If we don't, someday never comes.

This was my story. Thank you for letting me share it with you.

Dan Blewett

ACKNOWLEDGEMENTS

So many of you built me up. Though I tried, I couldn't fit every piece into this crazy, 120,000 word puzzle. For those not mentioned, thank you for being a part of my life and this story.

I had no idea how hard the home stretch would be. Getting this book cleaned up and ready for the world truly took a village.

Thank you to my editors: Tom Jackson, JD Blewett, Joann Blewett, Bill Blewett, Tim O'Brien and Joe Nemetz.

To Annie, my closer: Wherever typos live, you are the bringer of doom, destroyer of worlds.

Lucas: The cover is perfect. Your Adobe sorcery brought this whole thing together.

I Humbly Ask For Your Help…

If you enjoyed my story, please leave an honest review.

This book will not reach those who need it without your help.

Thank you.

#13

The final chapter is yet to be written.

Follow up with me

——

I create video stories: www.youtube.com/c/danblewett

I'm on the interwebs: www.danblewett.com

I have social media: @CoachDanBlewett

Speaking: www.danblewett.com/education

People love my newsletter: www.danblewett.com/dan-blewett-newsletter

Send me your own letter: info@danblewett.com

Google me if you get lost.

.

.

Made in the USA
Columbia, SC
14 January 2020